Persons Names / Taxable property /
The 2d. List for 8 Gov'r / Capt. Watson Dist.

No	Persons Names	No of Acres of Land	White Polls	Black Polls	Lots in Elizabeth	Wheels of Pleasure	Stud Horses	Lots Wilmington	Lots Fayetteville	Military Lands & c	Fayetteville	Elizabethtown	
1	Joseph Kemp	1403		3									K
2	James Bradley & John Cowan	2028	3	17	3	1		1					B
3	David Russ	1340	2	1	1								R
4	Eliz'th Brown			2									B
5	Samuel McRee	270	1										M
6	John Ellis	610	1										E
7	Robert McConkey	550		2									M
8	William Bryan	350	1	1									B
9	Samuel Baxter	640	1										B
10	Joseph Kemp Jun'r	50	1										K
11	Mathew R. White	300	1	1									W
12	Philip Cattle	52	1										C
	John White	2070	2	8									W
13	for James White	200											W
	for the Estate of D. Wm. Ross	420											R
	for the Estate of D.a Morley	200											M
14	Richard Salter	1060	3	4									S
15	William Chisher	460	1										C
16	James Moorhead	3452	1	8				2	1	660			M
17	Lucy Smith	640		3									S
18	Isaac Jones	1500	1	2									J
19	John Kister	424	1										
20	David Owen		1										O
21	John Owen	640	1	2									O
22	Dan'l Shaw	350	1										S
23	William Jas. Watson	2780	1	4	1			1					W
24	Colo. Thos. Owen	7360	1	20	2						1	2	O
25	for the Estate Inc. Owen	2395	1	9	1								O
26	Mary White	750		1									W

Bladen County Tax List for 1789

BLADEN COUNTY NORTH CAROLINA

TAX LISTS

1775 THROUGH 1789

VOLUME II

William L. Byrd, III

HERITAGE BOOKS
2007

HERITAGE BOOKS
AN IMPRINT OF HERITAGE BOOKS, INC.

Books, CDs, and more—Worldwide

For our listing of thousands of titles see our website
at
www.HeritageBooks.com

Published 2007 by
HERITAGE BOOKS, INC.
Publishing Division
65 East Main Street
Westminster, Maryland 21157-5026

Copyright © 2000 William L. Byrd, III

Other Heritage Books by William L. Byrd, III:

Against the Peace and Dignity of the State: North Carolina Laws Regarding Slaves, Free Persons of Color, and Indians
Bladen County, North Carolina Tax Lists: 1768 through 1774, Volume I
Bladen County, North Carolina Tax Lists: 1775 through 1789, Volume II
For So Long as the Sun and Moon Endure: Indian Records from the North Carolina General Assembly Sessions, & Other Sources
In Full Force and Virtue: North Carolina Emancipation Records, 1713-1860
North Carolina General Assembly Sessions Records: Slaves and Free Persons of Color, 1709-1789
North Carolina Slaves and Free Persons of Color: Chowan County, Volume One
North Carolina Slaves and Free Persons of Color: Chowan County, Volume Two
North Carolina Slaves and Free Persons of Color: Pasquotank County
North Carolina Slaves and Free Persons of Color: Perquimans County
Villainy Often Goes Unpunished: Indian Records from the North Carolina General Assembly Sessions, 1675-1789

Other Heritage Books by William L. Byrd, III and John H. Smith:

North Carolina Slaves and Free Persons of Color: Burke, Lincoln, and Rowan Counties
North Carolina Slaves and Free Persons of Color: Hyde and Beaufort Counties
North Carolina Slaves and Free Persons of Color: Iredell County
North Carolina Slaves and Free Persons of Color: Mecklenburg, Gaston, and Union Counties
North Carolina Slaves and Free Persons of Color: McDowell County
North Carolina Slaves and Free Persons of Color: Stokes and Yadkin Counties

All rights reserved. No part of this book may be reproduced or transmitted in any form or by any means, electronic or mechanical, including photocopying, recording or by any information storage and retrieval system without written permission from the author, except for the inclusion of brief quotations in a review.

International Standard Book Number: 978-0-7884-1426-8

TABLE OF CONTENTS

INTRODUCTION V

ACKNOWLEDGEMENTS VII

CHAPTER 1 1
   BLADEN COUNTY LOOSE PAPERS *1*

CHAPTER 2 33
   BLADEN COUNTY TAX LISTS OF 1775 .... *33*

CHAPTER 3 43
   BLADEN COUNTY TAX LISTS OF 1776 .... *43*

CHAPTER 4 99
   BLADEN COUNTY TAX LISTS OF 1778 .... *99*

CHAPTER 5 105
   BLADEN COUNTY TAX LISTS OF 1779 .... *105*

CHAPTER 6 161

BLADEN COUNTY TAX LISTS OF 1786 .... *161*

CHAPTER 7 191
   BLADEN COUNTY TAX LISTS OF 1787 .... *191*

CHAPTER 8 195
   BLADEN COUNTY TAX LISTS OF 1789 .... *195*

APPENDIX A 227
   NORTH CAROLINA LAW *227*

INDEX 235

INTRODUCTION

This volume completes the tax lists and loose papers transcribed and abstracted from manuscripts located at the University of North Carolina at Chapel Hill. Hopefully, more records will eventually surface, and raise the shroud of mystery surrounding Bladen County and its colonial population.

Bladen County was formed from New Hanover Precinct in 1734. At this time it existed as a precinct of Bath County. In 1800 and 1893 Courthouse fires destroyed most of Bladen's court records and some of the land deeds.[1] The devastation of Bladen County's records by these fires has created a void for historians and genealogists alike. These early tax lists and loose papers provide information and insight into many of the early families that would have otherwise been lost to posterity. Several of the lists gives the names of sons and other family members. Mixed blood families and a myriad of slave names abound throughout the lists.

When Bladen County was first formed it covered a large territory from which other counties eventually came into existence. Anson County was formed from Bladen County in 1750, and part of Orange County was formed from Bladen in 1752. In 1754, Cumberland County was formed from Bladen, and later, in 1764, Brunswick County was formed from Bladen and New Hanover County. Twenty three years later, in 1787, Robeson County was formed from Bladen.[2]

The Bladen County records in this volume were obtained from the ***Thomas David Smith McDowell Papers***, collection #460. They are a part of the vast collection housed in the **Southern Historical Collection** at the Wilson Library of the University of North Carolina at Chapel Hill. There are three thousand items and five volumes contained in this collection alone.

The first part of this volume contains full transcriptions of loose papers from Bladen County. Most of them are confiscations of property for acts of treason against the State, and failure to take the oath of allegiance to the newly formed country during the Revolutionary War. Individuals who refused to take the oath were forced to leave the State by the issuing of Departure Bonds. One such Loyalist (Maturin Colville) refused to give up the records of the county to newly appointed officials. As a result of this the General Assembly of North Carolina actually passed a law in 1777 demanding that he give up the records. This law along with laws pertaining to treason can be found in **Appendix A** at the back of this book.

The remaining part of this volume consists of tax lists for the years 1775 through 1789. As with the first volume some years are missing. Other lists are torn or partial. Many of the lists were badly damaged and could not be copied, and had to be transcribed in the Manuscript Department. There is, however, enough information to shed new light on an otherwise burned county. This volume should be of interest to historians, and genealogists alike.

Old Bladen County was also home to many of the ancestral families of the Lumbee Indians of North Carolina. They will be found listed variously as Whites, Mulattoes, and Mixt Bloods. Bound together by common ancestry, they have survived to this day as a unified group.

Free Persons of Color are listed in italics in the various tax lists in this volume. It should be of note that the wives and other females in this group are given as taxables. This policy originated from a statute passed by the General Assembly in 1723 as a result of so many mixed blood people who were moving into the colony and intermarrying with Whites. Inter-racial marriages were forbidden by an earlier statute passed by the General Assembly in 1715. This same statute was again confirmed in 1741.

---

[1] *Guide to Research Materials in the North Carolina State Archives: County Records*, eleventh rev. ed. (Raleigh: Division of Archives and History, Department of Cultural Resources, 1997): 31.
[2] David Leroy Corbit, *The Formation of the North Carolina Counties: 1663-1943* (1950, reprint, Raleigh: Division of Archives and History, Department of Cultural Resources, 1987): 27-31.

The statute of 1723 wherein mixed bloods and their wives and daughters were both considered taxables was again confirmed in 1749.

In 1755 a petition was submitted to the General Assembly praying relief from the 1723 statute, but no results came from it. Five years later, in 1760, an act passed by the General assembly again reaffirmed the 1723 statute. This resulted in another petition being filed with the General assembly in 1762 by sundry inhabitants of several North Carolina Counties protesting the paying of taxes on their wives and daughters. This statute, however, remained on the books, and Free Persons of Color were still paying taxes on their wives and daughters in 1774.

It should also be noted that Patrollers were also exempt from taxes. The first statute defining Patrollers (or Searchers) was enacted by the General Assembly in 1753. This statute gave the Patrollers broad powers to search slaves and their quarters for guns, swords, clubs, or any other weapons. The laws passed by the North Carolina General Assembly regarding the taxing of Free Persons of Color, and of Patrollers can be found in the appendix of volume one of Bladen County tax lists

Another confusion factor for Bladen County stems from a border dispute with South Carolina. This problem was addressed in a Guide to South Carolina Genealogical Research and Records by Brent Holcomb.

> **The North Carolina-South Carolina border east of the Catawba River was surveyed in 1764, and west of of the Catawba River in 1772. Prior to these surveys, much of the territory in the north-central and north-western part of South Carolina was considered to be North Carolina. The South Carolina Counties of Marlboro, Chesterfield, Lancaster, York, Chester, Union, Spartanburg, Cherokee, and portions of Greenville, Laurens and Newberry are involved. There are three, or in some cases, four North Carolina counties to be considered: Bladen ca. 1745-1749, Anson 1749-1764, Mecklenburg 1763-1772, and Tryon 1769-1772. The researcher should consider persons in that area as though they were residents of North Carolina and search the appropriate records in that state**[3]

Considering the above excerpt, the tax lists in this volume should be of interest to North Carolina and South Carolina researchers alike. Adjacent border research (especially across state lines) has routinely been overlooked by many researchers.

---

[3] Brent Howard Holcomb, *A Guide to South Carolina Genealogical Research and Records* (Privately printed, 1986): 39.

ACKNOWLEDGEMENTS

The publishing of this second volume of Bladen County, North Carolina tax lists, and loose papers, was made possible by the kind permission of Richard A. Shrader, Reference Archivist, of the Manuscripts Department at the University of North Carolina at Chapel Hill. They are part of the ***Thomas S. McDowell Papers***, collection #460. They have an excellent and knowledgeable staff, and it is always a pleasure to do research there.

CHAPTER 1

BLADEN COUNTY LOOSE PAPERS

Land Deed

John McVicker Deed to Duncan McKeithan
Paid A.R. 66 Acres
June Session 1799
This Deed was proved by Alexr Ballantine
and Ordered to be Registered
Attest J S Purdie Cl.
Registered in the Regst. office of Bladen
in Book (G) page (222) 29th Augt. 99
J. Ellis Regr.

Sold & the Timber Reserved
Tho: Smith

know all men by these presents that I John McVicker of the County of Bladen in the State of North Carolina for and in Consideration of the sum of fifty pounds North Carolina Currency paid to me by Duncan McKeithen of Bladen County in the State of North Carolina have bargained sold conveyed unto and by these presents do bargain Sell convey unto the aforesaid Duncan McKeithen a certain tract or parcel of Land lying and being in Bladen County aforesaid and containing Sixty Six Acres fifty Acres of which Land was patented by Isabella McKeithen Deceased lying and being between Duncan Blews and Duncan McKeithen to have and to hold the aforesaid bargained premises with all the woods waters mines minerals Hereditaments and Appurtenances thereto belonging unto him the said Duncan McKeithen his heirs and Assigns forever and I the said John McVicker my heirs and Assigns executors and administrators will forever warrant and defend unto the aforesaid Duncan McKeithen his heirs and Assigns all the aforesaid tract with all woods waters mines minerals thereto belonging against all Claims and demands that shall or may arise from any person or persons whatever against the aforesaid tract or parcel of Land in witness whereof I have hereunto set my hand and Affixed my seal this sixth Day of September in the Year of Our Lord one thousand seven hundred and ninety seven --

John McVicker (Seal)

Signed Sealed }
and Delivered }
in presence of }
Alexdr. Ballantine
Daniel McKeithen

****

Petition

To the Worshipful the County Court of Bladen at June Term 1801
The Petition of Richard and John Singletary respectively sheweth that in the Year 1790 Danl Schaw Esqr. Surveyed for them 100 Acres of Land which was Measured and Marked as per Certificate to

Chapter 1: Bladen County Loose Papers

the plat Annexed, but that in Makeing out the Plat, it is Eroneously State in the Second line to run No 40 West Whereas it should have been stated to run South 50 East & West in the [Faded] and last line it is stated to run South 40 East it should have been described as Appears from the Plat to run direct to the begining Which course is different from the line that was run the whole of which appears to be the Mistake of the Surveyor. Your Petitioners Pray Your Worships to Order the Errors aforesaid to be Corrected as the Act of Assembly in that case has provided

Richd. Singletary
Jno Singletary

****

Petition

Petition of Nicholas Parker
for correcting an Error in a Grant

25th of April 1801
I hereby Certify
That I have this
Day Serv'd a Coppy of this

To The Worshipful the Justices of the Court of Pleas and Quarter Sessions held for the County of Bladen, on the first Monday in June 1801.

The Petition of Nicholas Parker Humbly Sheweth

That in the Year one Thousand seven hundred and Eighty four One John Sugg Obtained a Patent from the State for One Hundred Acres of Land Lying in The County of Bladen in the forks of David Gam branch, Begining at A large Pine and Runing North forty Chains to a Stake, then West Twenty five Chains to a Stake, then South forty Chains to a Stake, then East Twenty five Chains to the Begining, References being had to the Patent will fully appear, that your Petitioner is now the Owner of said Tract or Parcel of Land here described.

Your Petitioner further States That he Obtained a Grant from the State for Fifty Acres of Land lying in Bladen County on the East side of Turnbull Begining at A Stake the North East corner of John Suggs hundred Acres Survey (which is the one before described) and Runs on that line West 15 Chains & 82 links to a stake, thence South 31 Chains and 63 links to a [Blank], thence East 15 Chains and 82 links to a stake, thence North 31 Chains and 63 links to the Begining &c the Grant dated 17th December 1796.

Your Petitioner further states that either by a Mistake in the surveyor in making his return to the Secretary, or the Secretary in Making out the Grant, for the above fifty Acres; that the same, is thrown altogether within the lines of the Hundred Acre survey before mentioned, owing to the Begining corner of the fifty Acre tract calling for the North East corner of the Hundred Acre survey, which it ought to have done and which was the intention of your Petitioner and which intention will be made appear to your Worships by the surveyors field Book and other Testimony in due time.

Your Petitioner prays this Worshipfull Court that his Grant of fifty Acres may be altered in the following Manner, Vizt. that in lieu of Begining at the North East Corner of Suggs Hundred Acre Survey, That it <u>Begin at the Stake by four Pines John Suggs North West Corner, Thence West 15 Chains & 82 links to a Stake, thence South 31 Chains 63 links to a Stake, thence East 15 Chains and 82 links to a Stake, then direct to the Begining;</u> in Consequence of which your Petitioner will obtain relief agreeable to an Act of the General Assembly in such Case made and provided; this being Agreeable to the Survey made, as also the Surveyors field Book, and your Petitioner in Duty Bound &c --

June Term 1801 }
Bladen County }

Chapter 1: Bladen County Loose Papers

***

Warrant

North Carolina }
Bladen County }

George the third by the Grace of God of Great Brittain France & Ireland king Defender of the faith &c. To the Sheriff of Bladen County greeting, Whereas Alexander Stewart hath Complained To me on Oath that Samuel Hughes Senr. late of our County is Justly Indebted to him the Sum of Twenty Pounds procl. And Oath having also been Made That the said Samuel Hughes hath removed himself privately Out of our said County or to Abscond, and Conceals himself That the Ordinary process of Law Cannot Be Served on him, and having Given Bond and Security Agreeable to Law.

We therefore Command you that you Attatch the Estate of the Said Samuel Hughes if to be found in your Bailiwick or so much thereof Repleviable on bond & Security Given as shall be of Value Sufficient to Satisfie the said Debt [Torn] Damages according to the Complaint & Costs and such [Torn] so Attached in your hands to Secure or so to provide that the Same May be liable to further proceedings Thereupon to be had at our Next Court to be held for the County aforesaid at the Court house in Bladen the [Blank] Tuesday In February next So as to Compell the Said Samuel Hughes to Appear and Answer the Above Complaint, When and Where you Shall Make known to our said Court How you Shall have Executed this Writ Witness Hugh Waddell one of his Majesties Justices of our said County of Bladen This First day of Jany. In the year of our Lord one thousand Seven hundred and Seventy One

H Waddell

***

Land Transfer

Joseph Howard to Titus Howard

Joseph Howard }
     to }
Titus Howard }

Deed dated the 6th January 1761 for a piece of land containing 110 Acres lying on the East Side of Black river in Newhanover County and Province of North Carolina, Begining at a pine by black river runing So. 20 Et. 25 chains to a pine by William Ashburns line, thence down his line So. 55 Et. 44 chains to a gum by black River to the first Station, Pattented by Sd. Howard 23d October 1761

North Carolina }
Newhanover County }Ss.

I hereby certify that the above is a true Copy of the Courses as appears upon record in my Office 8th October 1772
Jas. Moran register

***

Land Transfer
Joseph Howard Junr. to Titus Howard

Chapter 1: Bladen County Loose Papers

Joseph Howard Junr.   }
       to   }
Titus Howard   }

    Deed dated 22d August 1767 for 200 acres of Land in Newhanover County in the Province of North Carolina on the East Side of Black River nearly opposite to John Howards Landing; Begining at a pine in open ground on a bluff thence runing No. 60 Et. 66 chains & 66 links to a pine thence North 30 Wt. 30 chains to a Pine So. 60 Wt. 66 chains and 66 links to a Cypress by the River & down the river to the first Station, Pattented by Wm. Ashburn M[Torn] 17th in 32 year of his Majesties Reign George the Second 1759 and transferred to the said Joseph Howard Junr.

North Carolina   }
Newhanover County   } Ss.

    I hereby certifie that the above is a true Copy of the Courses as appears upon record in my Office 8th October 1772

Jas. Moran register

****

Warrant

North Carolina   }
Bladen County   }

(Seal)

    This Day appeared before me Jane Yates & Complained that Jesse Howard Did abuse & Scandalise greatly her Caracter, and also laid violent hands on her & tore her Cloaths greatly

These are Commanding you in his Majesties Name to Cause the said Howard to appear before me to answer the above Complaint herein fail not and this shall be your warrant given under my hand and seal this 21 august 1774

                                                                                   Thos. Owen

To any Lawful Officer
To Execute & return

****

Petition

North Carolina Ss.
    To the worshipfull the Justices of Bladen County Now Sitting in Court on the Third day of may in the Year of our Lord 1774

    The petition of Thomas Robeson Senr
Humbly Sheweth

    That whereas there is an Action now Depending in this Court on an Appeal from the Judgment of Hector McNeill Esqr of the sd County to this Court wherein Joseph Wood is plaintiff and Thos Robeson Senr. is Defend -- the Defendt prays your Worships that the said Appeal may be Continued Over to the Next Court by Reason that your petitioner hath Applied for Summonsed to Summons his Evidence in the best manner he Could to this Court but Could not Obtain the Summons to have his Evidences here to

Chapter 1: Bladen County Loose Papers

Attend And further your petitioner is vary lame and is not able to Attend this Court without Suffering much paign Youe petitioner therefore prays your worships that the said appeal may be Continued over to the Next Court and your petitioner as in Duty bound shall pray

Thos Robeson Senr.

****

Settlement

Settlement of Partnership between

Gibson an King

State of North Carolina   }
Bladen County   } Eliza. Town 5th Aprill 1777

    Know all Men by these presents That Whereas there are Certain Accompts between Walter Gibson and John King both of said County Arising from their being equally concerned as Commissarys for the first Regmt. of Militia Commanded by Genl. Ash in the Year 1776 -- Disputes between them Arising about Selling Said accompts they chose us Subscribers as Arbitrators to Settle Said Accts. and disputes between them as may appear by their Bond Bearing date the **[Blank]** day of **[Blank]** where each became bound to the other in the Sum of One thousand Pounds to stand to and abide by our determination and award -- We the said Arbitrators having Duly examined and Stated their Accts. finds a proffit arising from said Copartnership of One thousand and Sevebty three pounds Twelve shills. & 3d Proc. money and of that Sum of said proffits a Ballance is due to John King of Thirty three pounds Nine Shillings and Sevenpence three farthings Proc. -- Now know Ye that we the said Arbitrators give it as our award that the said Ballance Shall well and truly be paid by said Walter Gibson to said John King upon demand -- And we do also further award that Bonds of Indemnification shall be given from each to the other in the Sum of One thousand Pounds proc. money Obliging each of them to abide by and Settle what Accompts are passed to their respective Credits in their Accts. with the Company which may be out standing bring **[Faded]** as already paid -- We do also award that if the nine head of Cattle belonging to said Copartnership (that was Lost) or any part of them Shall hereafter come to hand or be found they shall be equally divided between said Walter Gibson & John King as also what Leather belonging to said Copartnership is in the hands of William McRee Esqr. -- Lastly (upon performance of the above arbitriment) we award that each perfect and deliver to the Other proper Releases to be drawn for the purpose of discharging each other.

Signed Sealed & delivered in presence of	John White Senr.	(Seal)
William McRee Junr	Jno White	(Seal)
	Jas Smith	(Seal)

****

Bond for Departure

State of North Carolina   }
Bladen County   }

    Know all Men by these presents that we John Seller Robert McMillen Samuel Bozman Edward Reves and Christopher Sutton all of Said County are held and firmly Bound unto Richard Caswell Esquire Governor & his Successors in the Sum of Five hundred Pounds Proc. money **[Torn]** true payment whereof

Chapter 1: Bladen County Loose Papers

we bind ourselves our heirs and assigns Sealed with our Seals and dated this **[Torn]** 1777 **[Torn]** Independence.

The Condition of the Above Obligation is Such that if the above Bound John Sellers and Robert McMillan do Depart this State in Sixty Days from the Date hereof Agreeable to An Act of Assembly made and provided for People refusing the Oath of Allegiance to this State that then the above Obligation to be Void and of non effect otherwise to remain in full force and Virtue

Signed Sealed and Delivered		
in presence of	John Sellars	(Seal)
in open Court	his	
John White Senr.	Robt X McMillan	(Seal)
	mark	
	Saml. Bosman	(Seal)
	Edward Reeves	(Seal)
	Christopher Sutton	(Seal)

****

Bond for Departure

State of North Carolina }
Bladen County }

Know all men by these presents that we Duncan McAllester, Anguish McAlestar, Daniel McMillan, Archibald Sellers, Robert Stewart, Iver McMillan, and Archibald Sellers all of said County Are held and firmly Bound unto Richard Caswell Esqr. Governour and his Successors in the Sum of One thousand five hundred Pounds Proc. money **[Next Line Torn]** our heirs and assigns Sealed with our Seals and Dated this 5th Day of Novr. 1777 And in the Second Year of our Independence

The Condition of the above Obligation is Such that if the above bound Duncan McAllister Anguish McAllister Danl. McMillan and Archibald Sellers do Depart this State in Sixty Days from this Date Agreeable to an Act of Assembly made and provided for People Refusing the Oath of Allegiance to this State that then the above Obligation to be Void and of non Effect Otherwise to remain in full force & Virtue

Signed Sealed and Delivered		
in presence of	Duncan McAlester	(Seal)
in open Court	Angus McAlester	(Seal)
John White Senr.	Daniel McMillan	(Seal)
	Archibald Sellers	(Seal)
	his	
	Iver X McMillan	(Seal)
	mark	
	Archibald Sellars	(Seal)

****

Petition

To the Worshipfull Justices of Bladen County Now Sitting

The Petition of Charity Stevens Humbly Sheweth
That about 5th Day of April 1781[2] A certain Stephen Godwin Alexander Godwin William Strickland Junr. Mark Ronalds saml. Andress Moses Coleman Son of Jno. Coleman decd.[?] Jno.

Chapter 1: Bladen County Loose Papers

Harrison With Others Came to the house of the Late Barnabas Stevens Deceasd. and Did With force and Arms Burn, Rob and take Away from Me Sundry Articles Contrary to Law Which Articles is hereto Anext Which I hope your Worships in your Wisdoms and Acording to Law Will Order an Alowance and your Petitioner in Duty bound Shall Ever pray

****

Summons

Fayette-Ville District, SS.

STATE OF NORTh-CAROLINA.

To the Sheriff of Sampson County, Greeting.

You are hereby commanded to summon Curtis Ivey personally to appear before the Judges of the Superior Court of Law, to be held at Fayette-Ville, on the 23d day of June next, then and there to testify and the truth to say, on behalf of Jacob Rhodes in a certain matter of controversy in the said court depending, and then and there to be tried, between John Den plaintiff, and Richard Fen defendant, and this you shall in no wise omit under the penalty by law.

Witness Richard Henderson, Clerk of the said court, at Fayetteville the 20th day of Decr. in the xiii year of independence, and Anno Domini 1788

R. Henderson

****

Petition

To the Worshipfull Court of Pleas & Quarter Sessions for the County of Bladen Now Sitting

The Petition of Jno Plummer Humbly sheweth that Some time in the month of June 1781 that Certain Danl. McPharsion Levy Glass Charles MeLoy Daniel Meloy Danl. Patterson John Megloklin Anguish Brown **[Torn]** **[Torn]** the Command of Duncan Ray and Hector McNeill With sundry Others Plundered him of Certain Articles Which Will appear by the Annext Inventory and Petitioner therefore Humbly pray that you will afford him Such Relief as by Act of the General Assembly in such Case has Provided and your Petitioner as in Duty bound Shall pray

John Plummer

Articles taken by the Torys Under the Command of Hector McNeel and Duncan Ray From John Plummer Viz

	£	Sh	d
1 Horse Saddle and bridle	34	0	0
1 Hunting Shirt	1	10	0
1 blanket	2	0	0
1 Stock buckle	0	10	0
	39	0	0

This Day John Plummer Came before me and made Oath that the Above mentioned Articles Was taken from him by the Torys under the Command of Hector McNeel an Duncan Ray Sworn to before me this 7th Day of Novemr. 1782
Saml. Cain

****

Petition

Chapter 1: Bladen County Loose Papers

To the worshipfull the County Court of Bladen, Augt. 1782
    The Humble petition of Robert Baker of said County
        Sheweth That your petitioner hath a just Claim against the estate of Maturin Colvil decd. Your Petitioner prays the same be inquired pursuant to the Act of the General Assembly in such cases made and provided and your petitioner shall pray &c.

****

Deposition

Bladen County }
This Day Daniel Flinn personally appeared Before me John Yates and Being Duly Sworn Saith that Some time in September 1781 he Saw William White have a Bay mare in his possession the property of John Flinn Which mare Was onbranded the Deponant Saith and further Saith Not Sworn to Before me the 26th of October 1782
John Yates
                                                            Daniel Flinn

****

Petition

State of North Carolina }
Bladen County   }Febry Sessions 1783

    The Petition of Thomas Hadley Administrator of the Estate of Thomas Hadley deceased --
Sheweth
    That Your petitioner hath a just claim against the estate of William Maulsby late of Bladen County who hath forfeited his estate for having joined the enemies of America which claim is by book delet due in the life time of the said Thomas Hadley deceased
    Your Petitioner prays the same be inquired pursuant to the Act of the General Assembly in such cases made and provided and Your Petitioner Shall pray &c
                                                            Thos Hadley

Wm. Maulsby Dr.
To Book Acct. £73.13.4

****

Articles taken by Tories

Articles taken by the Torys under the Command of David Fanning & Samuel Andres from Wm. Clark Viz

	£	S	d
1 Bridle and Saddle	8	0	0
1 New fur hatt	4	0	0
1 fine Shirt	4	10	0
1 New homespun Coat	3	10	0
1 New Wejcoatl	1	0	0
1 Pair of breechess	1	0	0
1 Pair of Over alls	1	0	0
3 Pair of Stokings	3	0	0
1 Pair of Shoes	0	16	0
	27	6	0

This Day William Clark Came before Me & made Oath that the Above Mentiond. Articles was taken from him by the Tories under the Command of David Fanning

Chapter 1: Bladen County Loose Papers

Sworn to before Me this 6th Day of Novemr. 1782
Saml. Cain

****

Statement

That at Bladen Court February Term 1782 William McRee esquire and my self Qualified as executors of the Last will of Maturin Colvill decd. immediately after which I Took the Charge of the Deceased's Marsh Plantation and part of the Negroes And continued the Overseer imployed by Faithfull Graham on the same Terms Graham had imployed him (said Graham being put in care of Colvills Estate some time before by Col. Thomas Robeson at the Decease of Colvill) Mr. McRee at the same time taking charge of the Deceased's River Plantation and the Other part of the Negroes belonging to said estate And imployed his Nephew William McRee Junior Overseer of said Plantation and Negroes.

That I as Executor of the Deceased Maturin Colvill was Summoned by James Council, John King and John Yates esquires Commissioners of Confiscated property to appear at Bladen August Term 1782 to shew cause why the Estate of the said Maturin Colvill deceased Should not be Confiscated, The first Day of which Term One of the Lawyers retained by me for the Defence of said Estate and my self were assaulted in open Court Dangerously wounded and together with the Other Lawyer (retained as aforesaid) Drove off from thence; After which said Court Proceeded to Confiscate said Colvills Estate I not having an Opertunity by my self Or Lawyer to Offer any Reasons why said Estate should not be Confiscated, Shortly after the Aforesaid James Council Esquire as Commissioner of Confiscated Property took possession of that part of said Estate that was in my possession which has never since been Delivered to me.

That at the August Court aforesaid Sundry Petitions were Prefered and Several Judgments had and Obtained against said Colvills Estate in Consequence of said Confiscation as appears by the records now in my Possession, which proceedings were called up and and still remains before the Honourable the Superior Court.

That at the Bladen November Term following I was re-Admitted Clerk of said Court at which Term Several Petitions were prefered and Judgments Obtained against said Estate And altho I Was then present my Situation was Such that I could not with Safety interfere which is a fact of Great Notoriety; The Same Reasons Opperated to hinder me from forbiding the Sales made in Consequence of the last mentioned Judgments which is also A Matter of Notoriety.

That as a friend to the Heirs of the Deceased Colvill and in hopes that the Confiscation aforesaid would not take effect I have since as much as was consistent with my Safety endevoured to keep together what remained of said Estate.

****

Petition

The Claim of Patk. Travers against Hecto McNeill & others
Petition to the Court
£369..8..2
1782

To the Worshipful The County Court of Pleas & quarter Sessions for Bladen County,

The Petition of Patrick Travers Sheweth, That in the month of March 1781 Hector McNeill, James Bartly, Benjamin Wood, Danl. Patterson, Charles Mulloy, Anguish Mulloy, Solomon Glass, Danl. Mcferson with several others, whose names are yet unknown, did with force of Arms enter the House of Thomas Gadby in Cumberland County and did take & carry away fifty seven thousand five hundred pounds Continental currency, forty two thousand State dollars, twenty five thousand pounds in Loan office certificates, sundry clothing & Papers with a certain large bay horse the property of your Petitioner.

Chapter 1: Bladen County Loose Papers

Your Petitioner therefore humbly prays that the Same may be enquired of pursuant to the Act of assembly in such case made & provided and your Petitioner shall pray &C.

Patrick Travers

***

Petition

To the worshipful the county court of Bladen

The Petition of John Flinn, humbly sheweth

That he has just claim against William White, who has attached himself to the enimies of this State, and your petitioner being a good Citizen, prays proceedings thereon in manner as by act of assembly directed, in such cases made & provided and your petitioner shall pray.

***

Petition

To the Worshipfull Court of Pleas & Quarter Sessions for the County of Bladen Now Setting

The Petition of William Clark Humbly Sheweth that Some time in the Month of August 1781 that Matthew Moor John Sawyer Solomon Glass and Philemon Tarel and Sundry Others Under the Command of David Faning & Samuel Andrew Plundered your Petitioner of Sertain Articles Which will appear By the Anext Invatory and your Petitioner therefore humbly Pray that you will afford him Such Relief as by Act of the general Assembly in such Cases has Provided and your Petitioner as in Duty Bound Shall Pray.

Wm Clark

***

Petition

To the Worshipful the court of Bladen now setting

The Petition of Mary Lyon humbly pray,
    That your worships will take into consideration the deplorable case of your humble petitioner, who is the widow of the late unhappy George Lyon, whose estate is liable to confiscation, which only consists of 640 acres of land 3 indifferent Negroes, one Mare, one Cow & calf & one Bed -- and your petitioner [?] some of the said property now under execution --
    And as your petitioner is a helpless woman with two small Children prays that your worships will pursuant to an Act of Assembly impowering courts for that purpose, decree for your petitioners & Children as you shall in your wisdom think proper -- And your petitioner will ever pray

Mary Lyon

[?] Lightfoot
Atto.

***

Petition

Chapter 1: Bladen County Loose Papers

To the Worshipfull Justices of Bladen now sitting

The petition of Wm. McRee[?] humbley sheweth that about the last of July and the first of August 1781 A certan John Slingsby David Goddin William White cordwander Duncan Morrison Josiah Lewis Junr. Charles Baldwin John Harrison junr. and William Harrison did come to my house as well as to the hous and plantation called Brumpton which plantation my son Wm. McRee decd. had rented with a banditte of toreys about 300 and did with force and arms did take away from sundry articles of provision contrary to law which Articles is hereunto anexed which I hope your worships in your wisdom and according will order me an allowance for and your petitioner as in duty bound shall ever pray

Wm. McRee

the articles taken (Viz)

Article	£	s	d
240 bushells of corn taken and destroyed at 4/6 pr Bushel	54	0	0
the oats of 18 acres at Brumpton at 20 bushell P acre is 368 bushells at 4/ Pr Bushell	73	12	0
25 bushells of oats at my house at 4/ P Bushel	5	0	0
destroy & took away about 4 bushells [?]	1	0	0
25 pounds of butter at 1/6 Pr lb	1	17	6
5 head of Beef cattle at £[?] Pr head	20	0	0
grabeled and destroyd about 8000 potato hills	33	15	0
all the beef bacon flower meal and fowls could be found in my house or on my plantation	[?]8	0	0
Rubd. and destroyed out of two taner bats about 20 sides of lether 10 or 12 sheep skins and about as many calf skins	22	14	0
£	219	16	6

of Mr. Stons property they took of one father bedd and one side of tand lether with sundry other articles

Benj Stone Acct.   3 16 0

***

Damage Assessment

State of No. Carolina }
Bladen County }

We the Subscribers being Calld. by Capt. Peter Robeson to ascertain the Damages which he has Sustaind. by the Insurgents Commanded by David Fanning & Other -- We on our Oaths Do say that the Said Peter Robeson has Sustaind. Damages (by Fire & Otherwise) to the Amount of three Hundred Pounds Specie -- In witness whereof we have hereunto set Our hands this 3 Day August, Anno Dom. 1782

Sworn to before me this 3d Day
of August 1782
Saml. Cain

Saml. Cain
David Lindsay White
Peter Byrns[?]
John Le Compt
Samuel Richardson
M.R. White

***

Memorandum of an Agreement

Chapter 1: Bladen County Loose Papers

Memorandum of an Agreement made, and concluded upon this 25th Day of July in the Year of our Lord 1772 between Saml. Watters of the County of Brunswick and Province of North Carolina of the one part and Elizabeth Hall of the County and province aforesaid of the other part.
Whereas Elizabeth Blenning Died Seised of a considerable Chattle Estate Intestate, and Samuel Watters in Right of his Wife and Elizabeth Hall in Right of her son William Hall are equal Claimants, It is agreed and concluded between the said Samuel and Elizabeth in manner following (That is to say) that an Indian Wench belonging to the Estate of the said Elizabeth Blenning named Hannah shall be and remain with the said Samuel Watters; That Seventy Pounds Proclamation money shall be paid Miss Lucy Hall out of the money Due from the said Samuel Watters to the Estate of the said Elizabeth as a Legacy; and that the Remainder of the money Due from the said Samuel to the said estate shall be equally Divided between the said Samuel Watters and William Hall.
It is Likewise further agreed between the sais Samuel and Elizabeth that a Bond Due from the said Elizabeth to the above mentioned estate now in the possession of the said Samuel shall by him be Delivered to Docter Thos. Hall in Trust for the said William Hall.
It is also further agreed by the parties that the said Elizabeth Hall shall have one half of a Bond Due from Robert Horse Esqr. to the said Elizabeth Blenning, with one half the Interest Due upon the said Bond, and that the said Samuel Watters shall be accountable to the said Elizabeth for one half the money Due upon the said Bond, or Deliver the said Bond to the said Elizabeth Hall.
In Witness whereof the parties have set their Hands and Seals the Day and Year above written

| Test Joshua Bowman | Eliza. Hall | (Seal) |
| Alfred Moore | S. Watters | (Seal) |

****

Petition to the Court

Willm. Kirkpatrick's Petition to the Court
Against Benjn. Wood and Others

To the Worshipful the Magistrates of Bladen Court
The Humble Petition of Wm. Kirkpatrick Humbly Sheweth

That on the 7th Day of March 1781 The Tories or Persons inimical to the American Cause came to my House and after Shooting me & Leaving me for Dead, Rob'd me of the underneath Articles which together with the Costs & expence of my Cure & the Loss of Time has been of Very Great Damage to me. Your Petitioner is Clearly of Opinion that David Godwin & Levi Glas, James Bartley, and Benjamin Wood was the Sole instigation of my Loss and Damage which Your Petitioner can Support with Sufficient Reasons &c

Your Petitioner therefore Prays Redress against the Estates of the Said David Godwin, Levi Glass, James Barkley & Benjamin Wood agreeable to the Act of Assembly in Such Case made and Provided, And Your Petitioner &c

One Suit Broad Cloth Cloaths	30	0	0
One Coat -- Do	5	0	0
1 pair fine Linen Sheets	3	0	0
1 pair Double Rose Blankets	4	0	0
1 Black Silk Apron	3	4	0
Parull[?] Ribbon	2	0	0
2 Bushells Allum Salt	10	0	0
1 Gold Diamond Ring & One Plain ring	40	0	0
8 Silver Tea Spoons	3	0	0
About 2 Cts Solid Silver	10	0	0
1 Pair Silver Sugar Tongs	2	10	0

Chapter 1: Bladen County Loose Papers

1 Pair Gold Sleeve Buttons	2	10	0
1 Pair Silver Knee buckles	1	10	0
1 Pair Plated Spurs	2	0	0
1 Pistol	2	0	0
1 Good Note of hand with Interest for 10 Years £8[?]	12	16	10
1 Do with Interest for £14.10	24	18	0
£6,000 State Currency at 100 for One	60	0	0
The Doctor's Bill	25	0	0
The Board of my Self wife & Negroe Wench for 42 Days in Cross Creek	33	16	0
	£276	10	0
Bladen County }			
5th Augt. 1782 }twp pare of Silver Shoe Buckles	4		
Add for Spurs	1	4	0
	£281	14	

****

Petition to the Court

Petition of Thos. Henderson to Bladen Court
August Sessions 1782

these accounts & a defa[?] take for Doctor James White, to be [?] first and both together, the jury need not leave the Bar

To the worshipful the county court of Pleas and quarter Sessions for the county of Bladen

The petition of Thomas Henderson humbly sheweth,

That the estate of Maturin Colvill & Henry Graham both confiscated to the use of this State, are justly indebted to Your petitioner in the following sum
The estate of Maturin Colvill in the sum of forty three pounds ten Shillings specie and the Estate of Graham in the sum of Eleven pounds three Shillings & two pence specie, for which your petitioner prays an allowance and your petitioner shall ever pray

W. Lightfoot
Alls. for Petr.

****

Petition

To the worshipful the county court of pleas and quarter Sessions, held for Bladen

November Term 1782

The petition of Robert Council humbly sheweth,
That he has a just complaint against Levi Glass who has attached himself to the enemies of this State, and your petitioner prays proceedings thereon in manner as by law directed in such cases, and your petitioner shall pray.

****

Chapter 1: Bladen County Loose Papers

State Of North Carolina
To the worshipful the justices of the county court of Bladen November Session 1782

The humble petition of David Lindsay White and Thomas White Humbly sheweth

That your petitioners are faithful citizens of said State and residents of said County and have a just claim against Levi Glass for the sum of £203.1.7 Specie

Your Petitioners pray the same be inquired pursuant to the Act of the General Assembly in such Cases made and provided and Your Petitioner shall Pray &c
David L. White
Thos. White

****

Petition

To the Worshipfull Court of Pleas & Quarter Sessions for the County of Bladen Now Setting

     The Petition of Jno. Plummer Humbley sheweth that some time in the month of June 1781 that Certain Danl. McPhersion Levy Glass Charles MeLoy Daniel Meloy Danl. Patterson John Megloklin Anguish Brown **[Torn]** **[Torn]** the Command of Duncan Ray and Hector McNeil With Sundry Others Plundered him of Certain Articles Which Will appear by the Annext Inventory and Petitioner therefore Humbley prays that you will afford him such relief as by Act of the General Assembly in such Case has Provided and your Petitioner as in Duty bound Shall pray

                                                                                                 John Plummer

****

Petition

To the Worshipfull the Justices of Bladen County the Petition of William Smith Humbley sheweth that on 29 of August 1781 that Partey of the Tories Commanded by Colo. John Slingsbey Did take to of my Prime oxen and kill them for the use of the said Tories

     Your Petitioner Prays Redress against the said Estate of John Slingsbey, as he can make it appear that he was the sole instragation of my Damage

     Your Petitioner applys to the act of the General Assembly Made and Provided for that Purpose
     Your Pettiner shall Pray &c

To 2 Prime oxen   £20.0

                                                                                                  William Smith Sr.

****

Whereas Sundry Negroes are Advertised for Sale by Richard Bradley (as Attorney for Saml. Rogers late of this Province) by Virtue of a Mortgage from Hezekiah Done to him wch Said Negroes Vzt Casar, Pompey, Cato & Flora wth. her Increase were Sold by said Saml. Rogers to Sd. Hezekiah Done; This is therefore to forewarn any person from purchasing the Said Negroes above Mentioned as they are the property of Mary Shephard left her by the Will of the late John Malsby deceased

Chapter 1: Bladen County Loose Papers

Novr. 30th 1770
Mary Newton
Executrix to the Will of John Malsby

***

Petition

State of North Carolina
To the Worshipful the justices of the County Court of Bladen November Sessions 1782

The Humble Petition of Thomas Locke Humbly sheweth
    That your Petitioner is a faithful Citizen of said State and a resident of said County and hath a Just Claim against Isaiah Powel Michael Ikener and Philemon Tyrell for Trespass
    Your Petitioner prays the same be inquired pursuant to the act of the General Assembly in such cases made and provided and your petitioner shall pray &C

                                                                  Thos Locke

***

Petition

To the Worshipful the county court of pleas and quarter Sessions held for Bladen

November Term 1782

The petition of Joseph White humbly sheweth,
    That Archibald McKay late of Cumberland county is justly indebted to your petitioner as he is able to make appear, and your petitioner humbly conceives the same to be within the express meaning of an Act of the General Assembly in such cases made and provided, and therefore prays proceedings thereon, and your petitioner shall pray as in duty bound.

***

Petition

State of North Carolina

    To the worshipful the justices of the Court of pleas and quarter sessions for Bladen County - November Session 1782.

    The humble petition of James Eglestor

Humbly sheweth
    That your Petitioner is a faithful Citizen of the said State and a resident of said County and that your petitioner hath a just demand against Maturin Colville for Debt who hath forfeited his estate for having attached himself to the enemies of the United States.

    Your petitioner prays the same be inquired pursuant to the act of the General Assembly in such cases made and provided and your petitioner shal pray.
J Speller Atty   J Eglestor

***

Petition

Chapter 1: Bladen County Loose Papers

Olive Cain Petition
1782

To the worshipful the Court of Bladen

The petition of Olive Cain humbly sheweth

That she as representative of William Cain Dec.d & has just claims against Peter Mallett[?], and prays proceedings thereof in manner as by law directed, in such cases made & provided and your petitioner shall pray, as in duty bound

April the 2d. vizt. -- & Destroyd.
Articles taken By the Brittish & Tories from William Cain

330,	Pannets of Fince Burnt	£0	[?]	0
500,	Gallons of Syder Destroyd.	£150	0	0
Between 13 & 15 Bushels of Salt		£28	0	0
500 Bushels of Grain		£100	0	0
1 Still & Worm		£35	0	0
2 Guns		£9	10	0
3 Horses & 2 Saddles		£60	0	0
		£388	10	0

Besides a Number of Other Articles too tedious to Mintion

      This Day Mrs. Olive Cain Came before me & made Oath that the Above Mintiond. Articles was taken & Destroyd. by the Brittish & Tories
Sworn to before me this 6th Day of
Novemr. 1782   Wm. Moore

****

List of Articles Taken

Articles taken By the torys Under the Command of Hector McNeal and Duncan Ray from Zachariah Plummer Viz

1 horse Saddle and bridle	£60	0	0
2 Mairs	£65	0	0
1 New fer hat	£04	0	0
1 Pair of Silver Shew Buckles	£02	0	0
1 Silver Stock Bukle	£01	4[?]	0
1 Pair of Shews	£0	16	0
1 pair of Spirs	£0	16	0
1 great Coat	£06	10	0
Damage for being Wounded	£50	10	0
	£190	16	0

This Day Came before Me Zachariah Plumer & Made Oath that the Above Mentioned Articles ware taken from him by the torys Under the Command of Hector McNeal and Duncan Ray.
Swore to before Me this 6th Day of Novemr. 1782
Saml Cain

****

Chapter 1: Bladen County Loose Papers

Petition

State of North Carolina

To the worshipful the justices of the county court of pleas and quarter sessions for Bladen County November Session 1782

The humble petition of John Odum
Humbly sheweth

    That your petitioner is a faithful citizen of said State and a resident of said County and hath a just claim against the estates of Robert Jones John Thompson William Brown and Matthew Jones for a trespass as will be proved by your petitioner

    Your petitioner prays the same be inquired pursuant to the Act of the General assembly in such cases made and provided And your petitioner shall pray

                                                                 John Odum

****

Petition

To the worshipfull, the county court of Bladen

    The Petition of Richard Smith Esquire
Sheweth,
    That your petitioner hath a just claim against the estates of John Slingbley, Charles Baldwin, John Baldwin & David Godwin for the damage he sustained in losing the enclosed articles.

    Your Petitioner Prays that the same be inquired into by a Jury, Pursuant to the act of General Assembly in such case made and Provided & your Petitioner shall Pray &c
Augt. 1782

****

Petition

The Petition of Colo Brown
to the Court

The worshipful the County Court of Pleas and Quarter Sessions for Bladen County Aug. Term 1782

The humble Petition of Thomas Brown Sheweth

That your Petitioner hath a just Claim Against the Estates of John Baldwin Junr Archibald Taylor Duncan Morrison William White John McKinsey William Maultsby and David Godwin whose estates are forfeited to the State
Your Petitioner prays that the same be inquired pursuant to the act of the General assembly in such cases made and provided and your petitioner shall pray

                                                         Thomas Brown

The Verdict Given in favr. to Colo Brown and the Damages said to be £282--8

Chapter 1: Bladen County Loose Papers

The Negro pomp Valued to £200 and David Godwin not Guilty of taking him the Negroe Quash not to Be paid for   1782

****

Dividing Line Between Bladen & Robeson

To the Worshipfull the County Court of Bladen

    Whereas by an Order or Ordering by the aforesaid Counties of Bladen & Robeson to Appoint William Moore & William Byrd of the part of Bladen and John Hawthorn and Philip Blount of the part of Robeson To run or Adjudge a Temporary line between the Aforesaid Countys of Bladen & Robeson Agreeable to an Act of Assembly &c. And in pursuance of the said Orders & Agreeable to the Said Act have Measured Five Miles Westardly from the Bluff Bridge as the Road Now Stands And then do agree that Those On the Verge of the Said Countys between the Mouth of the Great Swamp & the Road at the point of the said Five Miles End, Resides as follows that is to Say Cader Hawthorn & Richmond Ferrell in the Said County of Bladen And John Cook & Alexander McArthur in the County of Robeson And between the Said Road & Cumberland County Touching by Stewarts Mill On Rockford Creek - Ralph Regan Neil McClpan[?] Hugh Brown John Councill & John Stewart in the Said County of Bladen And Henry Taylor Shadrick Lee James Stevens Henry Mercer & John McFall in the said County of Robeson - Which We & Either of us have hereby Agreed On - The 29th of May 1787

W Moore
William Bird
Philip Blount

****

Mary Singletary's Declaration

Bladen County to wit

Whereas at the next Court after my Husband William Singletarys decease & in open Court relinquished my part in his Will and Claimed my dower Agreeable to Law, which was granted and is on record in Said Court, at which Court James Councill Esquire Qualified as Executor of my said Husbands Will and Obtain'd an order of Court to sell as much of the perishable part of his estate as would pay his just debts; in consequence of which order Mr. Council called a Vendue and sold a number of cattle and horses for which sales Mr. Council has Never yet settled with the said Court so as to strike a ballance between the debts due and the said sales which was his indispensible duty as executor in return for said order Granted, in order, that if it should appear to the said Court that there was Just debts still unpaid the Court might order a further sale, Notwithstanding all which Irregularities he presuming upon his old order of Court Never yet fairly settld. has put the above Advertisement.

    I therefore forbid the said executor to sell as above advertised and also every person whatsoever from purchasing any part of said estate untill the said executor shall settle as above with said Court and obtain a further order.

Bladen 16th March 1788   Mary Singletary

****

Division of Richard Singletary's Land

Chapter 1: Bladen County Loose Papers

Robert Rayford   James Moorehead C.C.

This plat Represents the Survey of Land Claimed by the Sons of Richd. Singletary   Benjamin and Richd. Singletary William Singletary's part Deceased agreeable to an Order at Cort by the Directions of the jurers Aponted for the same beatween Mary his wife and Council his Son Surveyed agreeably to the [?] in Sd. plot Pr. Isaac Jones
This [?] November 1788

Robt. Raiford
John McKay
Richd. Callum

[Transcriber's note: This tract of land was divided between Richd. Singletary, Benjamin Singletary, Council Singletary, and Mary Singletary, wife of William Singletary deceased.]

****

Petition

To the worshipful the Court of the County of Bladen

The petition of Cullen Connelly humbly sheweth

That he had a grant for fifty acres of land in said County No. 507 dated 28th February 1789 but that in the surveyor's Certificate annex'd to the said grant there exists a mistake which on examination goes near to rob him of the whole benefit of his Entry which Mistake lies in the distance from the 2d Corner and in the Course from the Third. The alledged Course & Distance from the second Corner South ten degrees east Sixty Chains, thence No. forty degrees East Eight chains & fifty links, thence No. 70 Deg West 50 Chains to the beginning. Whereas it will be found that So. 10 Deg East from the second corner Eight Chains, thence So. Eighty degrees west fifty chains thence So. Sixty six Degrees East, ten Chains thence North 80 Deg East thirty Chains thence No. forty Degrees East 17 Chains to the beginning will correspond with the Survey & marked lines[?]   While the other Courses run alltogether excepting about five acres or six at most on your Petitioners old patent [?] and are not supported by one marked tree or other boundary other than in the first line which is conformable to what was equally run & is now claimed

    Your petitioner therefore prays your Worships to take his Cause into Consideration & grant him such relief as is allowed by the act or acts of the general assembly in such case made & provided & your petitioner as in duty bound shall ever pray &c

Cullen Connelly

****

Bond for Departure

State of North Carolina} }
Bladen County   }

    Know all men by these presents That we Ignatious Flowers, John Yates esquire and Benjamin Sellers are held and firmly bound unto Richard Caswell Esqr. and his successors in the sum of five hundred pounds Proc. money for the true payment whereof we bind Our selves our Heirs and assigns Sealed with our Seals and Dated this 5th Day of November 1777 and in the Second Year of Our Independence.

Chapter 1: Bladen County Loose Papers

The Condition of the above Obligation is such that if the above bound Ignatious Flowers do depart this State in Sixty days from the date hereof Agreeable to an Act of Assembly made and provided for People Refusing to take the Oath of Alegiance to this State that then the above Obligation to be Void and of non effect Otherwise to remain in full force and virtue.

Signed Sealed and	Ignatious Flowers	(Seal)
delivered in Open Court	John Yates	(Seal)
Test John White	Benjn. Sellers	(Seal)

****

Bond for Departure

State of No Carolina }
Bladen County }

Know all men by these presents that we Daniel Mcfhassion Hugh Brown and Malcolm McFatter all of Sd. County are held and firmly bound unto Richard Caswell Esqr Governor and his Successors in the sum of Five Hundred pounds proclamation Money for the True payment where of we bind our Selves our Heirs Executors Administrators and Assigns Jointly and Severally firmly by these presents Seald with our Seals and Dated this 5th Day of November 1777 & in the Second Year of our Independence.

The Condition of the above obligation is Such that if the above bounden Daniel Mcphersion do Depart this State in Sixty Days from the Date hereof agreeable to an Act of assembly made and provided for People Refusing to take the Oath of Allegiance to this State - That then the above Obligation to be Void and of None Effect otherwise to Remain in full force and Virtue.

Signed Sealed and Delivered	Daniel McPherson	(Seal)
in the presence of us	Hugh Brown	(Seal)
in Open Court	Malcolm McFatter	(Seal)
David Lindsay White		
John White Senr.		

****

Land Warrant

Elizabeth Cade came into Court and made it appear to the Satisfaction of Said Court that John Cade had Entered 200 acres of Land on the South Side of Mitchell Swamp and Joining the province line as appears by the location dated February the 3d. 1779

The Warrant being lost or mislaid that no Grant issue for want of Said Warrant -- For remedy Whereof-- Ordered that the Clerk of the County Court of Bladen Issue a Warrant for Said Land agreeable to the location on the Entry Takers Books as the Law directs

No 962   February the 3d 1779

200 Acres   }
John Cade Esqr } on the So. Side of Mitchell Swamp & Joining the Province line

****

Bond for Departure

Chapter 1: Bladen County Loose Papers

State of North Carolina }
Bladen County }

    Know all men by these Presents that we William McDonald, Archibald Campbell and Iver McCollom all of said County are held and firmly bound unto Richard Caswell Esqr. Governour and his Successors in the sum of Five hundred Pounds Proc. money for the true payment where of we Jointly and Severally bind our Selves our Heirs and assigns Sealed with our Seals and dated this 5th Day of November 1777 and in the Second Year of Our Independence

    The Condition of the above Obligation is Such that if the above bound William McDonald do depart this State in Sixty days from the Date hereof agreeable to an Act of assembly made and provided for People refusing to take the Oath of Allegiance to this State That then the above Obligation to be Void and of non effect Otherwise to remain in full force and Virtue.

Signed Sealed and }	William McDonald	(Seal)
delivered in open Court }	Archd. Campbell	(Seal)
Test John White	his	
	Iver X McCollum	(Seal)
	mark	

****

Appearance Bond

State of No. Carolina }
Bladen County }

    Know all men by these presents that we William Stevens, George Knowles and James Campbell all of the County and State aforesaid are all held and firmly bound unto Elisha Morse his certain Attorney, his Heirs, Executors &c for the true payment whereof, we and each of us hereby bind ourselves, our heirs, Executors and Assigns, Jointly and severally, firmly by these presents, Sealed with our Seals and dated this 5th day of June 1799

    The Condition of the above Obligation is such that if the above bounden William Stevens shall well and truly make his personal appearance before the Justices of the County Court of Bladen at the Court house in Eliza. Town to be held on the first Monday in September next, and then and there to stand and abide the Judgment of the said Court, and not to depart the same without leave, to Answer Joseph Wingate in a plea of trespass, which he is there charg'd with then this Obligation to be Void and of none effect, otherwise to be and remain in full force power and Virtue

Sign'd Seal'd & delivered }
in presence of }
J. Lewis

William Stevens	(Seal)
Geo: Knowle	(Seal)
James Campbell	(Seal)

****

Bond

State of No. Carolina
Bladen County
We Jesse Jones & Jared Irwin promise and bind our selves our heirs &c to pay Jas. Pender Clerk of the County Court of Bladen in the sum of fifty pounds to be paid upon Condition that the above Jesse Jones shall prosecute his suit in said Court against William Ellis with effect or in case he fail therein pay all

Chapter 1: Bladen County Loose Papers

such Cost and Damages as may be therein awarded against him by the said County court   Witness our hands and seal this 4th of April 1799
J. Ellis

         his
      Jesse H Jones (Seal)
        mark
      Jared Irwin (Seal)

****

Petition

To the Worshipfull Justices of Bladen County Now Sitting

The Petition of Charity Stevens Humbley Sheweth That about 5th Day of April 1781 A certain Stephen Godwin Alexander Godwin William Strickland Junr. Mark Ronalds Saml. Andress Moses Coleman Son of Jno. Coleman and Jno. Harrison With Others Came to the house of the Late Barnabas Stevens deceas'd and Did with force and arms Burn Rob and take Away from Me Sundry Articles Contrary to Law Which Articles is hereto Annext Which I hope your worships in your Wisdoms and According to Law Will Order an Allowance and your Petitioner in Duty bound Shall Ever Pray.

****

Petition

The Petition of Thos.
Hains to the Court
1781

To the Worshipfull the Justices of Bladen County The Humble Petition of Thos. Haynes.
  Humbly Sheweth

That on the 30 Day of August 1781 there was a great Number of the People Call'd Tories, had taken possession of this Town and my House Field and garden, greatly to the Damage of Your Petitioner.

  Your Petitioner is well informed that David Godwing and Charles Baldwin was the sole instragation of my Damages which your Petitioner Can support with several reasons &c

  Your Pettitioner therefore Prays Redress against the Estate of the said David Goding & Charles Baldwin agreable to the act of the general assembly in such Case Made and Provided

And your Petitioner shall Pray &c

                   Thos. Haynes

Augt. 30, 1781

To 1 field of Corn and Peas 5 acres grounds	£10
To 1 Petato Patch and Quantity of Cotten	£7
To Cutting & Distroying of Apple Trees	£2
To Plundering Destroying of garden	£10
To 1 large Fish Sain Destroyed	
To Quantity of Lead taken from the [?]	£10
To Ransacking of my House and Damage Done	£39

Chapter 1: Bladen County Loose Papers

The within Acct. Dated
and Verdict say he shall have £39

****

Will of Duncan Munro

Copy of Duncan Monro's Will

In the Name of God Amen

    I Duncan Monro of Bladen County North Carolina & Brown Marsh being Very Sick and weak in Body but of Sound Mind and Memory do make and Ordain this my Last Will and Testament Viz

    First I Give and Bequeath to my dearly beloved Wife the third part of my Estate and One Cow Over and Above her part to be raised and levied out of my estate together with my debts.

    Also I give to my well beloved son Angus Monro two parts of my Estate after Reduction of the above Cow of the above Mentioned Estate; And I do hereby Utterly disallow revoke and disanull all and every Other former Testament Wills Legacies Bequests and Excsutors by me made Ratifying and Confirming this and No Other to be my Last will and Testament in Witness whereby I have hereunto Set my hand and Seal this first day of december in the Year of Our lord One thousand Seven hundred and Seventy Seven.

Signed   Duncan Monro   (Seal)

Signed Sealed published pronounced }
published & Delivered by the said }
Duncan Monro as his last will & }
Testament in the presence of us }
who in his presence & in the presence }
of Each Other have hereto set our names }

                                            a Copy P

Donald McCollum Witness }   John White
Neil Curry Witness }

Inventory of the Estate of Duncan Monro Del. Augt. 1778
5 Cows, 3 Yearlings, Money £42.16, 1 Bed & Bedstead, 2 Blankets, 1 Sheet, 1 Bolster, 1 Setant, 2 Coats mostly worn, 2 Jackets one Mounted with Silver Buttons, 1 pr. **[Faded]**, 1 Hat, 1 pair plated Buckles, 1 Hide Tanned Leather, **[Faded]** making of one pair Shoes of do., 2 Broad Axes, 1 Club do., 1 F[?], 1 Coulter, 2 Hoes, 3 planes, 3 Chizels, 1 Gaudge, 1 Adze, 1 Hammer, 2 Chests, 1 Barrell, 1 Buck, 7 Spoons, 1 pothook, 1 flesh fork, 1 Skillet, 1 Brass Candlestick, 1 Chest Lock, 1 Snuff box, 3 Quart Bottles, 1 Beem[?], 1 looking Glass, 1 Silver Shirt Buckle, 1 Sadle & Bridle, 1 Belt, 1 Tub, 2 pigens, 2 Lime [?], 1 Linen Wheel, 1 Bag.

Copy P John White CC

****

Petition

Petition to sale
ferriages &c

[Transcriber's Note: The below excerpt is located on the first page of the document.]
Thy works of Glory mighty Lord that sale the **[Faded]**
Metal Spark of heavenly flame

Chapter 1: Bladen County Loose Papers

Quit O quit this mortal frame
Fumbling, hoping, lingring, flying
O the pain the bless of dying
Cease fond nature cease the strife
let me languish unto life
Hark they whisper
Angels say sister spirit wave away
The world recedes it disappears
Hea[?] [?] on my eyes my ears
With [...?...] ceraphim sing
Lend lend your wings I mount I fly

> To the Worshipful Court of Bladen County
> The Petition of Sundry

the Inhabitants of said County Humbly Sheweth

    That your petitioners, on occurrent business frequently have to cross Waddles Ferry and also others from local situation to attend Public business in Elizabeth Town for which (with all original propriators) they have stipulated by the year on terms satisfactory to themselves and as they conceved fully adequate to the trouble of the Propriator. The present Propriator will not stipulate with your petitioners but on terms the most exorbitant and Oppressive, and such as they cannot think of Complying with-- they are therefore constrained to pay the accustomed rate or ferriage (Eight pence for man and horse) which they conceive rather extravagant, and by which they and all passengers generally sustain loss -- as there is no Current money of that sum nor any by which that change can be made and the ferryman is seldom disposed to sustain loss upon his part. Your petitioners therefore humbly pray that your Worships will take their particular hard case into your sincere consideration and grant them relief, by redeeming the present rated ferrage of eight pence for man and horse to six pence which will be greatly to the relief of them; and other passengers in general
And your Petitioners as in duty Bound Will ever Pray
Novr. 4th 1793

Hugh Murphy	William Saltar	Richd. Saltar
Bailey Sutton	Ambross Wilson	James Campbell
Robert MacMillan	Jno. McKay	Donald Callum
James Cromarte	J. Ellis	Th[?] Thomas
John Robertson	John Smith	V [?] White
Wm. Cromartie	Josiah Sikes	John Cowan
John Sutton	Daniel Melvin	John Campbell
John Sillars	Benja. Fitzrandolph Senr.	
John McMillan	Benjamin Singletary	
William Cromartie	Jas. Singletary	
John McEacharn	Edward Jones	
Danl. McI[?]	Wm Chishire	
Even Currie	Jonathan Th[?]	
Wm Led	Jos. Singletary	
Eleaser Russ	Benja. Fitzrandolph Junr.	
William Mac Ourrich	Philip Hill	
Joseph Russ	Ithamar Singletary	
Alexr. Strahan	Musgrove Jones	
James Hendry	Thomas Russ	
Charles Hendry	Charles Roberson	
Francis Thomas	Alexander Hendry	

Chapter 1: Bladen County Loose Papers

George Thomas	Dugal Blue	
David Loyd	Duncan McCoulsky	
John Taylor	Benjamin Lock	Charles McAlestar
Philemon Bryan	William Bryan	James Evers
John Singletary	Jos. Smith	

****

Petition

To the Worshipfull Court of Pleas & Quarter Sessions for the County of Bladen Now Siting

    The Petition of Zachariah Plummer Humbly Sheweth that Some time in the Month of June 1781 that Daniel Mcfarshen Levy Glass Daniel Paterson Charles Meloy Daniel Meloy John Meglohlen Anguish Brown and Neal Smith with others under the Command of Hector McNeal & Duncan Ray Wounded and took Your Petitioner Prisoner & Plundered him of Certain Articles which will Appear by the Anext Inventory and your petitioner therefore Humbly Pray that you will Afford him such Relief as by Act of the General Assembly in Such Cases has Provided and your Petitioner as in Duty Bound shall Pray

                                                                    Zachariah Plumer

****

Petition

To the Worshipful The County Court of Bladen

The Petition of Patrick Travers Sheweth
    That Thomas Trul late of Annson County is Justly Indebted to your Petitioner the sum of Sixty three pounds, and whereas the said Thos. Trull has attached himself to the enemies of this Country your Petitioner prays for such redress as by act of Assembly he is intituled to

                                                                      P. Travers

****

The State of North Carolina

To the County of [Blank]   in the Commonwealth of Virginia

    Whereas Francis Lucas of Bladen County in the State of North Carolina Planter has produced a Deed of Conveyance made to him from William Garrat and Mary his Wife John Marshall and Sarah his wife William Simpson and Elinor his wife William Powell and Tillah his wife Richard Simpson and Ann his wife Of a Certain Tract or Parcel of Land lying and being in the County of Bladen in the State of North Carolina and procured [Torn] to be proved in [Torn] of the said County of Bladen, And it being Represented to the Said Court that the Said Mary [Torn] Sarah Marshall Elinor Simpson Tillah Powell and Ann Simpson are inhabitants of the Common wealth of Virginia and cannot Travel to the Court of the Said County of Bladen to be privily examined as to their free consent in executing the said Conveyance.
    Know Ye that we in Confidence of Your prudence an fidelity have Appointed You the Said **[Blank]** and by these presents do give unto you the said **[Blank]** or any two of You full power and Authority to take the private Examination of the said Mary Garret Sarah Marshall Elinor Simpson Tillah Powell and Ann Simpson Concerning their free Consent in their executing the said Conveyance

Chapter 1: Bladen County Loose Papers

And therefore we command You the said **[Blank]** or any two of You that at such Certain day and place as You shall think fit You Go to the said Mary Garret &C if they cannot conveniently come to you and privily and apart from their Respective Husbands examine them the Said Mary Garret &C whether they executed the said Conveyance freely and of their Own Accord without force or compulsion of their Said respective Husbands; And the examination being distinctly wrote on the said deed or on some paper Annexed thereto and when you have so taken the said Examination You are to send the same closed up under the Seals of You or any two of You together with this writ unto the Court of the said County of Bladen on the first Monday in February Next Ensuing Witness **[Torn]** Clerk of the said Court of Bladen County at Elizabeth Town the first day of November in the Year of Our Lord 1779 and in the fourth Year of American Independence.

****

Bond for Departure

Know all men by these Presents that we John Hanna, William Macteer, William McRee, William McNeil & John Slingsby are held & firmly bound to Richard Caswell Esqr. Governor of this State or his Sucessors in the sum of One Thousand Pounds Current Money of said State to be Paid to the said Richard Caswell or his Sucessors.

The Condition of the above Bond is such, that if the Above Nam'd John Hanna & William Macteer, departs the State of North Carolina, or the United States of America in Sixty days from this date or does their outmost endeavours to that Purpose, then and in that Case the above Bond Shall be Void, otherwise to be in full force.

State of North Carolina }	John Hanna (Seal)
Bladen County the 7th of }	William Macteer (Seal)
August 1777 }	Wm. McRee (Seal)
Test	Wm. McNeil (Seal)
John White C.C.	John Slingsby (Seal)

****

Deed of Gift

John Smith Deed of Gift
to Samuel Smith
A Copy
for T C Smith

To all christian people to whome these presents shall come I John Smith of Bladen County and province of North Carolina do send greeting Know ye that I the said John Smith for and in consideration of the love and good will & affection I have and do bear to my well beloved son Samuel Smith of the County and provence aforesaid have given granted Demised and bequeath to my said Son Samuel two pieces of land Both Containing Six hundred and forty acres be the same more or less lying and being in the County of Bladen and province aforesaid on the No. Et. Side of the No. West branch of Cape Fear River Beginning at a Birch on the river So. 60 Degs E 456 poles to a pine thence No. 30 degs W. 116 poles to a pine thence So. 60 degs 456 poles to a red oak on the river then the various Courses of the river to the first Station, the other piece beginning at the upper line at a red oak on the river thence No. 60 degs E. 456 poles to a pine thence No. 30 Degs W. 116 poles to a pine thence So. 60 Degs W. 456 poles to a red oak on the river thence the various Courses of the river to the first Station with the buildings Improvements and apputenances there unto belonging   To have and To hold to him my Son Samuel Smith his heirs & assigns forever Only reserving to my self any part or so much of the said pieces of land Timber and

Chapter 1: Bladen County Loose Papers

Building during my natural life as I shall think proper to Make use of   In Witness whereof I hereunto Set my hand and Seal this 22 day of July and in the year of Our Lord One Thousand Seven hundred and Seventy Seven

Signed Sealed & delivered in the presence of   John Smith   (Seal)
Wm. McRee Jr
John Bloeker

        Bladen November Term 1777   This deed was acknowledged in open Court and ordered to be registered   John White CC

I do Certify the above to be a true Copy from the registers Office of Bladen County
D Lewis regr.

****

Road Petition

Petition for Road leading
to fair Bluff
Septr Term 1749

To the Worshipful Court of the County of Bladen   We your petitioners humbly beg leave to represent to your Worships the inconvenience we lay under for want of a Road leading from Fair Bluff up the North Side of Gap way [**Torn**] to join the new Road lately opened in the County of Brunswick to the line & to beg relieve   We therefore beg of your Worships to Grant us an Order for said Road to be laid of by jury & your petitioners as in duty bound will ever pray.

T.N. Gautier	Clo[?] S Carright
Benj Lewis	John Mcfashion
Abraham Jernigan	Richard Carright
Berryman Watts	Martain Hanchey
Theophilus Coleman	Solomon Cartright
John Simmons	Thomas Simmonds
Jesse Simmons	Samuel Williams
Demcy Simmons	Lige nebe[?]
Jacob Crowson	Simmon Smith
Joseph Sols	
Benjamin Sols	
Benedict Williams	
Tobe Galano	
Joseph Nobles	
Joshua Williams	
John Slaughter	
Samuel Lewis	
Samuel Holliman	
Nicholas Worley	
James Sineth	
John Edwards[?]	
Joseph Caright	

Jury to lay out the within mentioned Rhode
Theophilus Coleman
Ni. Worley

Chapter 1: Bladen County Loose Papers

Thomas S. Gautier
John Coleman
Moses Tyler
Berryman Watts
Benj. Lewis
Thomas Simmons
John Simmons
Benj. Soules
Philon Strickland
Joshua Williams
Jacob Crowson
Abraham Gernagan
Joseph **[Faded]**

****

Bond

State of North Carolina }
Bladen County }

  Know all Men by these Presents that we Saml. Baker Jno. Ellis esqr Jno. McKay Robert Harvey Benj Lock Overton Daniel Patrick Kelly and Snowden Singletary are held and firmly bound unto the high Sheriff or Coroner of the County and State aforesaid in the Sum of two Hundred Pounds N. Carolina Currency of sd State to be paid to the Shff or Coroner aforesaid or their Successors in office which payment well and truly to be done We bind Ourselves Our heirs Exrs. and Admrs. Jointly and Severally firmly by these Presents Seald With Our Seals and dated this 18th of March 1797.

  The Condition of the above Obligation is Such that Whereas the above bound Samuel Baker has been Committed to Goal for Debt: at the Instance of the Admrs. of John Harvey Decd. and from thence Admitted to bounds Now if the sd Baker shall and do keep within the Bounds laid of by the Court of sd County then this Obligation to be Void otherwise to remain in full force and Virtue.

Saml. Baker	(Seal)
J. Ellis	(Seal)
Jno. McKay	(Seal)
Robt. Harvey	(Seal)
Benj. Lock	(Seal)
O. Daniel	(Seal)
P. Kelly	(Seal)
S. Singletary	(Seal)

****

Petition

To the Worshipful **[Faded]** of Bladen County **[Torn]**

  The humble Petition of John Wilson Senr. humbly sheweth that whereas your Petitioner is now in An Advanced time of life (viz) Seventy seven years of Age, and Not above two years since he had the Misfortune of having a Tree fall on him, by which Accident he had his Skull fractured, and at Certain times is rendred Delirious by that hurt, to the great Damage of him with respect to his supporting himself and Family, having no Other dependance for Support but what he is oblidged to Labour for, and hoping

Chapter 1: Bladen County Loose Papers

that your Worships will take the same into your Consideration and Cause him to be Exempted from paying any kind of Publick Taxes, and your Petitioner as in Duty bound shall ever Pray

his
John X Wilson
mark

Witness
James Bailey

This day came before me John Wilson Senr. who made Oath on the Holy Evangelist that he is upwards of Seventy Seven Years of Age this 2d day of Febuary Anno Domini 1773

****

Statement

On the Night of Tuesday the 12th of December 1820 I was in Mr. James Cook's House and called for some Brandy, which James Cook brought and set on the table; Then James Cook and myself drank with each other - He then pointed to a chair for me to set in and taking another for himself we both set down before the fire tolerable close to each other -- Where after a short time I asked him -- If he did not tell Mr. Enoch Daniel that I whipt John Daniel (Enoch's Son) wrongfully for James Benson's Lies -- As Enoch Daniel told me a few Days before then that he did -- James Cook said then that he never told Enoch Daniel no such thing -- I then told James Cook that there must be a Lie depending between himself and Enoch Daniel ---- He then (without any further Notice) got up and with his fist struck me over the left Eye with such force as sent me and the Chair that I sat in along the Floor --When I got up James Cook and his Wife and Mr. John Edwards all of them appeared not to be satisfied until I should be further Beatten -- And had not Stephen Cook interfered I know not what the Consequences might have been before they would have been satisfied -- I was so frightened in Consequence of what was going on between James Cook and his Wife and John Edwards after I got up that I scarcely knew what I was doing for I never met with such treatment before in my life -- I was cut over the left Eye and also on the outside of it and the whole side of my head ached and pained me very much for six or seven Days afterwards --

A.G. Campbell

****

Deed of Gift

State of North Carolina }
Bladen County }

To all Christian people to whom these presents shall come I Benjamin Fitzrandolph send Greeting in the name of our lord God Everlasting

Know ye that I Benjamin Fitzrandolph of the County and state aforesaid for and in consideration of the love good will and consideration and affection Which I have and do bear toward my son in law Jamy McRee the three Negroes Jamy Bess and Peg, to the said Jamy Mcree the said negroes Jamy Bess and Peg, to his heirs Executors administrators and assins forever without any manner of consideration as I the said Benjamin Fitzrandolph have absolutely and of my own accord and put in further testimony in Witness hereunto I have set my hand and seal this twenty third of March one thousand Eight hundred and fifteen

Signed Sealed and delivered   Benjamn. Fitzrandolph   (Seal)
  his
Mark M Phillips

Chapter 1: Bladen County Loose Papers

    mark
Robt. Baker

****

Petition

Petition from Sundry People to Court to Counteract a petition for working on the Waccamaw Lake.

Septr. Term 1802

To the worshipfull the Justices of Bladen County

Be it known to You, That we Your petitioners consider ourselves in Danger of being Compelled to a Worke incompetent to our circumstances, In consequence of a Petition now in hand that will be presented to You At the Insuing Court, for the purpose of Opening And making the Waccamaw Stream Navigable for Boats And Rafts, which will only be Advantagious to a few Citizens having Lands Joining Thereunto

We are already compelled to worke the Public Roads which we consider our Duty, Should we also be compelled to Worke on Said River which will not be profitable to us or the Public, we should consider ourselves Imposed on, We therefore pray that Your Worships take us into consideration, And if their Petition be granted that it should not Extend so as to compell us to worke on Said River, Is the Desire of Your Humble petitioners Which they are in Duty bound Doth ever pray for

Thomas Brantly	James Freeman	Edward Byar
Henry Jones	Peter P[?]	Simon Jones
William Stevens	James Ellis	John Simpson
Solomon Simpson	Jonathan Bryan	John Richeson
		Thomas Richeson
T Arthur Smith		William Penny
John Redgister		Zakariah Murrell
Benja. Sasser		Samuel Murrel
Demsey Reynolds		William Lewis
Brittain Hargrove		Hanson Lewes
Bennet Bryan		Henry [?] Stevens
Jacob Simpson		Joseph Hobbs
Joseph Baldwin		James Right
George Stubbs		James Mim
Tire McShaw		[?] Ray
Surrel Simpson		Frederic Sasser
Jno. Clark		Jas Sasser
John Baldwand		Drure haddock
John Baldwin		Robt Newcombe
Richard Stubbs		Richd. Reynolds
John Dimery		Moses Richeson
John Tokes		John Chang
Kinchen Pritchet		Jas. Redgister
David Clark		Jonathan Pierce
James Clarke		James Smith
Elisha Jay		John Cambeskon
Richard Runalds		Samuel Smith
Shadrach Daniel		Elexander Bird
Henry Parker		Jonn Wright

Chapter 1: Bladen County Loose Papers

Josiah Jones
Charles Edwards

Job Bacon
David Counsel
Samuel Wells
Henry Smith
Newit Smith
John **[Faded]**
[Faded] Wright
Marten **[Faded]**
Shaderick Jacobs
John Chavous
James Jacobs
Jesse [?] Bridges
Joseph Marshingal
William Wilkinson
John Parker
Benjamin Smith
Samuel Jacobs
Nathen Thomas

Henry haddock
Josiah Wright
[Faded]
Jese Smith
Thomas Chancey
[?] marten
Moses Pittman
Samuel Swindall
Abram Freeman
Henry Swindall
Samuel **[Faded]**
Isaac Hobbs
Robert Beasly
Daniel Shaw Junr.
Esau high
Lewis Goff
Aaron Parker
William Chavers
Daniel Patrick

CHAPTER 2

BLADEN COUNTY TAX LISTS OF 1775

BLADEN COUNTY TAX LIST OF 1775

A Just And True List of The Masters and Mistresses of Every Family & Overseer of Every Plantation within my District June ye 29th 1775

There are no Headings in this list.

Thos. Amis
Joshua Stevens
Jacob Hanchy
John Butler
Luke Barefield
William Boyit
Gabriel Parker
Michael Whitman
Dempsey Dawson
William Strickland
Moses Coleman
Coleman Nickols
John Yates
Nehemiah Johnston
John Rogers
Edward Wilson
John Branton
Ignatious Flowers
Sirthy Hays

Summon'd to give in their List of Taxables Before Mr. John Turner, Ten Days Before Next Court By Me Jno. Coleman

Summon'd in Henry Boswell's District By me Jno Coleman
Abraham King
Joseph Noble
James Wilson
David Clark
Simon Bright
William Boyces
David Godwin

****

A List of Taxables in Bladen County for the Year 1775

Headings for this list include: Whites, Black Males, Black Females, Boys, & Total

John Adair	
Whites	1
Total	1
Samuel Andrews	
Whites	3
Total	3

Samuel Andrews, Constable

Jacob Alford	
Whites	1
Black Females	1
Total	2
Thomas Amis	
Whites	3
Black Males	8
Black Females	2
Total	13
John Atkins	
Whites	1
Total	1
William Atkinson	
Whites	1
Total	1
Benjamin Arington	
Whites	1
Black Males	1
Black Females	1
Total	3
Stephen Anders	
Whites	2
Black Males	4
Black Females	1
Total	7

Chapter 2: Bladen County Tax Lists of 1775

Joseph Anders
Whites 1
Total 1

John Anders Senr.
Whites 3
Black Males 4
Black Females 1
Boys 1
Total 9

John Anders
Whites 1
Total 1

Willm. Anders
Whites 1
Total 1

Thomas Atkins
Whites 1
Total 1

Thomas Ard
Whites 2
Black Males 1
Black Females 1
Total 4

James Ard
Whites 1
Black Males 1
Total 2

Reuben Ard
Whites 1
Black Males 1
Total 2

Simon Burney
Whites 1
Total 1

Archibald Bradley
Whites 1
Total 1

Dugald Blue
White 1
Total 1

George Brown Esqr
Whites 2
Black Males 1
Black Females 2
Boys 1

[Next nine names torn out]

Joshua Bowman
Whites 1
Total 1

Robert Baker
Whites 1
Black Males 1
[Rest of entry torn]

John Butler
Whites 1
[Rest of entry torn]

John Branton
Whites 3
[Rest of entry torn]

William Brown
Whites 1
[Rest of entry torn]

Simon Bright
Whites 1
[Rest of entry torn]

[Name torn from document]

Henry Boyswell, Constable

Nathaniel Baldwin
Whites 1
Total 1

James Baldwin
Whites 1
Black Males 2
Black Females 1
Total 4

Charles Baldwin
Whites 1
Black Males 1
Black Females 2
Total 4

Willm. Burney Senr.

Chapter 2: Bladen County Tax Lists of 1775

Whites	1
Black Males	2
Black Females	2
Total	5

John Baldwin Senr.
Whites	2
Black Males	4
Black Females	3
Total	9

Morria Beven
Whites	2
Total	2

William Barefoot
Whites	1
Total	1

William Burney Junr.
Whites	1
Black Males	1
[Rest of entry torn]	

Joseph Baldwin
Whites	1
Total	1

[Half of the next page is missing, & household numbers are missing and torn]

Headings for this list include: Whites, Black Males, Black Females, Under 16, Over 60, & in All.

Tho. Walters & Jonah Lewis
John Walters
Saml. Branton
Saml. Branton Jr.
Jacob Johnson
[?] Parker
Joshua Stevens & Oliver Stephens
John Yeats
Coleman Nichols
William Stricklin, Philip Stricklin & William Stricklin Junr.
William Johnson
David Marlow
John Johnson Senr. & Simon his son
Edward Wall & his son Richard
Aaron Tomlinson

Thomas Hardiwick and his Two sons Allan and Linville
Thomas Robison
John Johnson Junr.
Israel Thomlinson
Henry Bossell, Constable
Duncan Morrison
John Wingate
Nathaniel Baldwin
Thomas Johnson
John Chicken
Solomon Dyson
Thomas Hardiwick Junr.
Daniel Flinn
James Money, his Two Brothers & Benjamin & John
David Godwin & Eleazr Godwin
Amelia Morley, Alexr: Woodside
John Eless and his Sons Willm and James
John Cohone, Will Cohone
[Torn] Green
[Torn] Carver
[Torn]
[Torn] Baldwin
Jas Green
John Ellis Junr.
Hill Green
Charles Baldwin
Will Starkey
Frederick Dores, John Dores
Will Burney Senr.
John Baldwin, Will Baldwin

[The next page is badly torn on the left side.]

Headings for this list include: Whites, Black Males, Black Females, Under 16, Over 60, & In All

[Torn] Claraday & Jos. Smith
Whites	2
Black Males	3
Black Females	3
In All	8

[Torn] Thos. Jones
Whites	2
In All	2

[Next three names are torn & missing]

[Torn] Constable John Tolor
Whites	2

Chapter 2: Bladen County Tax Lists of 1775

Black Males	1
Black Females	1
In All	4

[Name torn & missing]

[Torn] H. Lewis Junr.
Whites	2
Black Males	1
Black Females	2
In All	5

[Torn]am Russel
Whites	2
Black Males	6
Black Females	5
In All	13

[Name torn & missing]

[Torn] Smith
Whites	1
Black Females	1
In All	2

[Torn]hson Richd., Laml. son
Whites	2
Black Females	1
In All	3

[Next six names torn & missing]

[Torn] and his son Steven
Whites	2
Black Females	6
Under 16	2
In All	10

[Name torn & missing]

[Torn] his son John[?] Junr.
Whites	2
In All	2

[Next four names torn & missing]

[Torn]ed Richard Runals
Whites	2
In All	2

[Name torn & missing]
[Torn] Willm. Sanders
Whites	2
Black Females	2
In All	4

[Name torn & missing]

[Torn] Zachriah Chancey
Whites	2
In All	2

[Torn]enr. & John Powell Junr.
Whites	2
Black Males	3
Black Females	1
In All	6

[Torn] Pavey and Two Sons & wife
Black Males	4
In All	4

[Indicates Free Persons of Color]

[Torn]ham Freeman
Black Males	3
In All	3

[Indicates Free Persons of Color]

[Torn] Webb
Black Males	3
In All	3

[Indicates Free Persons of Color]

Willm. Freeman
Black Males	2
In All	2

[Indicates Free Persons of Color]

John Blankes
Black Males	1
In All	1

[Indicates Free Person of Color]

[Right side of next page torn & missing]

Barnabas Stevens and sons Willm. Stevens and James Sutton
John Baldwin
Absalom Powell
Thos. Dawson
Tax List of Taxables Took by me for the Year 1775 Jn. Turner

****
BLADEN COUNTY TAX LIST OF 1775

Chapter 2: Bladen County Tax Lists of 1775

A List of the Taxables Taken by Thos. Brown from the County Line to Whites Creek for the year 1775

Headings in this List include: Whites, Black Males, Black Females, Boys, & Total

Whites: Ralph Miller, James Pemberton	2
Black Males: York, Peter & James	3
Black Females: Florow, Darcus & Doll	3
Total	8

Whites: Jacob Mezick & Jacob Mezick Junr. 2
Total 2

Whites: Turner Davis 1
Total 1

Whites: William Maultsby & Thos. Drybrow 2
Black Males: Tom & Jupiter 2
Black Females: Ameritta 1
Total 5

Whites: Joseph White, Patroller
Black Females: Nan & Bet 2
Total 2

Whites: John Tailor, Constable
Total 0

Whites: John Jones & William Jones 2
Black Males: Tomboy 1
Black Females: Bellow, Juda & Silvia 3
Total 6

Whites: James Carver & John Pointer Junr. 2
Total 2

Whites: Frances Lucas 1
Black Males: Tom, Bob, Venter, Secas, & Manuel 5
Black Females: Sutina, Mary, Nan & Lucy 4
Total 10

Whites: Jeremiah Dofford 1
Black Males: Black Billy 1
Black Females: Hagar & Penney 2
Total 4

Whites: John Rowan, James Wood & Francis Wood 3
Total 3

Whites: John Cambell, Anguish Cambell, Archible Tailor & Macum McBri[**Torn**] 4
Total 4

Whites: Moses Homes, John Homes & John Lamb 3
Total 3

Whites: Benony Claton 1
Total 1

Whites: Benjamin Benbow, Thomas Benbow & Thomas Maultsby 3
Black Males: Sanco 1
Black Females: Nell 1
Boys: Noco & Bristoe 2
Total 7

Whites: Levi Young 1
Black Males: Harris 1
Black Females: Money 1
Total 3

Whites: Basil Manly 1
Black Males: Peter, Stepny, Tom, Isick, Cockney, Pompey, Jenny, Isaik, Tom, Tony, Quacoe, Samboe, Mood, & Dick 14
Black Females: [**Torn**], Care, Hagar, Moriah, Ambor, Mary, Doll, Molly, Nancey, Moll, Poja, Len & Addie 13
Boys: Poiny, Hendrick & Joney 3
Total 31

Whites: William Purcell, Joseph [**Torn**] & Daniel McNemarr 3
Total 3

Whites: Daniel Curry & Jonadab Russ 2
Total 2

Whites: William How[?], John Conerly & Willm: Standfast 3
Boys: Dick 1
Total 4

Whites: Ezekiah Davis 1
Black Males: Catoe 1
Black Females: Sarah & Nancy 2
Boys: Will 1

Chapter 2: Bladen County Tax Lists of 1775

Total   5

Whites: Mary Moore & George Lucas   1
Black Males: Robin, Rentes, Joney, Quash, Jackoe, Will, Jack, Toney, Attey & Joe   11
Black Females: Philis, Cater, Clareda, Besse, Bellah, Dianna, Sarah, Lucy, Hannah, Judah, Peggy, Selah, Bellah, Hannah, Dilly & Sethra   16
Boys: Peter, Sam, Nat, Sam & Cane   5
Total   33

Whites: Thos. Lucas   1
Black Females: [Not named]   1
Total   2

Whites: Harbert Tailor   1
Total   1

Whites: Thos. McGuire & James Campbell 2
Black Males: Old Jack, Old Toney, Jemmy, Cesar, Cymen, Isaac, Quaco, March, Emanuel, Dirnboe, Jetang, Greenwick, Glasgow, Jack, Alfred & Cuffey   16
Black Females: Old Betty, Old Nany, Philis, Amilia, Jubah, Kate, Young Nanny, Judey, Amy, Bobbit, Molly, Priscilla, Casinda, Perthene, Nancy, Cloe, Elsey, Silvia & Belinda   19
Boys: Boy Ned   1
Total   38

Whites: Thos. Brown & John Brown   2
Black Males: Old Jack, Pomp, Catoe, Shields, Jack & Lonzoe   6
Black Females: Old Cloe, Balindah, Grace, Albrow, Agnis, Amy & Little Cloe   7
Total   15

Whites: John White   1
Total   1

Whites: John Pointer   1
Black Males: [Not named]   2
Total   3

Whites: John Nicholson   1
Total   1

True Copy Taken pr. Thos. Brown
[The next list is attached to the above list of Thomas Brown]

A list of the Names of the house keepers between Whites Creek & the county line Summon'd by John Tailor 1775

John Pointer
Willm Flow
Moses Holmes
John Nicleson
Ralph Miller
Anguish Campbel
Jeremiah Daffor
Frances Lucas
Jacob Messack
Joseph White
Henry Graham
Willm: Maultsby
John Rowan
John Grange
Thos. McGayer
John Campbell
Harbert Tailor
Mary Moore
Thos. Benbow
Turner Davice
Daniel Curry
Benony Claton
Benjamin Benbow
Bassel Manly
John Jones
John White
Thos. Brown

John Tailor Made Oath that he Summon'd all the Masters Mss and Over Seeor of Families from the County Line to Whites Creek: Thos: Brown

****

Bladen County Tax List of 1775

Constables Lists for 1775
A List of Taxables Summoned by William Singletary & Returned to Will. McRee Esqr.

There are no headings in this list.

Richard Singletary
Mary M Fatter
Alexander McLary
John Campbell
Daniel Robeson
William Smith
Duncan McKeithan
John Canady

Chapter 2: Bladen County Tax Lists of 1775

Stephen White
Gilbert McKeithan
Daniel McKeithan
Benjamin Stone
Christopher Goodwin
John Adare
Robert M Conkey
Neil Shaw
Thomas Hester
John Hill
Archibald Darrah
William Forrester
John Taylor
Alexander Harvey
Sarah Seymore
Archibald Taylor
George Brown
Alexander Graham
Dugald Bleu
Archd. McBride
Danie McFatter
Samuel Roots
John McMullin
Edward Davis
Angus Sellars
John White Mercht.
Thomas Haynes
John Leveston
David White
Elizabeth Bailey
Niel Thompson
John Lennon
James White
John Reess
Thomas Cox
Mary Weir
Edmund Chancey
Daniel Curry
[Torn] McKay
[Torn]rgt. Pemberton
[Torn] Boyd
[Torn]ham Gray
[Torn] M Clelland
John McKewn
Simon Burney
Maturin Colvill
Charles McNaughten
John M Claron
Archibald Shaw
Daniel Shaw
Archibald M Coulskey
Archd. Bradley
John Gibbs

Neil McCoulskey
John Pemberton
William Purcel
Thomas M Clelland
James Murphey
John Shaw
Alexander M Gillop
John Smith
Benjamin Humphreys
Unity Hays
William Hendon
William McRee
William Davis
Ann Maultsby
Ester Doan
John Gunn
Henry Graham
Arch. M Keithan
Mary Singletary
Sarah Singletary
John Drydon
Benjamin Fitzrandolph
Edward Bryan
Amey Bryan
Jean Bryan
Phillemon [Torn]
Jacob Munts
John Bently
William Dowlace[?]
John White
Richard Small
Francis Child
James Smith
Thomas Howard
Moses Walker

****

Bladen County Tax List of 1775
A List of Taxables taken by Thomas Owen 1775

Headings for this list include: White Men, Negro Men, Negro Wenches & Negro Boys

Joseph White
White Men	2
Negro Men	3
Negro Wenches	4

Joseph Thims
White Men	2
Negro Men	2

Chapter 2: Bladen County Tax Lists of 1775

Negro Wenches | 1

Turtle McNeal
White Men | 1
Negro Men | 3
Negro Wenches | 2

Laughlin McNeal
White Men | 1
Negro Men | 1

Joseph Price
White Men | 3

David Young
White Men | 2

John Berry
White Men | 2

Ambrois Powell
White Men | 1

William Moor
White Men | 1

Childs Powell
White Men | 1

Danold McEachern
White Men | 1

John Barefield
White Men | 1

Hecter McNeal
White Men | 1
Negro Men | 2
Negro Wenches | 1

John Little
White Men | 1

Neal Culbreath
White Men | 1

James McNeal
White Men | 1
Negro Men | 2
Negro Wenches | 1

Archibald Little
White Men | 1

Danold Patterson
White Men | 1

Thomas Stephens
White Men | 1

Daniel Matthias
White Men | 1

John Dormand
White Men | 1

William Godfrey
White Men | 1

Seth Due
White Men | 1

William Kirkpatrick
White Men | 3
Negro Men [Torn]
Negro Wenches [Torn]

Robert Rayford
White Men | 2
Negro Men | 1
Negro Wenches | 1

John Johnston
White Men | 1

Duncan [Torn]
White Men | 2

Neal [Torn]
White Men | 2

Danold [Torn]ntagard
White Men | 1

William McMuling
White Men | 1

William Blue
White Men | 1

William Butler
White Men | 2

Isaac Canady
White Men | 1

Chapter 2: Bladen County Tax Lists of 1775

Gilberd Ramsey
White Men 2

William Smith
White Men 1

William Taylor
White Men 3
Negro Men 1

William McDonald
White Men 1

Peter McBean
White Men 2

Samuel Evers
White Men 1

Absolem Legett
White Men 1

Benjamin Britt
White Men 1

Talley Douge
White Men 1

Robert Sims
White Men 1

Lauthren Camren
White Men 1

Levey Glass
White Men 3
Negro Men 1
Negro Wenches 2

Lewis Monrow
White Men 2
Negro Men 1

John Legett
White Men 7
Negro Men 3
Negro Wenches 2

Lazarus Johnston
White Men 2

Richard Elwell
White Men 1

Thomas Atkins
White Men 1

Thomas Finney
White Men 1

Thomas Ard
White Men 2
Negro Men 1
Negro Wenches 1

James Ard
White Men 1
Negro Men 1

Ruben Ard
White Men 1
Negro Wenches 1

Godfrey McNeal
White Men 1

Christopher McKey
White Men 2

Judith Corbet
White Men 1

Samuel Canady Senr.
White Men 1
Negro Men 1
Negro Wenches 1

Duncan Bosey
White Men 2

Joseph Cooper
White Men 1
Negro Wenches 1

Sampson Carver
White Men 1
Negro Men 1
Negro Wenches 1
Negro Boys 1

John Mclaughlin
White Men 1

Daniel McDuffy
White Men 1

Chapter 2: Bladen County Tax Lists of 1775

John McNeal
White Men 1

James Forguson
White Men 2

Peter Simpson
White Men 1

James Ellis
White Men 2
Negro Men 5
Negro Wenches 1

Abel Colbert
White Men 1

Benjamin Sims
White Men 1

William Cruis
White Men 1

John Newberry
White Men 2
Negro Men 3
Negro Wenches 1

Henry Mercer
White Men 1
Negro Men 1
Negro Wenches 1

John Ba[Torn]
White Men 1

Andre [Torn]
White Men 1

Isaac [Torn]
White Men 2
Negro Men 2

John Smith
[Rest of entry torn]

James Smith
White Men 1

Philip Ikner
White Men 3

Tobias Sealah
White Men 1

Jesse Thims
White Men 1
Negro Men 1

Elias Fort
White Men 1
Negro Wenches 1

Archebald Bone
White Men 1

John Moore
White Men 2

Malcolm Bovey
White Men 1

Jesse Newberry
White Men 1
Negro Men 6
Negro Wenches 4
Negro Boys 1

Elizabeth Newberry
Negro Wenches 1

John McFarson
White Men 4
Negro Men 2
Negro Wenches 2

Hector McNeal, sailor
White Men 1

Peter McArthur
White Men 2

Mordach McLoud
White Men 1

Danold McSwainey
White Men 2

CHAPTER 3

BLADEN COUNTY TAX LISTS OF 1776

BLADEN COUNTY TAX LIST OF 1776

George Browns List of Taxables for the year 1776

Headings in this list include: White, Black Males, & Black Females

William McNeil
Whites 1
Black Males: Duncan, Marky & Dick 3
Black Females: Clorey & Veanus 2

John Campell
Whites 1

Josiah Lewis
Whites 1
Black Males: London 1
Black Females: Molly 1

Dugal Blue
Whites 1

Archibald Shaw
Whites 1
Black Males: Tom 1

John Simson
Whites 1

James Murphy
Whites 1

Archibald Bradly
Whites 1

Matthew Kelly
Whites 1
Black Males: Limbrick, Will & Jack 3
Black Females: Jude & Sal 2

James Lewis & James Lewis & Jerry [?]
Whites 3

Archibald Campbell
Whites 1

Simon Burny
Whites 1

Anguish McKay & John
Whites 2

Robert Walker & John
Whites 2

Daniel Shaw, John Shaw & Duncan
Whites 3
Black Males: Lewis 1
Black Females: Febe 1

John Kelly
Whites 1

Frances Lawson
Whites 1

Neil McCoulsky
Whites 1
Black Males: Jack 1
Black Females: Filis 1

Solomon Lewis
Whites 1

Neil Kurry
Whites 1

Andrew Mclelland
Whites 1
Black Males: Siras 1
Black Females: Febe 1

John McCleland
Whites 1

William Bryan & John

Chapter 3: Bladen County Tax Lists of 1776

Whites 2
Black Females: Molly 1

John McLaren & Darby
Whites 2

Daniel Turner[?]
Whites 1

Daniel Shipman, James & Daniel Junr.
Whites 3
Black Males: Sam & Sesar 2

Benjamin Aranton
Whites 1
Black Males: Sesar 1
Black Females: Joan 1

George McGee
Whites 1

Joseph Wigens & Son
Whites 2

Thomas Browder & James Sutton
Whites 2

Joshua Hays
Whites 1
Black Males: Markes 1
Black Females: Dinah & Veanus 2

John Mckown & Robert Mckown
Whites 2

Duncan Henderson
Whites 1

Thomas Simson
Whites 1
Black Males: Harglus, Harry & Sam 3
Black Females: Jean & Amaretta 2

Ever McMullin & Dugal McMullin
Whites 2

William Brown
Whites 1

Archibald Kelly
Whites 1

Jeremiah Bigford & William Bigford
Whites 2
Black Males: Jude 1

Archibald Sellors
Whites 1

Daniel McCollem
Whites 1

Thomas Bryan
Whites 1
Black Males: Jo 1
Black Females: Grace 1

Barneby Steavens & Abraham Steavens
Whites 2
Black Males: Aberdeen, Aro, Tom & Bob 4
Black Females: Dinah 1

Dennis Lenning
Whites 1

Joseph Powers
Whites 1

Ezekiel Busby
Whites 1

Thos. Hayes & Joshua Hayes Junr.
Whites 2

Simon Brit, Richard Brit & Isams Brit
Whites 3

****

BLADEN COUNTY TAX LIST OF 1776

List of Taxables taken for the Year 1776 by John Turner

Headings for this list include: White Males, Black Males, Black Females, Boys, Over Sixty & Total.

Daniel Flinn
White Males 2
Total 2

John Green
White Males 1
Black Males 1

Chapter 3: Bladen County Tax Lists of 1776

Total 2

Edward Wall
White Males 2
Total 2

Thomas Hardwick
White Males 3
Total 3

Thomas Saunders
White Males 1
Black Males 1
Black Females 1
Total 3

Thomas Dyson
White Males 1
Total 1

Christopher Saunders
White Males 1
Total 1

Thomas Robeson
White Males 2
Total 2

John Johnston Junr.
White Males 1
Total 1

Aaron Tomlinson Senr.
White Males 2
Total 2

John Johnson Senr.
White Males 2
Total 2

James Baldwin
White Males 1
Black Males 2
Black Females 1
Total 4

John Coleman, Constable
White Males 2
Total 2

Moses Coleman
White Males 2
Total 2

Thomas Johnston
White Males 1
Total 1

Coleman Nichols
White Males 2
Total 2

Jacob Hanchey
White Males 1
Total 1

William Busby
White Males 1
Total 1

Nehemiah Johnston
White Males 1
Total 1

Allen Hardwick
White Males 1
Total 1

Solomon Dyson
White Males 1
Total 1

Ezekiel Hill
White Males 2
Total 2

Thomas Hardwick Junr.
White Males 1
Total 1

Israel Tomlinson
White Males 1
Total 1

Ezekiel Bryant
White Males 1
Total 1

Henry Boswell, Constable
White Males 1
Total 1

John Rogers
White Males 2
Total 2

Chapter 3: Bladen County Tax Lists of 1776

Absalom Powell
White Males	1
Total	1

Charles Baldwin
White Males	1
Black Males	1
Black Females	2
Total	4

John Baldwin Senr.
White Males	2
Black Males	4
Black Females	3
Total	9

John Fokes
White Males	2
Total	2

John Williams
White Males	4
Total	4

Simon Sellers
White Males	1
Total	1

Jacob Fokes
White Males	1
Total	1

John Yates
White Males	1
Total	1

James Fokes
White Males	1
Total	1

Amelia Morley
Black Males	2
Black Females	1
Total	3

James Money
White Males	3
Total	3

Samuel Rourk
White Males	1
Black Males	1
Black Females	1
Total	3

Hanson Lewis Senr.
White Males	2
Black Females	1
Boys	1
Over Sixty	1
Total	5

William Burney Senr.
White Males	1
Black Males	2
Black Females	2
Total	5

Micajah Cohoon
White Males	1
Total	1

John Cohoon
White Males	2
Total	2

John Clark
White Males	1
Total	1

William Starkey
White Males	1
Total	1

David Mims
White Males	1
Black Males	1
Total	2

Thomas Mims Senr.
White Males	2
Black Males	2
Total	4

Joseph Baldwin
White Males	1
Total	1

Grace Smith
White Males	2
Black Males	1
Total	3

Nathaniel Baldwin
White Males	1
Total	1

Chapter 3: Bladen County Tax Lists of 1776

John Dores
White Males 2
Total 2

Thomas Richardson
White Males 2
Total 2

James Ellis
White Males 4
Black Males 3
Total 7

Richd. Stubbs
White Males 1
Total 1

John Stubbs Senr.
White Males 2
Total 2

Morriss Bevins
White Males 2
Total 2

John Elliss
White Males 1
Black Females 1
Total 2

John Atkinson
White Males 2
Total 2

Burwell Hargrove
White Males 2
Total 2

Edward Willson
White Males 1
Total 1

John Willson Junr.
White Males 1
Total 1

James Willson
White Males 1
Total 1

John Branton
White Males 3

Total 3

Ignatius Flowers
White Males 1
Total 1

Southy Hayes
White Males 1
Black Males 1
Total 2

William Strickland
White Males 3
Total 3

Eliza. Green
Black Males 2
Black Females 1
Total 3

Luke Barfield
White Males 2
Black Females 5
Boys 2
Total 9

Demcey Doboys
White Males 1
Total 1

John Crews
White Males 1
Total 1

Michael Whitman
White Males 1
Total 1

Benjamin Beesley
White Males 1
Total 1

William Lucas
White Males 1
Total 1

Robert Beesley
White Males 1
Total 1

Joshua Pevy
Black Males 3
Black Females 1

Chapter 3: Bladen County Tax Lists of 1776

Boys 1
Total 4
[Indicates Free Persons of Color]

Abraham Freeman
Black Males 1
Black Females 1
Total 2
[Indicates Free Persons of Color]

John Webb
Black Males 1
Black Females 2
Total 3
[Indicates Free Persons of Color]

Roger Freeman
Black Males 1
Black Females 1
Total 2
[Indicates Free Persons of Color]

William Burney Junr.
White Males 1
Black Females 1
Total 2

John Chancey
White Males 2
Total 2

William Freeman
Black Males 1
Black Females 1
Total 2
[Indicates Free Persons of Color]

James Clardy
White Males 1
Black Males 3
Black Females 3
Total 7

Arthur Smith
White Males 1
Total 1

Steven Smith
White Males 1
Total 1

William Wilkinson
White Males 1

Total 1

William White, Constable
White Males 1
Black Males 1
Black Females 1
Total 3

Thos. Amis
White Males 1
Black Males 8
Black Females 2
Total 11

Joshua Stevens
White Males 2
Black Males 2
Black Females 2
Total 6

Demcy Lawson
White Males 1
Black Males 2
Black Females 1
Total 4

John Buttler
White Males 1
Total 1

Jas. Dupree
White Males 2
Black Males 6
Black Females 5
Over 60 1
Total 14

Margaret Gibbs
Black Males 3
Black Females 3
Total 6

John Roberts
White Males 1
Total 1

David Godwin
White Males 3
Black Males 5
Black Females 2
Total 10

Abram King

Chapter 3: Bladen County Tax Lists of 1776

White Males	1
Total	1

Joseph Noble
White Males	1
Total	1

William Stevens
White Males	1
Total	1

Simon Green
White Males	1
Total	1

John Baldwin
White Males	1
Black Males	1
Black Females	1
Total	3

Duncan Morison
White Males	1
Black Males	5
Black Females	2
Total	8

****

BLADEN COUNTY TAX LIST OF 1776

List taken and Returned to Court this 7th Day of August 1776 pr John Smith

Headings for this list include: Whites, Black Males, Boys, Black Females & Total.

Thomas Russ & John Thomas
Whites	2
Black Males	2
Black Females	1
Total	5

Gilbert McKeithan
Whites	1
Total	1

George Thomas Senior
Whites	1
Total	1

James Benson
Whites	1
Total	1

Richard Huffam
Whites	1
Total	1

Hudnal Huffam
Whites	1
Black Females	1
Total	2

John Singletary & William Streite[?]
Whites	2
Black Males	1
Total	3

Brayton Singletary, John Russ & Benj. Singletary
Whites	3
Black Males	1
Total	4

Samuel McRee
Whites	1
Black Males	2
Total	3

George Thomas
Whites	1
Black Males	1
Total	2

David Lock Senior & Junior & Benj. Lock
Whites	3
Black Males	2
Black Females	2
Total	7

William Saltar
Whites	1
Black Males	8
Black Females	4
Total	13

Sarah Wilson & Richard Floyd
Whites	1
Black Males	1
Boys	1
Black Females	1
Total	4

Joseph Lock & Leonard Lock
Whites	2

Chapter 3: Bladen County Tax Lists of 1776

Black Males 1
Black Females 1
Total 4

Benjamin Elwell
Whites 1
Black Females 1
Total 2

Peter Broades
Whites 1
Black Males 3
Black Females 1
Total 5

Thomas [Torn]
Whites 1
Black Males 1
[Rest of entry torn & missing]

Hezekiah Davis
Whites 1
Black Males 1
Boys 1
Black Females 2
Total 5

Ephraim Mulford & Thos Mulford
Whites 2
Black Males 1
Boys 1
Black Females 3
Total 7

James Dowy & David Thomas
Whites 2
Total 2

Martha Campbell & Daniel Campbell
Whites 1
Black Males 3
Black Females 2
Total 6

John Slingsby, Donald Bain, John McNeil, John Young & Thos. Esom
Whites 5
Black Males 9
Black Females 7
Total 21

Jean Duboise
Black Males 6

Black Females 3
Total 9

David Lloyd
Whites 1
Total 1

James White
Whites 1
Black Males 6
Black Females 5
Total 12

William Shaw & James Shaw
Whites 2
Total 2

William Stuart & Duncan McLaron
Whites 2
Black Males 9
Boys 1
Black Females 9
Total 21

John Andres & two Sons & Ruben Treadwell
Whites 4
Black Males 3
Boys 1
Black Females 1
Total 9

Othniel Straughhan
Whites 1
Black Males 1
Black Females 2
Total 4

Moses Treadway & Israel Bourdoux
Whites 2
Black Females 1
Total 3

Robert Stewart
Whites 1
Total 1

Matthew Prigon & 2 Sons
Whites 3
Total 3

Hezekiah Howard
Whites 1
Total 1

Chapter 3: Bladen County Tax Lists of 1776

Daniel Cook
Whites	1
Total	1

John Howard and Son
Whites	2
Black Males	3
Black Females	2
Total	7

Duncan McAlister and Son
Whites	2
Total	2

Isaac Hays
Whites	1
Black Males	1
Black Females	1
Total	3

Samuel Freeman
Whites	1
Black Females	1
Total	2

Jeremiah Doane & Ephraim Doane
Whites	2
Total	2

[Torn]iah Sykes
Whites	1
Total	1

[Torn] McDaniel
Whites	1
Total	1

Joseph Andres & John Andres
Whites	2
Total	2

Nathan Maradith
Whites	1
Total	1

James Gardner
Whites	1
Total	1

William Sloan
Whites	1
Total	1

Jacob Sykes, James Gay & David Mason
Whites	3
Total	3

Beaumont Sutton & William Sutton
Whites	2
Black Males	1
Total	3

John Sutton, Constable

Michael Mixon
Whites	1
Total	1

Stephen Andres & Isaiah Sykes
Whites	2
Black Males	4
Boys	1
Black Females	1
Total	8

John Sykes
Whites	1
Total	1

John Monroe
Whites	1
Total	1

Jesse Barefoot
Whites	1
Total	1

****

BLADEN COUNTY TAX LIST OF 1776

A true List of the Taxables as given 1776 To Isaac Jones

Headings for this list include: Whites, Black Males, Black Females & Total. This list also has a column listing single persons living with the family.

William Cromarty
Whites	1
Black Males	2
Black Females	1
Total	4

Chapter 3: Bladen County Tax Lists of 1776

Evan Ellis
Whites	1
Black Males	1
Black Females	1
Total	3

William Ellis
Whites	1
Black Males	1
Total	2

James Isham
Whites	1
Black Males	1
Total	2

Prichard Harrison
Whites	1
Black Males	1
Total	2

Edward Reeves
Whites	1
Total	1

Christopher Sutton
Whites	1
Total	1

Sa[Torn] Boazman
Single Persons: David Moat
Whites	2
Total	2

[Next three names torn & missing]

[Torn]nard Salter
Whites	1
Black Males	2
Black Females	1
Total	4

[Torn]is Collemn
Whites	1
Total	1

[Torn] White, Widow
Single Persons: William White
Whites	1
Black Males	3
Black Females	3
Total	7

[Torn] [Torn]orth
Single Persons: Stephen Hollingsworth Junr.
Whites	2
Total	2

[Next two names torn & missing]

[Torn] & Wife
Black Males	1
Black Females	1
Total	2

[Indicates Free Persons of Color]

[Torn] [Torn]on
Whites	1
Total	1

[Torn] [Torn]gsworth Senr.
Whites	1
Total	1

[Torn] [Torn]
Single Persons: Archabald Sellers & Duncan Sellers
Whites	3
Total	3

[Next two names torn & missing]

[Torn] [Torn]
Single Persons: James Moorhead
Whites	2
Total	2

[Torn] [Torn] So. Rivers Senr. [Name torn from entry]
[So. River is actually South River, the residence of the missing name]
Single Persons: William Smith
Whites	2
Total	2

[Torn] Smith So. River Junr.
Whites	1
Total	1

Archabald McDaniel
Whites	1
Total	1

[Torn] Rogerson
Single Persons: Joseph Singletary
Whites	2

Chapter 3: Bladen County Tax Lists of 1776

Black Males 3
Black Females 2
Total 7

[Torn] [Torn]tary
Whites 1
Black Males 1
Total 2

[Torn] [Torn]see
Whites 1
Total 1

[Torn] [Torn]ll
Single Persons: John Nickleson
Whites 2
Total 2

Thomas Suggs
Single Persons: William Suggs
Whites 2
Total 2

Thomas Sessoms
Whites 1
Total 1

John McCollemn
Whites 1
Total 1

Peter Robeson
Whites 1
Black Males 4
Black Females 3
Total 8

Lawrence Byrne
Single Persons: Matthew Byrne
Whites 2
Total 2

Peter Byrne
Whites 1
Total 1

Wm McMaster
Single Persons: Alexr. McKeever
Whites 2
Total 2

Wm Plumer
Single Persons: Zachariah Plumer
Whites 2
Total 2

Jeremiah Plumer
Whites 1
Total 1

John Plumer
Whites 1
Total 1

Gidion Pricket
Whites 1
Total 1

Robt. Edwards
Whites 1
Black Males 2
Black Females 2
Total 5

James Beard
Single Persons: John Lock, Constable
Whites 1
Black Males 1
Black Females 1
Total 3

Nathaniel Reeves
Whites 1
Black Males 1
Black Females 2
Total 4

James McDaniel
Single Persons: Wm McDaniel
Whites 2
Black Males 1
[Rest of entry torn & missing]

John Barton Owel [Unclear whether Barton or Owel is the surname]
Whites 1
[Rest of entry torn & missing]

John Beard
Whites 1
Black Males 1
[Rest of entry torn & missing]

Benja. Clark
Whites 1
Black Males 4

Chapter 3: Bladen County Tax Lists of 1776

[Rest of entry torn & missing]

Saml. Carman
Whites   1
[Rest of entry torn & missing]

John Richardson Senr.
Whites   1
[Rest of entry torn & missing]

John Richardson Junr.
Whites   1
[Rest of entry torn & missing]

Wm Cain
Single Persons: Wm Cain Junr. & James Cain
Whites   3
[Rest of entry torn & missing]

Isaac Ray
Whites   1
Black Males   2
[Rest of entry torn & missing]

Wm Johnson
Single Persons: Saml. Johnson
Whites   2
[Rest of entry torn & missing]

Saml. Boazman
Single Persons: Saml. Boazman Junr. & Joseph Boazman
Whites   3
[Rest of entry torn & missing]

Henry Bullard
Whites   1
Total   1

Michal Thomas
Whites   1
Total   1

James Bennet
Whites   1
Total   1

David McDaniel
Whites   1
Total   1

Benja. Clark   So. River
Whites   1

Total   1

Wm Owens
Whites   1
Black Males   2
Black Females   1
Total   4

Robt. Richardson
Whites   1
Total   1

Thos. Avert
Whites   1
Total   1

Ezekiah Jones
Whites   1
Total   1

Isaac Jones
Single Persons: Edward Jones & Isaac Jones Junr.
Whites   3
Black Males   3
Black Females   2
Total   8

****

BLADEN COUNTY TAX LIST OF 1776

List of Taxables Taken by Wm McRee for the Year 1776

Headings for this list include: Whites, Fellows, Wenches, Under 16 & Total

William Smith
Whites   2
Fellows   5
Wenches   2
Total   9

John Adair
Whites   1
Total   1

David Lindsay White
Whites   1
Fellows   2
Wenches   1
Under 16   1

Chapter 3: Bladen County Tax Lists of 1776

Total	5

William Wishart
Whites	1
Fellows	1
Wenches	1
Total	3

Thomas Kindlow
Whites	2
Total	2

Jacob Muns
Whites	1
Total	1

Saml. Curry
Whites	1
Total	1

Wilm. Dowlas
Whites	1
Total	1

Lewis Thomas
Whites	1
Total	1

Stephen Bryan
Whites	1
Total	1

John Lessley & J.S Lesley
Whites	2
Total	2

Cannon Cumbo
Whites	2
Wenches	1
Under 16	1
Total	3

Elizabeth Bailey
Fellows	1
Wenches	2
Total	3

Edward Davis
Whites	1
Fellows	2
Wenches	2
Total	5

Margt. Byrn
Fellows	4
Wenches	6
Total	10

Wm Russ
Whites	1
Total	1

David B[?]wn
Whites	1
Total	1

John Hill, Constable
Total	0

George Brown
Whites	2
Fellows	2
Wenches	2
Under 16	1
Total	7

Neil Shaw
Whites	2
Fellows	2
Wenches	2
Total	6

Wm. Forster
Whites	1
Total	1

Wm. Hendon
Whites	2
Fellows	1
Wenches	1
Under 16	1
Total	5

John White
Whites	1
Total	1

[Torn] Harrison Junr.
Whites	3
Fellows	1
Wenches	2
Total	6

[Torn] McKoy
Whites	1
Fellows	4

Chapter 3: Bladen County Tax Lists of 1776

Wenches 5
Total 10

[Torn] Pemberton
Whites 1
Total 1

Margt. Pemberton her Son James
Whites 1
Wenches 1
Under 16 1
Total 3

Duncan McKeithan
Whites 1
Fellows 1
Total 2

Donald McFatter
Whites 1
Total 1

John Shaw & Gibba & Jno. McMullen
Whites 3
Total 3

Archd. McBride
Whites 1
Total 1

Archd. McKeithan & Son Duncan
Whites 2
Total 2

Donall McKeithan and father
Whites 1
Total 1

Duncan Lemmon [Lennon?]
Whites 1
Total 1

John Owen & Richd. Thomas
Whites 2
Fellows 5
Wenches 4
Total 11

Iver McCullam
Whites 1
Total 1

Alexr. Graham

Whites 1
Total 1

Jo Wood, Wm. Willkinson & Joseph Freeman
Whites 3
Fellows 2
Total 5

Robt. McKonkey
Whites 1
Fellows 1
Wenches 3
Total 5

Ann Maulsby & Sons James & Anthony
Whites 2
Fellows 1
Wenches 2
Under 16 2
Total 7

Donall McKeithan
Whites 1
Total 1

Abraham Gray
Whites 1
Total 1

John Drydand
Whites 1
Total 1

Phillm. Bryan & two Sons
Whites 3
Fellows 1
Total 4

Edwd. Bryan and Son Idam[?]
Whites 2
Under 16 1
Total 3

Arch. Daragh and son John
Whites 2
Fellows 1
Total 3

James Washburn & Ithamor Singletary
Whites 2
Total 2

Jos. Handon

Chapter 3: Bladen County Tax Lists of 1776

Whites	1
Fellows	1
Wenches	1
Total	3

Jo Campbell
| Whites | 1 |
| Total | 1 |

Anguish Campbell
| Whites | 1 |
| Total | 1 |

John Campbell Junr.
| Whites | 1 |
| Total | 1 |

Thos Howard
| Whites | 1 |
| Total | 1 |

Archd. Taylor and 3 sons
| Whites | 4 |
| Total | 4 |

John Taylor
| Whites | 1 |
| Total | 1 |

John Bentley
| Whites | 1 |
| Total | 1 |

James White ar[?]
| Whites | 1 |
| Total | 1 |

Phillip Wood
| Whites | 1 |
| Total | 1 |

John Boyd and son Jon
Whites	2
Wenches	1
Total	3

John McKinzey
| Whites | 1 |
| Total | 1 |

Anguish Sellers and son Anguish
| Whites | 2 |
| Total | 2 |

Donnal Downey
| Whites | 1 |
| Total | 1 |

Thos Owen Esqr and James Agelston
Whites	2
Fellows	8
Wenches	4
Total	14

James Singaltary
Whites	1
Wenches	1
Total	2

Ammey Bryan
Fellows	1
Wenches	2
Total	3

Thomas Sorevin
| Whites | 1 |
| Total | 1 |

Joel Allen
Whites	1
Wenches	1
Total	2

Benjm. Singaltary & Wm. Singaltary, Constable
Whites	1
Fellows	4
Wenches	2
Total	7

Stephen Hestors
| Whites | 1 |
| Total | 1 |

John Russ Senr.
| Whites | 1 |
| Total | 1 |

Sam Gytan
| Whites | 1 |
| Total | 1 |

Robt. Baker and son Saml.
Whites	2
Fellows	1
Total	3

Chapter 3: Bladen County Tax Lists of 1776

John King
Whites	1
Fellows	1
Wenches	1
Total	3

Wm Cain and son John
Whites	2
Fellows	10
Total	12

Saml. Cain
Whites	1
Fellows	2
Total	3

Wm Moorehead
Whites	1
Fellows	2
Wenches	1
Total	4

Peter Lord and son Wm & Wm Jonston
Whites	3
Fellows	3
Wenches	2
Total	8

Thos Robeson Esqr
Whites	1
Fellows	8
Wenches	5
Under 16	3
Total	17

Benjm. Humphrey & Joe
Whites	2
Wenches	1
Total	3

James Cain
Whites	1
Total	1

Archd. McCoulsky and James
Whites	2
Wenches	2
Total	4

Donall Robison Archd. McGillup
Whites	2
Total	2

John Lennon
Whites	1
Wenches	2
Total	3

Thos. Holt
Whites	1
Total	1

Benj. Stone & John Cudington
Whites	2
Fellows	5
Wenches	2
Under 16	2
Total	11

Robt. Wells
Whites	1
Fellows	4
Wenches	3
Total	8

David White & James Ervin
Whites	2
Fellows	2
Total	4

Mary Singaltary & son Joe
Whites	1
Fellows	1
Wenches	1
Total	3

Sarah Singaltary
Fellows	1
Wenches	1
Total	2

Wm Davis
Whites	1
Total	1

Charels McNauton
Whites	1
Fellows	6
Total	7

Edmond Chansey and Rekum Reding
Whites	2
Wenches	1
Total	3

Robt. McRee and son Wm.

Chapter 3: Bladen County Tax Lists of 1776

Whites	2
Total	2

Jos. Cain
Whites	1
Fellows	1
Wenches	1
Under 16	1
Total	1

James Giffard
Whites	1
Total	1

Faith Graham
Fellows	32
Wenches	28
Total	60

Davd. Russ, Wm. Russ & Daniel Sellers
Whites	3
Total	3

Alexr. Brodie, Monday & Letice
Whites	1
Fellows	1
Wenches	1
Total	3

Iam Smith, Sam Smith & 3 Negro Slaves
Whites	2
Fellows	3
Total	5

James Aitkin
Whites	1
Total	1

****

BLADEN COUNTY TAX LIST OF 1776

A true List of Taxables Taken by Thos. Owen 6th July 1776

Headings for this list include: White Men, Black Males, Black Females, Black Boys & Carriages

John Newbery
White Men	1
Black Males	3
Black Females	1

Judith Corbet & her son James
White Men	1

Godfrey McNeal
White Men	1

David Young
White Men	1

Joseph Thimes
White Men	1
Black Males	2
Black Females	1

Philip Ikner
White Men	1

Samuel Canady
White Men	1
Black Males	2
Black Females	2

Peter McKeller
White Men	1

Hugh McCrane
White Men	1
Black Males	1
Black Females	1

William Butler
White Men	1

Daniel Campbell
White Men	1

Ambruis Powel
White Men	1

John Barefield
White Men	1

John Ward
White Men	1

Samuel Butler
White Men	2
Black Males	3
Black Females	1

Jesse Newbery
White Men	2

Chapter 3: Bladen County Tax Lists of 1776

Black Males 6
Black Females 5
Black Boys 1

Joseph Price
White Men 2

Uriah Lambardson
White Men 1

Henry Mercer
White Men 2

James Ard
White Men 1

James Smith
White Men 1

Benjamin Brantly
White Men 1
Black Females 1

Charles [Brantly?]
White Men 1

Jesse Thimes
White Men 1
Black Males 1
Black Females 1

Daniel McEachern
White Men 1

Andrew Puff
White Men 1

John Sinclair
White Men 1

Daniel Paterson
White Men 2

Mordoch McLoud
White Men 1

James McNeal
White Men 1
Black Males 2
Black Females 1

Archibald Little
White Men 1

John Stewart
White Men 2

Neal McKay
White Men 2

Hecter Munro
White Men 1

Malcum Munro
White Men 1

Neal Thomson
White Men 1

Archibald Little
White Men 1

Neal McFall
White Men 3
Black Males 1
Black Females 1

Alexander McKay
White Men 2

John Little
White Men 1

Daniel McFarsion
White Men 2
Black Males 2
Black Females 2

Patty Ard
Black Females 1

Levy Glass
White Men 3
Black Males 1
Black Females 2

John Baughard
White Men 2

Duncan Boiey
White Men 1

Gilbird Ramsy
White Men 1

John Johnston

Chapter 3: Bladen County Tax Lists of 1776

<u>**White Men**</u>   1

Absolem Legett
<u>**White Men**</u>   1

James Biggs
<u>**White Men**</u>   1

Rachel Legett
<u>**Black Males**</u>   3
<u>**Black Females**</u>   3

John Storm
<u>**White Men**</u>   1

John Wilson
<u>**White Men**</u>   1

John Gates
<u>**White Men**</u>   1

James Gates
<u>**White Men**</u>   2

Thomas Creel
<u>**White Men**</u>   1

John Lock
<u>**White Men**</u>   2
<u>**Black Males**</u>   2
<u>**Black Females**</u>   3
<u>**Black Boys**</u>   1

George Willis
<u>**White Men**</u>   2

Agerton Willis
<u>**White Men**</u>   2
<u>**Black Males**</u>   14
<u>**Black Females**</u>   11

Benjamin Willis
<u>**White Men**</u>   2
<u>**Black Females**</u>   2

John Moore
<u>**White Men**</u>   1
<u>**Black Males**</u>   1

James Jackson
<u>**White Men**</u>   1
<u>**Black Males**</u>   2

John Harrison Senr.
<u>**White Men**</u>   1
<u>**Black Males**</u>   1

Leonard Lock
<u>**White Men**</u>   1
<u>**Black Males**</u>   2
<u>**Black Females**</u>   1

Joseph Cooper
<u>**White Men**</u>   2
<u>**Black Males**</u>   1
<u>**Black Females**</u>   1

Benjamin Fitchrandolph
<u>**White Men**</u>   1
<u>**Black Males**</u>   2
<u>**Black Females**</u>   2

Stephen Butlar
<u>**White Men**</u>   1
<u>**Black Males**</u>   1

Joseph Butlar
<u>**White Men**</u>   1
<u>**Black Males**</u>   1
<u>**Black Females**</u>   1

John Carter
<u>**White Men**</u>   1

Joseph Carter
<u>**White Men**</u>   2

Henry Clark
<u>**White Men**</u>   1

Henry Carter
<u>**White Men**</u>   1

Robert Grise
<u>**White Men**</u>   1

Samuel Hails
<u>**White Men**</u>   1

Jesse Carter
<u>**White Men**</u>   1

John Suggs
<u>**White Men**</u>   1

Richard Cheser

Chapter 3: Bladen County Tax Lists of 1776

White Men	1

****

BLADEN COUNTY TAX LIST OF 1776

A True List of Taxables for the year 1776 Taken by me Archd. McKissaks

Headings for this list include: Whites, Negroes, Molatoes & No.

Duncan McCarmaig
Whites	1
No.	1

John McCarmaig
Whites	1
No.	1

Archd. McCarmaig
Whites	1
No.	1

Hector McLean
Whites	1
No.	1

Archd. McGirt
Whites	1
No.	1

Daniel McLean Junr.
Whites	1
No.	1

Anguish Cammeron
Whites	1
No.	1

Duncan McColl & son Duncan
Whites	2
No.	2

David McColl
Whites	1
No.	1

Abram Paul
Whites	1
No.	1

Archd. McLean
Whites	1
No.	1

Neill Graham
Whites	1
No.	1

John McLean
Whites	1
No.	1

William Wilkinson
Whites	1
No.	1

James Wilkinson
Whites	1
No.	1

John Fiveash & Son Demsey
Whites	2
No.	2

John Clyburn
Whites	1
No.	1

Duncan McEachern
Whites	1
No.	1

Gilbert McCarmaig
Whites	1
No.	1

Archd. McGill
Whites	1
No.	1

John Cairsey & son Jacob & a Negroe fellow Brunswick
Molatoes	2
Negroes	1
No.	3

Jacob Alford & Negroe wench Lettice & a boy Hardy
Whites	1
Negroes	2
No.	3

Peter McArthur
Whites	1

Chapter 3: Bladen County Tax Lists of 1776

No. 1

Duncan Campbell son Hugh & a Negroe fellow Champion
Whites 1
Negroes 1
No. 2

Alexr. McArthur
Whites 1
No. 1

Neill McNeill & Negroe fellows Peter & Billy & a wench Fiby
Whites 1
Negroes 3
No. 4

Hector McNeill, Sailor & John Hart & a Negroe fellow Quash
Whites 2
Negroes 1
No. 3

[Next entry torn & missing]

Daniel [Torn] & a Negroe fellow Dan
Whites 1
Negroes 1
No. 2

Lewis Hall & Isaac Hall Senr.
Whites 2
No. 2

James Lowry & two Negroe fellows Hansom & Jack
Molatoes 1
Negroes 2
No. 3

Isaac Hall Junr. & John Johnston
Whites 2
No. 2

William Beaty
Whites 1
No. 1

Enuch Hall
Whites 1
No. 1

Lewis Hall Junr.
Whites 1
No. 1

Anguish Rea
Whites 1
No. 1

Laughlan Campbell
Whites 1
No. 1

Lazarus Creal & son Lazarus
Whites 2
No. 1

John Jackson
Whites 1
No. 1

John McCrainey & Archd. Clark & a Negroe Boye Sam
Whites 2
Negroes 1
No. 3

Neill Brown
Whites 1
No. 1

Malcom Buey
Whites 1
No. 1

John Gilchrist
Whites 1
No. 1

John McaNewer[?] & a Negroe fellow Lingo & a wench Cloe
Whites 1
Negroes 2
No. 3

Anguish, Archd. & Neill Wilkinson
Whites 3
No. 3

John McLean, Taylor
Whites 1
No. 1

John Fairley & sons Alexr., Reuben & Archd.

Chapter 3: Bladen County Tax Lists of 1776

Whites	4
No.	4

Daniel Mc aNewer[?] & John
Whites	2
No.	2

William McFauter & Iver Mc aNewer[?]
Whites	2
No.	2

Malcum McFauter
Whites	1
No.	1

Daniel McFauter
Whites	1
No.	1

Duncan McMillan
Whites	1
No.	1

Neill McGill
Whites	1
No.	1

Elisha Sweetin, white or migst or not I don't know
Molatoes	1
No.	1

John Cheves & Wife
Molatoes	2
No.	2

Dudeley Lockeliar
Molatoes	1
No.	1

Joab Stapbleton & Solomon
Whites	2
No.	2

Richd. Smith & Jacob Odom & two Negroe wenches Cloe & Tinis
Whites	2
Negroes	2
No.	4

John Moore
Whites	1
No.	1

Duncan Little & son Neill
Whites	2
No.	2

Gutterage Lockeliar
Molatoes	1
No.	1

John Paul; I appointed him as Const. to warn the people
Whites	1
No.	1

John Cade & William McTigre & a Negroe fellow Jacob & Wenchis Nell & Katherin
Whites	2
Negroes	3
No.	5

Isaac Groom
Molatoes	1
No.	1

Aaron Strikland & sons Abram & David
Whites	3
No.	3

Ephraim Driggers
Molatoes	1
No.	1

John Sizemore
Molatoes	1
No.	1

Edward Murffy a criple that Goes with Cruches
[No other information on this entry]

Neill McNeill & two sons Peter & Hector
Whites	3
No.	3

Daniel McLauchlan
Whites	1
No.	1

Abraham Barnes, Josiah Barnes & Elias Barnes & Negro wench Sue, Negro wench Pegg & Negro fellow Jack
Whites	3
Negroes	3
No.	6

Chapter 3: Bladen County Tax Lists of 1776

****

BLADEN COUNTY TAX LIST OF 1776

A List of Taxables taken by Abraham Barnes Returnable to August Term 1776

Headings for this list include: Whites, Molatoes, Negro Men & Negro Women

Samuel Andrews, Asa Andrews, John Andrews & Robert Andrews
Whites   4

Henry Taylor Senr., Henry Taylor Junr., & Thomas Taylor
Whites   3

William Freeman
Whites   1

William Cook
Whites   1

Benjamin Freeman
Whites   1

Lewis Jenkins
Whites   1

Benjamin Freeman
Whites   1

John Regan & Richard Regan
Whites   2

Philemon Terril
Whites   1

Thomas Ivey
Whites   1

John Hammon
Molatoes   1

Thomas Ard, James Ard & Simon
Whites   2
Negro Men   1

Samuel Andrews, Constbl.
Whites   1

William Moore
Whites   1

Jeremiah Ivey
Whites   1

Solomon Whitly
Whites   1

Edmund Baxley
Whites   1

Moses Butler
Whites   1

Hugh & William Brown & Sall
Whites   2
Negro Women   1

Joseph Baggett
Whites   1

John Rozar
Whites   1

Milsby Muselwhite
Whites   1

Thos Jackson
Whites   1

Nathan Muselwhite
Whites   1

Isham Ivey
Whites   1

William Baxley
Whites   1

Robert Upton
Whites   1

Elisha Harrell & Phillis
Whites   1
Negro Women   1

Neill Brown
Whites   1

Will Jones
Molatoes   1

Chapter 3: Bladen County Tax Lists of 1776

Richard Hammon
Molatoes   1

Thomas Starling
Whites   1

John Baxley
Whites   1

David Rozar
Whites   1

Richard Baley
Whites   1

Thomas Oliver
Whites   1

Phillip Blount
Whites   1

Shadrach Lee
Whites   1

John Lee
Whites   1

John Sawyer
Whites   1

Joseph Williams
Whites   1

Reuben Rozar Senr., Reuben Rozar Junr. & Robert Rozar
Whites   3

John Blount & York
Whites   1
Negro Men   1

James Blount & John Smith
Whites   2

Jesse Pittman
Whites   1

John Bell
Whites   1

Henry Pope & Luke, Joe, Spencer, Beck & Tock
Whites   1
Negro Men   3
Negro Women   2

Sampson Pope
Whites   1

Charles Barker
Whites   1

Samuel Edwards
Whites   1

Thomas Carsey & William Horn & Dick & Quash
Molatoes   2
Negro Men   2

Edward Flowers, John Flowers, Drewry Flowers, Arick[?] Flowers & William Flowers
Whites   5

Jesse Baker
Whites   1

John Harper
Whites   1

Thomas Smith & Joseph Smith
Whites   2

Andrew Griffin Senr., Andrew Griffin Junr., James Griffin & Tull
Whites   3
Negro Men   1

Joseph Regan & Quocco, Sam, Patience & Lucy
Whites   1
Negro Men   2
Negro Women   2

Jesse Harrel, Jacob Mangam & Bandy
Whites   2
Negro Women   1

Thomas Musselwhite & Harry
Whites   1
Negro Men   1

Ralph Regan & Will
Whites   1
Negro Men   1

Thomas Jackson & John Jackson

Chapter 3: Bladen County Tax Lists of 1776

Whites	2

Joseph Fort & Harry, Jacob, Jude, Patt, Seley, Samson & Will
Whites	1
Negro Men	4
Negro Women	3

Thomas Litle
White	1

Malachi Mercer
Whites	1

Chambers Humphrey
Whites	1

Jesse Musselwhite
Whites	1

Solomon Mercer Senr., & Christopher Mercer Junr. & Limrick
Whites	2
Negro Men	1

Green Bodiford
Whites	1

William Bird
Whites	1

Solomon Mercer Junr. & Absalom Andrews
Whites	2

George Harrel & Fortune
Whites	1
Negro Women	1

Solomon James
Molatoes	1

George Young Sr. & George Young Jr.
Whites	2

Jacob Blount
Whites	1

Jacob Odom
Whites	1

Isaac Rozar Senr., Daniel Rozar & Isaac Rozar Junr.
White	3

David Braveboy
Molatoes	1

Noah Mercer
Whites	1

John Scot
Molatoes	1

Israel Scot
Molatoes	1

William Sawyer
Whites	1

Solomon James
Molatoes	1

James Moore
Whites	1

John Rowland & George & Phillis
Whites	1
Negro Men	1
Negro Women	1

Charles Barfield & William Griffin
Whites	2

Joseph Brigers
Whites	1

Dempsey Barfield
Whites	1

Charles Bullock
Whites	1

John Odom Senr., John Odom Junr., William Odom & Aaron Odom
White	4

William Lamb
Whites	1

John Phillips & James Phillips
Whites	2

John Starling, Isaac Starling, Joel Wells & Bess
Whites	3
Negro Women	1

Chapter 3: Bladen County Tax Lists of 1776

Gilbert Cox
Molatoes   1

Simon Cox
Molatoes   1

John Cox
Molatoes   1

Zachariah Lee
Whites   1

Silas Adkins & Daniel McGee
Whites   2

Archibald McKissak Sr., Archd. McKissak Jr. & Pegg & *Bud Chavers & Major Wiggins*
Whites   2
Molatoes   2
Negro Women   1

George Ivey & Adam Ivey
Whites   2

Caroway Oates & Phillis
Whites   1
Negro Women   1

Robert Cliburn & Joshua Cliburn
Whites   2

William Cliburn
Whites   1

James Carter Senr., Isaac Carter & Mark Carter
Molatoes   3

Moab Stephens
Whites   1

Isom Pitman
Whites   1

Thomas Russell
Molatoes   1

John Bullard
Whites   1

Daniel Willis Senr., Daniel Willis Junr., Constable & John Willis & Sam; *William Wilkins & wife Constant*
Whites   3
Negro Men   1
Molatoes   2

Charles Thompson
Whites   1
Negro Men   1
Negro Women   1

Thomas Townsend
Whites   1

Edward Grantham & Hampton
Whites   1
Negro Men   1

Richard Grantham, Constable
Whites   1

Jonathan Taylor & William Taylor
Whites   2

Hardy Inman
Whites   1

Jacob Faircloth
Whites   1

Nathan Horn & Richard Horn
Whites   2

Thomas Low
Whites   1

James Rowland, Nathan Rowland & Samuel Rowland
Whites   3

Hardy Horn
Whites   1

William Jones
Whites   1

Edmund Brown & Thomas Brown
Whites   2

James Carter Junr.
Molatoes   1

Arthur Lamb & Meedy Lamb
Whites   1
Molatoes   1

Chapter 3: Bladen County Tax Lists of 1776

James Inman, Henry Flowers & William Flowers
Whites 3

Thomas Rowland
Whites 1

Alexander McDaniel, Benjamin Daniel & John Daniel
Whites 3

Joel Pitman
Whites 1

Francis Ivey
Whites 1

Benjamin Ivey
Whites 1

Lewis Ivey
Whites 1

William Runalds, Mark Runalds & Jack & Hannah
Whites 2
Negro Men 1
Negro Women 1

Thomas Pitman & Sion Pitman
Whites 2

William Perrit
Whites 1

Nathan Cliburn
Whites 1

Belitha Hays & Robert Hays
Whites 2

Micael Barnes
Whites 1

Lemuel Brit
Whites 1

Zachariah McDaniel
Whites 1

John Smith
Whites: [Not Given]

Boltimoor, Daniel, Old Pompy, Young Pompy, Haywood, Old Frank, Young Frank, Peter, Wat, Mingo, Joseph, Tom, Brigs, Natt, Doll, Feebe, Binah, Amy, Sall, Dill, Tinah, Tamer, Lucy, Nell, Hannah, Phillis & Jenney
Negro Men 14
Negro Women 13

William Edwards
Whites 1

Stephen Gleer & Jane
Whites 1
Negro Women 1

Robert Jones
Whites 1

William Caps
Whites 1

Samuel Smith & Peter & Cloe
Whites 1
Negro Men 1
Negro Women 1

William Toler
Whites 1

****

[This list appears to be a complete county wide tax list for the year 1776.]

BLADEN COUNTY TAX LIST OF 1776

List of Taxables in Bladen in 1776

Headings for this list include: Whites, Mixt Blood & Free Negroes, Male Slaves, Female Slaves, Boys & Total

John Adair
Whites 1
Total 1

Joel Allen
Whites 1
Female Slaves 1
Total 2

Benjamin Arrenton
Whites 1

Chapter 3: Bladen County Tax Lists of 1776

Male Slaves 1
Female Slaves 1
Total 3

Jacob Alford
Whites 1
Female Slaves 1
Total 2

William Anders
Whites 1
Total 1

Thomas Avert
Whites 1
Total 1

John Atkinson
Whites 2
Total 2

Thomas Amis
Whites 1
Male Slaves 8
Female Slaves 2
Total 11

Thomas Ard
Whites 1
Total 1

Patty Ard
Female Slaves 1
Total 1

Samuel Andrews
Whites 4
Total 4

Thomas Ard
Whites 2
Male Slaves 1
Total 3

<u>Saml. Andrews, Constable</u>

Silas Adkins
Whites 2
Total 2

John Andres
Whites 4
Male Slaves 3
Female Slaves 1
Boys 1
Total 9

Joseph Andres
Whites 2
Total 2

Stephen Andres
Whites 2
Male Slaves 4
Female Slaves 1
Boys 1
Total 8

James Aitkin
Whites 1
Total 1

Stephen Bryan
Whites 1
Total 1

Elizabeth Bailey
Male Slaves 1
Female Slaves 2
Total 3

Margaret Byrn
Male Slaves 4
Female Slaves 6
Total 10

David Bryan
Whites 1
Total 1

George Brown
Whites 2
Male Slaves 2
Female Slaves 2
Boys 1
Total 7

Phillemon Bryan
Whites 3
Male Slaves 1
Total 4

Edward Bryan
Whites 2
Female Slaves 1
Total 3

Chapter 3: Bladen County Tax Lists of 1776

John Bently
Whites 1
Total 1

John Boyd
Whites 2
Female Slaves 1
Total 3

Amey Bryan
Male Slaves 1
Female Slaves 2
Total 3

Robert Baker
Whites 2
Male Slaves 1
Total 3

Alexander Brodie
Whites 1
Male Slaves 1
Female Slaves 1
Total 3

Willm. Bryan
Whites 2
Female Slaves 1
Total 3

Thoms. Browder
Whites 2
Total 2

William Brown
Whites 1
Total 1

Jeremiah Bigford
Whites 2
Female Slaves 1
Total 3

Thomas Bryan
Whites 1
Male Slaves 1
Female Slaves 1
Total 3

Ezekiel Buzby
Whites 1
Total 1

Simon Bright
Whites 3
Total 3

Sarah Bowen
Male Slaves 16
[Rest of entry torn & missing]

Thomas Benbow
White 1
Male Slaves 1
Female Slaves 1
Total 3

Dugald Blue
Whites 1
Total 1

Archd. Bradley
Whites 1
Total 1

Simon Burney
Whites 1
Total 1

Benjamin Benbow
Whites 1
Male Slaves 2
Total 3

Thomas Brown
Whites 2
Male Slaves 5
Female Slaves 7
Total 14

Willm. Beatty
Whites 1
Total 1

Neill Brown
Whites 1
Total 1

Malcom Buey
Whites 1
Total 1

Abram Barns
Whites 3
Male Slaves 3

Chapter 3: Bladen County Tax Lists of 1776

Saml. Bozman
Whites 2
Total 2

Daniel Beard
Whites 1
Total 1

Lawrence Byrn
Whites 2
Total 2

Peter Byrn
Whites 1
Total 1

James Beard & John Lock, Constable
Whites 1
Male Slaves 1
Female Slaves 1
Total 3

Owel John Barton
Whites 1
Total 1

John Beard
Whites 1
Male Slaves 1
Total 2

Samuel Boazman
Whites 3
Total 3

Henry Bullard
Whites 1
Total 1

James Bennet
Whites 1
Total 1

James Baldwin
Whites 1
Male Slaves 2
Female Slaves 1
Total 4

William Busby
Whites 1
Total 1

Ezekiel Bryant
Whites 1
Total 1

Henry Boswell, Constable

Charles Baldwin
Whites 1
Male Slaves 1
Female Slaves 2
Total 4

John Baldwin Senr.
Whites 2
Male Slaves 4
Female Slaves 3
Total 9

William Burney Senr.
Whites 1
Male Slaves 2
Female Slaves 2
Total 5

Joseph Baldwin
Whites 1
Total 1

Nathaniel Baldwin
Whites 1
Total 1

Morris Bevens
Whites 2
Total 2

John Branton
Whites 3
Total 3

Luke Barefield
Whites 2
Male Slaves 5
Female Slaves 2

Benjamin Beasley
Whites 1
Total 1

Robert Beasley
Whites 1
Total 1

Chapter 3: Bladen County Tax Lists of 1776

William Burney Junr.
Whites	1
Female Slaves	1
Total	2

John Butler
Whites	1
Total	1

John Baldwin Junr.
Whites	1
Male Slaves	1
Female Slaves	1
Total	3

William Butler
Whites	1
Total	1

John Barefield
Whites	1
Total	1

Samuel Butler
Whites	1
Male Slaves	3
Female Slaves	1
Total	5

Benjamin Brantly
Whites	1
Female Slaves	1
Total	2

John Baughard
Whites	2
Total	2

Duncan Buey
Whites	1
Total	1

James Bigs
Whites	1
Total	1

Stephen Butler
Whites	1
Male Slaves	1
Total	2

Joseph Butler
Whites	1
Male Slaves	1
Female Slaves	1
Total	3

Jessey Barefoot
Whites	1
Total	1

James Benson
Whites	1
Total	1

Peter Broades
Whites	1
Male Slaves	3
Female Slaves	1
Total	5

Greens Bodiford
Whites	1
Total	1

Edmund Baxley
Whites	1
Total	1

Moses Butler
Whites	1
Total	1

Hugh Brown
Whites	2
Female Slaves	1
Total	3

Joseph Bagget
Whites	1
Total	1

William Baxley
Whites	1
Total	1

Neill Brown
Whites	1
Mixt Blood & Free Negroes (Male)	1
Total	2

John Baxley
Whites	1
Total	1

Chapter 3: Bladen County Tax Lists of 1776

Richard Bailey
Whites	1
Total	1

Philip Blount
Whites	1
Total	1

William Bird
Whites	1
Total	1

Jacob Blount
Whites	1
Total	1

David Braveboy
Mixt Blood & Free Negroes (Male)	1
Total	1

Charles Barefield
Whites	2
Total	2

Joseph Briggers
Whites	1
Total	1

Dempsey Barefield
Whites	1
Total	1

Charles Bullock
Whites	1
Total	1

John Bullard
Whites	1
Total	1

Edmund Brown
Whites	2
Total	2

Michael Barnes
Whites	1
Total	1

Samuel Britt
Whites	1
Total	1

John Blount
Whites	1
Male Slaves	1
Total	2

James Blount
Whites	2
Total	1

John Bell
Whites	1
Total	1

Charles Barker
Whites	1
Total	1

Jesse Baker
Whites	1
Total	1

Samuel Curry
Whites	1
Total	1

Cannon Cumbo
Mixt Blood & Free Negroes (Male)	2
Female Slaves	1
Boys	1
Total	4

John Campbell
Whites	1
Total	1

Angus Campbell
Whites	1
Total	1

John Campbell Junr.
Whites	1
Total	1

William Cain
Whites	2
Male Slaves	10
Total	12

Samuel Cain
Whites	1
Male Slaves	2
Total	3

Chapter 3: Bladen County Tax Lists of 1776

James Cain
Whites	1
Total	1

Edmund Chancy
Whites	2
Female Slaves	1
Total	3

Joseph Cain
Whites	1
Male Slaves	1
Female Slaves	1
Boys	1
Total	4

John Campbell
Whites	1
Total	1

Archd. Campbell
Whites	1
Total	1

Daniel Curry
Whites	1
Total	1

Benoni Clayton
Whites	2
Total	2

Anguish Cameron
Whites	1
Total	1

John Clyburn
Whites	1
Total	1

John Carsey
Mixt Blood & Free Negroes (Male)	2
Male Slaves	1
Total	3

Duncan Cambelson
Whites	1
Male Slaves	1
Total	2

Laughlin Campbell
Whites	1
Total	1

Lazarus Creel
Whites	2
Total	2

John Cheves
Mixt Blood & Free Negroes (Male)	1
Mixt Blood & Free Negroes (Female)	1
Total	2

John Cade
Whites	2
Male Slaves	1
Female Slaves	2
Total	5

William Cromerty
Whites	1
Male Slaves	2
Female Slaves	1
Total	4

Dennis Coleman
Whites	1
Total	1

Joseph Chason
Whites	1
Total	1

William Crowson
Whites	1
Boys	1
Total	2

Benjamin Clark
Whites	1
Male Slaves	4
Female Slaves	1
Total	6

Saml. Carman
Whites	1
Total	1

William Cain
Whites	3
Total	3

Benjamin Clark
Whites	1
Total	1

Chapter 3: Bladen County Tax Lists of 1776

Maturin Colvill
Whites 1
Male Slaves 13
Female Slaves 11
Boys 2
Total 27

John Coleman, Constable
Whites 2
Total 2

Moses Coleman
Whites 1
Total 1

Micajah Cahoon
Whites 1
Total 1

John Clark
Whites 1
Total 1

John Crews
Whites 1
Total 1

John Chancy
Whites 1
Total 1

James Clardy
Whites 1
Male Slaves 3
Female Slaves 3
Total 7

William Cook
Whites 1
Total 1

Gilbert Cox
Whites 1
Total 1

Simon Cox
Whites 1
Total 1

John Cox
Whites 1
Total 1

Robert Cliburn
Whites 2
Total 2

William Cliburn
Whites 1
Total 1

James Carter
Mixt Blood & Free Negroes (Male) 3
Total 3

James Carter Junr.
Mixt Blood & Free Negroes (Male) 1
Total 1

Nathan Cliburn
Whites 1
Total 1

William Caps
Whites 1
Total 1

Thomas Carsey
Mixt Blood & Free Negroes (Male) 2
Male Slaves 2
Total 4

Judith Corbit
Whites 1
Total 1

Samuel Cannady
Whites 1
Male Slaves 2
Female Slaves 2
Total 5

Danl. Campbell
Whites 1
Total 1

Thomas Creel
Whites 1
Total 1

Joseph Cooper
Whites 2
Male Slaves 1
Female Slaves 1
Total 4

Chapter 3: Bladen County Tax Lists of 1776

John Carter
Whites 1
Total 1

Joseph Carter
Whites 2
Total 2

Henry Clark
Whites 1
Total 1

Henry Carter
Whites 1
Total 1

Jesse Carter
Whites 1
Total 1

Richard Cheshire
Whites 4
Total 4

Daniel Cook
Whites 1
Total 1

Martha Campbell
Whites 1
Male Slaves 3
Female Slaves 2
Total 6

Thomas Dyson
Whites 1
Total 1

Solomon Dyson
Whites 1
Total 1

John Dores
Whites 2
Total 2

Demsey Doboys
Whites 1
Total 1

Dawson Demsy
Whites 1
Male Slaves 2
Female Slaves 1
Total 4

James Dupree
Whites 2
Male Slaves 6
Female Slaves 5
Total 13

Ephraim Driggers
Mixt Blood & Free Negroes (Female) 1
Total 1

Jeremiah Doane
Whites 2
Total 2

Thomas Dawson
Whites 1
Male Slaves 1
Total 2

Hezekiah Davis
Whites 1
Male Slaves 1
Female Slaves 2
Boys 1
Total 5

James Dowey
Whites 2
Total 2

Jane Dubois
Male Slaves 6
Female Slaves 3
Total 9

Turner Davis
Whites 1
Total 1

William Dowlas
Whites 1
Total 1

Edward Davis
Whites 1
Male Slaves 2
Female Slaves 2
Total 5

John Dryden

Chapter 3: Bladen County Tax Lists of 1776

Whites	1
Total	1

Archd. Darrach
Whites	2
Male Slaves	1
Total	3

Donald Downey
Whites	1
Total	1

William Davis
Whites	1
Total	1

Benjamin Elwell
Whites	1
Female Slaves	1
Total	2

William Edwards
Whites	1
Total	1

Samuel Edwards
Whites	1
Total	1

Evan Ellis
Whites	1
Male Slaves	1
Female Slaves	1
Total	3

Willm. Ellis
Whites	1
Male Slaves	1
Total	2

Robert Edwards
Whites	1
Male Slaves	2
Female Slaves	2
Total	5

James Ellis
Whites	4
Male Slaves	3
Total	7

John Ellis
Whites	1

Female Slaves	1
Total	2

Daniel Flin
Whites	2
Total	2

John Fokes
Whites	2
Total	2

Jacob Fokes
Whites	2
Total	2

Ignatius Flowers
Whites	1
Total	1

Abraham Freeman
Mixt Blood & Free Negroes (Male)	1
Mixt Blood & Free Negroes (Female)	1
Total	2

Roger Freeman
Mixt Blood & Free Negroes (Male)	1
Mixt Blood & Free Negroes (Females)	1
Total	2

William Freeman
Mixt Blood & Free Negroes (Male)	1
Mixt Blood & Free Negroes (Female)	1
Total	2

John Fowler
Whites	1
Total	1

John Fiveash
Whites	2
Total	2

John Fairly
Whites	4
Total	4

Joseph Fort
Whites	1
Male Slaves	4
Female Slaves	3
Total	8

William Freeman

Chapter 3: Bladen County Tax Lists of 1776

Whites	1
Total	1

Benjamin Freeman
Whites	1
Total	1

Benjamin Freeman
Whites	1
Total	1

Jacob Faircloth
Whites	1
Total	1

Edward Flowers
Whites	5
Total	5

Saml. Freeman
Whites	1
Female Slaves	1
Total	2

Benjamin Fitz-Randolph
Whites	1
Male Slaves	2
Female Slaves	2
Total	5

William Forrester
Whites	1
Total	1

Alexander Graham
Whites	1
Total	1

Abraham Gray
Whites	1
Total	1

Saml. Guyton
Whites	1
Total	1

Jamie Giffard
Whites	1
Total	1

Faithfull Graham
Male Slaves	32
Female Slaves	28
Total	60

Henry Graham
Whites	1
Male Slaves	1
Female Slaves	1
Total	3

Levi Glass
Whites	3
Male Slaves	1
Female Slaves	2
Total	6

John Gates
Whites	1
Total	1

James Gates
Whites	2
Total	2

Robert Grice
Whites	1
Total	1

James Gardnier
Whites	1
Total	1

Edward Grantham
Whites	1
Female Slaves	1
Total	2

Richard Grantham
Whites	1
Total	1

Stephen Gleer
Whites	1
Female Slaves	1
Total	2

Andrew Griffin
Whites	3
Male Slaves	1
Total	4

Neill Graham
Whites	1
Total	1

Chapter 3: Bladen County Tax Lists of 1776

John Gilcriest
Whites 1
Total 1

Isaac Groom
Mixt Blood & Free Negroes (Male) 1
Mixt Blood & Free Negroes (Females) 1
Total 2

John Green
Whites 2
Total 2

John Green
Whites 1
Total 1

Eliz. Green
Male Slaves 2
Female Slaves 1
Total 3

Margaret Gibs
Male Slaves 3
Female Slaves 3
Total 6

David Godwin
Whites 3
Male Slaves 5
Female Slaves 2
Total 10

Simon Green
Whites 1
Total 1

John Hill, Constable

William Hendon
Whites 2
Male Slaves 1
Female Slaves 1
Boys 1
Total 5

John Harrison Junr.
Whites 3
Male Slaves 1
Female Slaves 2
Total 6

Josiah Hendon

Whites 1
Male Slaves 1
Female Slaves 1
Total 3

Thomas Howard
Whites 1
Total 1

Stephen Hestors
Whites 1
Total 1

Benjamin Humphreys
Whites 2
Female Slaves 1
Total 3

Thomas Holt
Whites 1
Total 1

Joshua Hays
Whites 1
Male Slaves 1
Female Slaves 2
Total 4

Duncan Henderson
Whites 1
Total 1

Thomas Hays
Whites 2
Total 2

Moses Holmes
Whites 2
Total 2

William How
Whites 2
Total 2

John Harrison Senr.
Whites 1
Male Slaves 1
Total 2

Samuel Hails
Whites 1
Total 1

Chapter 3: Bladen County Tax Lists of 1776

Hezekiah Howard
Whites 1
Total 1

John Howard
Whites 2
Male Slaves 3
Female Slaves 2
Total 7

Isaac Hays
Whites 1
Male Slaves 1
Female Slaves 1
Total 3

Richard Huffam
Whites 1
Total 1

Hudnal Huffam
Whites 1
Female Slaves 1
Total 2

Jesse Herrell
Whites 2
Female Slaves 1
Total 3

Chambers Humphrey
Whites 1
Total 1

John Hammon
Whites 1
Total 1

Elisha Herrell
Whites 1
Female Slaves 1
Total 2

Richd. Hammon
Mixt Blood & Free Negroes (Male) 1
Total 1

George Herrell
Whites 1
Female Slaves 2
Total 3

Nathan Horn
Whites 2
Total 2

Hardy Horn
Whites 1
Total 1

Balitha Hays
Whites 2
Total 2

John Harper
Whites 1
Total 1

Lewis Hall
Whites 2
Total 2

Isaac Hall Junr.
Whites 2
Total 2

Enoch Hall
Whites 1
Total 1

Lewis Hall Junr.
Whites 1
Total 1

Richard Harrison
Whites 1
Male Slaves 1
Total 2

John Hollingsworth
Whites 2
Total 2

Stephen Hollingsworth
Whites 1
Total 1

Thomas Hardwick
Whites 3
Total 3

Jacob Hunchy
Whites 1
Total 1

Allen Hardwick

Chapter 3: Bladen County Tax Lists of 1776

Whites	1
Total	1

Ezekiel Hill
Whites	2
Total	2

Thoms. Hardwick Junr.
Whites	1
Total	1

Burwell Hairgrove
Whites	2
Total	2

Southy Hays
Whites	1
Male Slaves	1
Total	2

John Jones
Whites	2
Male Slaves	1
Female Slaves	2
Total	5

Phillip Ikner
Whites	1
Total	1

Michael Ikner
Whites	1
Total	1

John Johnston
Whites	1
Total	1

James Jackson
Whites	1
Male Slaves	2
Total	3

Thomas Jackson
Whites	1
Male Slaves	1
Total	2

Lewis Jenkins
Whites	1
Total	1

Thomas Ivey

Whites	1
Total	1

Jeremiah Ivey
Whites	1
Total	1

Thomas Jackson
Whites	1
Total	1

Isham Ivey
Whites	1
Total	1

Soloman James
Mixt Blood & Free Negroes (Male)	1
Total	1

Soloman James
Mixt Blood & Free Negroes (Male)	1
Total	1

Hardy Inman
Whites	1
Total	1

William Jones
Whites	1
Total	1

Adam Ivey
Whites	2
Total	2

James Inman
Whites	3
Total	3

Francis Ivey
Whites	1
Total	1

Benjamin Ivey
Whites	1
Total	1

Lewis Ivey
Whites	1
Total	1

Robt. Jones
Whites	1

Chapter 3: Bladen County Tax Lists of 1776

Total 1

John Jackson
Whites 1
Total 1

James Isham
White 1
Male Slaves 1
Total 2

Isaac Jessop
Whites 1
Total 1

William Johnston
Whites 2
Total 2

Hezekiah Jones
Whites 1
Total 1

Isaac Jones
Whites 3
Male Slaves 3
Female Slaves 2
Total 6

John Johnston Junr.
Whites 1
Total 1

John Johnston Senr.
Whites 2
Total 2

Thomas Johnston
Whites 1
Total 1

Nehemiah Johnston
Whites 1
Total 1

Abraham King
Whites 1
Total 1

Joseph Kemp
Whites 1
Female Slaves 1
Total 2

Archibald Kelly
Whites 1
Total 1

Matthew Kelly
Whites 1
Male Slaves 3
Female Slaves 2
Total 6

John Kelly
Whites 1
Total 1

Neill Kurry
Whites 1
Total 1

Thomas Kinlow
Whites 2
Total 2

John King
Whites 1
Male Slaves 1
Female Slaves 1
Total 3

John Lessley
Whites 2
Total 2

Duncan Lemmon
Whites 1
Total 1

Peter Lord
Whites 3
Male Slaves 3
Female Slaves 2
Total 8

John Lennon
Whites 1
Female Slaves 2
Total 3

Josiah Lewis
Whites 1
Male Slaves 1
Total 2

Chapter 3: Bladen County Tax Lists of 1776

James Lewis
Whites 3
Total 3

Francis Lawson
Whites 1
Total 1

Solomon Lewis
Whites 1
Total 1

Denis Lennen
Whites 1
Male Slaves 1
Total 2

Uriah Lamberdson
Whites 1
Total 1

Archd. Little
Whites 1
Total 1

Archibald Little
Whites 1
Total 1

John Little
Whites 1
Total 1

Absolem Leggett
Whites 1
Total 1

Rachel Leggett
Male Slaves 3
Female Slaves 3
Total 6

John Lock
Whites 2
Male Slaves 2
Female Slaves 3
[Rest of entry torn & missing]

Leonard Lock
Whites 1
Male Slaves 2
Female Slaves 1
[Rest of entry torn & missing]

Thomas Little
Whites 1
Total 1

Shadarick Lee
Whites 1
Total 1

John Lee
Whites 1
Total 1

William Lamb
Whites 1
Total 1

Zachariah Lee
Whites 1
Total 1

Arthur Lam
Whites 1
Mixt Blood & Free Negroes (Male) 1
Total 2

James Lowry
Whites 1
Mixt Blood & Free Negroes (Male) 2
Total 3

Dudley Lockelair
Mixt Blood & Free Negroes (Male) 1
Total 1

Duncan Little
Whites 1
Total 1

Gutterage Lockelair
Mixt Blood & Free Negroes (Male) 1
Total 1

Thomas Lock
Whites 1
Male Slaves 2
Total 3

Hanson Lewis Senr.
Whites 2
Male Slaves 1
Female Slaves 1
Total 4

Chapter 3: Bladen County Tax Lists of 1776

William Lucas
Whites	1
Total	1

David Lock
Whites	3
Male Slaves	2
Female Slaves	2
Total	7

Joseph Lock
Whites	2
Male Slaves	1
Female Slaves	1
Total	4

David Loyd
Whites	1
Total	1

Francis Lucas
Whites	1
Male Slaves	4
Female Slaves	4
Boys	1
Total	10

George Lucas
Whites	2
Male Slaves	15
Female Slaves	14
Total	31

Ralph Miller
Whites	2
Male Slaves	3
Female Slaves	4
Total	9

Jacob Mezick Junr.
Whites	1
Total	1

Thomas McGuire
Whites	2
Male Slaves	15
Female Slaves	18
Boys	1
Total	36

William Maultsby
Whites	1
Male Slaves	2
Female Slaves	1
Total	4

William McRee
Whites	3
Male Slaves	9
Female Slaves	5
Total	17

Duncan McAllister
Whites	2
Total	2

John McDaniel
Whites	1
Total	1

Nathan Meredith
Whites	1
Total	1

Michael Mixon
Whites	1
Total	1

John Munro
Whites	1
Total	1

Gilbert McKeithan
Whites	1
Total	1

Saml. McRee
Whites	1
Male Slaves	2
Total	3

Ephraim Mullford
Whites	2
Male Slaves	1
Female Slaves	3
Boys	1
Total	7

Amelia Morley
Male Slaves	2
Female Slaves	1
Total	3

James Money
Whites	3

Chapter 3: Bladen County Tax Lists of 1776

Total	3

David Mims
Whites	1
Male Slaves	1
Total	2

Thoms. Mims Senr.
Whites	2
Male Slaves	2
Total	4

Duncan Morrison
Whites	1
Male Slaves	5
Female Slaves	2
Total	8

Danl. Melvin
Whites	1
Total	1

Archd. McDaniel
Whites	1
Total	1

Mathas Munce
Whites	1
Total	1

John McCollom
Whites	1
Total	1

William McMaster
Whites	2
Total	2

James McDaniel
Whites	2
Male Slaves	1
Female Slaves	1
Total	4

David McDaniel
Whites	1
Total	1

Duncan McCarmig
Whites	1
Total	1

John McCarmig
Whites	1
Total	1

Archd. McCarmig
Whites	1
Total	1

Hector McLean
Whites	1
Total	1

Archd. McGirt
Whites	1
Total	1

Daniel McLean Junr.
Whites	1
Total	1

Duncan McCall
Whites	2
Total	2

David McCall
Whites	1
Total	1

Archd. McLean
Whites	1
Total	1

John McLaine
Whites	1
Total	1

Duncan McEacharn
Whites	1
Total	1

Gilbert McCarmig
Whites	1
Total	1

Archd. McGill
Whites	1
Total	1

Peter McArthur
Whites	1
Total	1

Alexander McArthur
Whites	1

Chapter 3: Bladen County Tax Lists of 1776

| Total | 1 |

Neill McNeill
Whites	1
Male Slaves	3
Total	4

Hector McNeill, Sailor
Whites	2
Male Slaves	1
Total	3

Malcom McNeill
| Whites | 1 |
| Total | 1 |

Danl. McClain Senr.
Whites	1
Male Slaves	1
Total	2

John McRainey
Whites	2
Male Slaves	1
Total	3

John McAnewer
Whites	1
Male Slaves	2
Total	3

John McLean, Taylor
| Whites | 1 |
| Total | 1 |

Daniel McAnewer
| Whites | 2 |
| Total | 2 |

William McFater
| Whites | 2 |
| Total | 2 |

Malcom McFater
| Whites | 1 |
| Total | 1 |

Duncan McMillan
| Whites | 1 |
| Total | 1 |

Neill McGill
| Whites | 1 |

| Total | 1 |

John Moore
| Whites | 1 |
| Total | 1 |

Edwd. Murphy, a Criple
[Exempt from tax]

Neill McNeill
| Whites | 3 |
| Total | 3 |

Danl. McLaughlin
| Whites | 1 |
| Total | 1 |

Godfrey McNeill
| Whites | 1 |
| Total | 1 |

Peter McKeller
| Whites | 1 |
| Total | 1 |

Hugh McRainey
Whites	1
Male Slaves	1
Female Slaves	1
Total	3

Henry Mercer
Whites	2
Male Slaves	1
Female Slaves	1
Total	4

Daniel McEachern
| Whites | 1 |
| Total | 1 |

Murdoch McLoud
| Whites | 1 |
| Total | 1 |

Jams. McNeill
Whites	1
Male Slaves	2
Female Slaves	1
Total	4

Neill McKay
| Whites | 2 |

Chapter 3: Bladen County Tax Lists of 1776

Total	2

James McKay
Whites	1
Total	1

Hector Munro
Whites	1
Total	1

Malcom Munro
Whites	1
Total	1

Neill McFall
Whites	3
Male Slaves	1
Female Slaves	1
Total	5

Alexr. McKay
Whites	2
Total	2

Danl. McFarsion
Whites	2
Male Slaves	2
Female Slaves	2
Total	6

Thoms. Musstlewhite
Whites	1
Male Slaves	1
Total	2

Malachi Mercer
Whites	1
Total	1

Jesse Musstlewhite
Whites	1
Total	1

Solomon Mercer Senr.
Whites	2
Male Slaves	1
Total	3

Willm. Moore
Whites	1
Total	1

Milsby Musstlewhite
Whites	1
Total	1

Nathan Musstlewhite
Whites	1
Total	1

Solomon Mercer Junr.
Whites	2
Total	2

Noah Mercer
Whites	1
Total	1

James Moore
Whites	1
Total	1

Archd. McKissack
Whites	2
Mixt Blood & Free Negroes (Male)	2
Male Slaves	1
[Rest of entry torn & missing]	

Alexander McDaniel
Whites	3
Total	3

Zachariah McDaniel
Whites	1
Total	1

Robert McRee
Whites	2
Total	2

William McNeill
Whites	1
Male Slaves	3
Female Slaves	2
Total	6

James Murphy
Whites	1
Total	1

Anguish McKay
Whites	2
Total	2

Neill McCoulsky
Whites	1

Chapter 3: Bladen County Tax Lists of 1776

Male Slaves	1
Female Slaves	1
Total	3

Andrew McLelland
Whites	1
Male Slaves	1
Female Slaves	1
Total	3

John McLelland
Whites	1
Total	1

John McLaren
Whites	2
Total	2

George McGee
Whites	1
Total	1

John McKown
Whites	2
Total	2

Iver McMullan
Whites	2
Total	2

Danl. McCollom
Whites	1
Total	1

Jacob Munce
Whites	1
Total	1

Iver McKay
Whites	1
Male Slaves	4
Female Slaves	5
Total	10

Duncan McKeithan
Whites	1
Male Slaves	1
Total	2

Danl. McFater
Whites	1
Total	1

Archd. McBride
Whites	1
Total	1

Archd. McKeithan
Whites	2
Total	2

Donald McKeithan
Whites	2
Total	2

Iver McCollom
Whites	1
Total	1

Robt. McConkey
Whites	1
Male Slaves	1
Female Slaves	3
Total	5

Ann Maultsby
Whites	2
Male Slaves	1
Female Slaves	2
Boys	2
Total	7

Donald McKeithan
Whites	1
Total	1

John Mckinzie
Whites	1
Total	1

Willm. Moorhead
Whites	1
Male Slaves	2
Female Slaves	1
Total	4

Archd. McCoulsky
Whites	2
Female Slaves	2
Total	4

Charles McNaughton
Whites	1
Male Slaves	6
Total	7

Chapter 3: Bladen County Tax Lists of 1776

John Moore
Whites 1
Male Slaves 1
Total 2

John Newberry
Whites 1
Male Slaves 3
Female Slaves 1
Total 5

Jesse Newberry
Whites 2
Male Slaves 6
Female Slaves 5
Boys 1
Total 14

Coleman Nichols
Whites 2
Total 2

Joseph Noble
Whites 1
Total 1

Titus Overton
Mixt Blood & free Negroes (Male) 1
Mixt Blood & Free Negroes (Female) 1
Total 2

William Owens
Whites 1
Male Slaves 2
Female Slaves 1
Total 4

Thomas Oliver
Whites 1
Total 1

Jacob Odom
Whites 1
Total 1

John Odom
Whites 4
Total 4

Caraway Oats
Whites 1
Female Slaves 2
Total 3

John Owen
Whites 2
Male Slaves 5
Female Slaves 4
Total 11

John Pointer Junr.
Whites 1
Male Slaves 10
Female Slaves 8
Total 19

John Pointer Senr.
Whites 2
Male Slaves 1
Total 3

Mathew Prigeon
Whites 3
Total 3

Absolem Powell
Whites 1
Total 1

Joshua Pevey
Mixt Blood & Free Negroes 3
Female Slaves 1
Boys 1
Total 4

John Parnell
Whites 2
Total 2

Willm. Plummer
Whites 2
Total 2

Jeremiah Plummer
Whites 1
Total 1

John Plummer
Whites 1
Total 1

Gidion Pricket
Whites 1
Total 1

Abraham Paul

Chapter 3: Bladen County Tax Lists of 1776

Whites	1
Total	1

John Paul, Constable

John Phillips
Whites	2
Total	2

Isham Pittman
Whites	1
Total	1

Joel Pitman
Whites	1
Total	1

Thomas Pitman
Whites	2
Total	2

William Parret
Whites	1
Total	1

Jesse Pitman
Whites	1
Total	1

Henry Pope
Whites	1
Male Slaves	3
Female Slaves	2
Total	6

Sampson Pope
Whites	1
Total	1

Joseph Powers
Whites	1
Total	1

John Pemberton
Whites	1
Total	1

Margt. Pemberton
Whites	1
Male Slaves	1
Female Slaves	1
Total	3

Ambrose Powell
Whites	1
Total	1

Joseph Price
Whites	2
Total	2

Andrew Puff
Whites	1
Total	1

Daniel Patterson
Whites	2
Total	2

Thomas Russ
Whites	2
Male Slaves	2
Female Slaves	1
Total	5

Thomas Robeson
Whites	2
Total	2

John Rogers
Whites	2
Total	2

Samuel Rourk
Whites	1
Male Slaves	1
Female Slaves	1
Total	3

Thomas Richardson
Whites	2
Total	2

John Roberts
Whites	1
Total	1

Edwd. Reeves
Whites	1
Total	1

John Rogerson
Whites	2
Male Slaves	3
Female Slaves	2
Total	7

Chapter 3: Bladen County Tax Lists of 1776

Peter Robeson
Whites	1
Male Slaves	4
Female Slaves	3
Total	8

Nathaniel Reeves
Whites	1
Male Slaves	1
Female Slaves	2
Total	4

John Richardson Senr.
Whites	1
Total	1

John Richardson Junr.
Whites	1
Total	1

Isaac Ray
Whites	1
Male Slaves	2
Female Slaves	3
Total	6

Robert Richardson
Whites	1
Total	1

Anguish Rea
Whites	1
Total	1

Joseph Regan
Whites	1
Male Slaves	2
Female Slaves	2
Total	5

Ralph Regan
Whites	1
Male Slaves	1
Total	2

John Regan
Whites	2
Total	2

John Rozier
Whites	2
Total	2

David Rozier
Whites	1
Total	1

Ruben Rozier
Whites	3
Total	3

Isaac Rozier
Whites	3
Total	3

John Rowland
Whites	1
Male Slaves	1
Female Slaves	1
Total	3

Thomas Russell
Mixt Blood & Free Negroes (Male)	1
Total	1

James Rowland
Whites	3
Total	3

Thomas Rowland
Whites	1
Total	1

William Runalds
Whites	2
Male Slaves	1
Female Slaves	1
Total	4

William Russ
Whites	1
Total	1

John Russ Senr.
Whites	1
Total	1

Thomas Robeson
Whites	1
Male Slaves	8
Female Slaves	5
Boys	3
Total	17

Donald Robeson

Chapter 3: Bladen County Tax Lists of 1776

Whites	2
Total	2

David Russ
Whites	3
Total	3

Gilbert Ramsey
Whites	1
Total	1

James Smith
Whites	1
Total	1

John Sinclair
Whites	1
Total	1

John Stewart
Whites	2
Total	2

John Storm
Whites	1
Total	1

John Suggs
Whites	1
Total	1

William Smith
Whites	2
Male Slaves	5
Female Slaves	2
Total	9

Neill Shaw
Whites	2
Male Slaves	2
Female Slaves	2
Total	6

John Shaw
Whites	3
Total	3

Anguish Sellers
Whites	2
Total	2

James Singletary
Whites	1

Female Slaves	1
Total	2

Thomas Scrivin
Whites	1
Total	1

Benjamin Singletary
Whites	1
Male Slaves	4
Female Slaves	2
Total	7

Benjamin Stone
Whites	2
Male Slaves	5
Female Slaves	2
Boys	2
Total	11

Mary Singletary
Whites	1
Male Slaves	1
Female Slaves	1
Total	3

Sarah Singletary
Male Slaves	1
Female Slaves	1
Total	2

James Smith
Whites	2
Male Slaves	3
Total	5

Archd. Shaw
Whites	1
Male Slaves	1
Total	2

John Simpson
Whites	1
Total	1

Daniel Shaw
Whites	2
Male Slaves	1
Female Slaves	1
Total	4

Daniel Shipman
Whites	3

Chapter 3: Bladen County Tax Lists of 1776

Male Slaves	2
Total	5

Thoms. Simpson
Whites	1
Male Slaves	3
Female Slaves	2
Total	6

Archd. Sellers
Whites	1
Total	1

Barnabass Stevens
Whites	2
Male Slaves	4
Female Slaves	1
Total	7

Thomas Sterling
Whites	1
Total	1

John Sawyer
Whites	1
Total	1

John Scot
Mixt Blood & Free Negroes (Male)	1
Total	1

Israel Scot
Mixt Blood & Free Negroes (Male)	1
Total	1

William Sawyer
Whites	1
Total	1

John Sterling
Whites	3
Female Slaves	1
Total	4

Moat Stevens
Whites	1
Total	1

John Smith
Whites	1
Male Slaves	14
Female Slaves	13
Total	28

Saml. Smith
Whites	1
Male Slaves	1
Female Slaves	1
Total	3

Thomas Smith
White	2
Total	2

Elisha Sweetin
Mixt Blood & Free Negroes (Male)	1
Mixt Blood & Free Negroes (Females)	1
Total	2

Joab Stapleton
Whites	2
Total	2

Richd. Smith
Whites	2
Male Slaves	2
Total	4

Aaron Strickland
Whites	3
Total	3

John Sizemore
Mixt Blood & Free Negroes (Male)	1
Total	1

Christopher Sutton
Whites	1
Total	1

Richard Saltar
Whites	1
Male Slaves	2
Female Slaves	1
Total	4

John Sellars
Whites	3
Total	3

John Smith Senr. So. River
Whites	2
Total	2

Richd. Singletary
Whites	1

Chapter 3: Bladen County Tax Lists of 1776

Male Slaves 1
Total 2

Thomas Suggs
Whites 2
Total 2

Thomas Sessoms
Whites 1
Total 1

Thoms. Saunders
Whites 1
Male Slaves 1
Female Slaves 1
Total 3

Christopher Saunders
Whites 1
Total 1

Simon Sellers
Whites 1
Total 1

William Starky
Whites 1
Total 1

Grace Smith
Whites 2
Male Slaves 1
Total 3

Richd. Stubbs
Whites 1
Total 1

John Stubs Senr.
Whites 2
Total 2

Willm. Strickland
Whites 3
Total 3

Arthur Smith
Whites 1
Total 1

Steven Smith
Whites 1
Total 1

Joshua Stevens
Whites 2
Male Slaves 2
Female Slaves 2
Total 6

Willm. Stevens
Whites 1
Total 1

Willm. Stewart
Whites 2
Male Slaves 9
Female Slaves 9
Boys 1
Total 21

Othniel Straughan
Whites 1
Male Slaves 1
Female Slaves 2
Total 4

Robert Stewart
Whites 1
Total 1

Josiah Sykes
Whites 1
Total 1

Willm. Sloan
Whites 1
Total 1

Jacob Sykes
Whites 3
Total 3

Beaumont Sutton
Whites 2
Male Slaves 1
Total 3

John Sutton, Constable

John Sykes
Whites 1
Total 1

John Singletary
Whites 2

Chapter 3: Bladen County Tax Lists of 1776

Male Slaves 1
Total 3

Brayton Singletary
Whites 3
Male Slaves 1
Total 4

Willm. Saltar
Whites 1
Male Slaves 8
Female Slaves 4
Total 13

John Slingsby
Whites 5
Male Slaves 9
Female Slaves 7
Total 21

William Shaw
Whites 2
Total 2

Richard Small
Whites 1
Total 1

John Smith Ligs.[?]
Whites 2
Mixt Blood & Free Negroes (Male) 5
Mixt Blood & Free Negroes (Females) 5
Total 12

Moses Tredaway
Whites 2
Female Slaves 1
Total 3

George Thomas Senr.
Whites 1
Total 1

George Thomas
Whites 1
Male Slaves 1
Total 2

Aaron Tomlinson Senr.
Whites 2
Total 2

Israel Tomlinson
Whites 1
Total 1

Michael Thomas
Whites 1
Total 1

Henry Taylor Senr.
Whites 3
Total 3

Philemon Terrel
Whites 1
Total 1

Charles Thompson
Whites 1
Male Slaves 1
Female Slaves 1
Total 3

Thomas Townsend
Whites 1
Total 1

Jonathan Taylor
Whites 2
Total 2

William Toller
Whites 1
Total 1

Daniel Turner
Whites 1
Total 1

Lewis Thomas
Whites 1
Total 1

Archd. Taylor
Whites 4
Total 4

John Taylor
Whites 1
Total 1

Joseph Themes
Whites 1
Male Slaves 2
Female Slaves 1

Chapter 3: Bladen County Tax Lists of 1776

[Rest of entry torn & missing]

Jesse Themes
Whites 1
Male Slaves 1
Female Slaves 1
[Rest of entry torn & missing]

John Turner Esqr.
Whites 1
Male Slaves 5
Female Slaves 5
[Rest of entry torn & missing]

Neill Thompson
Whites 1
Total 1

Robert Upton
Whites 1
Total 1

Sarah Willson
Whites 1
Male Slaves 1
Female Slaves 1
Total 3

James White
Whites 1
Male Slaves 6
Female Slaves 5
Total 12

Joseph White
Whites 1
Female Slaves 1
Total 2

Edwd. Wall
Whites 2
Total 2

John Williams
Whites 4
Total 4

Edward Willson
Whites 1
Total 1

John Willson
Whites 1

Total 1

Jams. Willson
Whites 1
Total 1

Michael Whitman
Whites 1
Total 1

John Web
Male Slaves 1
Female Slaves 2
[Entry vague. John Web could be Mixt Blood or Free Negroe]

Willm. Wilkinson
Whites 1
Total 1

Solomon Wiley
Whites 1
Total 1

James Wilkinson
Whites 1
Total 1

Anguish Wilkinson
Whites 3
Total 3

Joseph Williams
Whites 1
Total 1

Willm. White, Constable

Mary White
Whites 1
Male Slaves 3
Female Slaves 3
Total 7

Danl. Willis
Whites 3
Mixt Blood & Free Negroes (Males) 2
Male Slaves 1
Total 6

Robert Walker
Whites 2
Total 2

Chapter 3: Bladen County Tax Lists of 1776

Joseph Wiggins
Whites 2
Total 2

David Lindsey White
Whites 1
Male Slaves 2
Female Slaves 1
Boys 1
Total 5

Willm. Wishart
Whites 1
Male Slaves 1
Female Slaves 1
Total 3

John White Senr.
Whites 1
Total 1

Joseph Wood
Whites 3
Male Slaves 2
Total 5

James Washburn
Whites 1
Total 1

Jams. White, Weaver
Whites 1
Total 1

Phillip Wood
Whites 1
Total 1

Robert Wells
Whites 1
Male Slaves 4
Female Slaves 3
Total 8

David White
Whites 2
Male Slaves 2
Total 4

John Ward
Whites 1
Total 1

John Willson
Whites 1
Total 1

George Willis
Whites 2
Total 2

Agerton Willis
Whites 2
Male Slaves 14
Female Slaves 11
Total 27

Benjamin Willis
Whites 2
Female Slaves 2
Total 4

David Young
Whites 1
Total 1

George Young
Whites 2
Total 2

John Yates
Whites 1
Total 1

Levi Young
Whites 1
Total 1

James Moore
Whites 1
Male Slaves 1
Female Slaves 1
Total 3

Isaac Simms
Whites 2
Male Slaves 2
Total 4

Total 1923
Jno Smith Esqr 12

CHAPTER 4

BLADEN COUNTY TAX LISTS OF 1778

BLADEN COUNTY TAX LIST OF 1778
Appears to be a partial list.

Returns of Assessmt. in William McRee Esqr.'s District 1778

Persons Taxable in William McRee's District

Headings for this list include: Cultivated Lands on the River, Uncultivated on the River, Back Lands Uncultivated, Lands in other Districts, No. of Negroes, No. of Horses, No. of Horn Cattle, Lotts in Eliza., Wilmington, Money, Money at Interest, Stock in Trade, Poll Taxables, Sum Total to be Taxed, Taxes 2.5 on the Pound two years, & Sundry Remarks

[Abbreviations will be used on the above headings]

Alexr. Harvey	
Uncultivated Lands	190
Bk. Lands Uncult.	10.5
No. Horses	1
No. Horn Cattle	5
Lotts in Eliza.	2
Sum Total	£168. 10
Taxes 2.5	£1.- 15. -1.25
Willm. Russ	
Bk. Lands Uncult.	640
No. Horses	1
No. Horn Cattle	7
Money	£130
Sum Total	£220
Taxes 2.5	£2.-5.-8
John Adair	
Cultivated Lands	75
No. Horn Cattle	3
Money	£24
Sum Total	£105
Taxes 2.5	£1.-1.-6.5
David Russ	
Cultivated Lands	100
Bk. Lands Uncult.	200
No. Negroes	1
No. Horses	3
No. Horn Cattle	16
Lotts in Eliza.	3
Money	£22
Sum Total	£322
Taxes 2.5	£3.-6.-2.5
George Brown	
Cultivated Lands	493
Lands in other Districts	680
No. Negroes	10
No. Horses	14
No. Horn Cattle	40
Money	£50
Sum Total	£1304.-13.-4
Taxes 2.5	£13.-11.-6
Sundry Remarks	Other Districts not Assessed
James Smith	
No. Horses	3
No. Horn Cattle	10
Lotts in Eliza.	2
Money	£80
Money at Interest	£20
Stocks in Trade	£60
Sum Total	£370
Taxes 2.5	£3.-16.-8.5
Benjn. Humphrey	
No. Horses	1
No. Horn Cattle	4
Lotts at Eliza.	4
Money	£15.-2.-6
Sum Total	£131.-2.-6
Taxes 2.5	£1.-6.-10.75
Margt. Weir	
Lands in other Districts	150
No. Horses	2
No. Horn Cattle	13

Chapter 4: Bladen County Tax Lists of 1778

Lotts in Eliza.	2
Money	£10.-2
Money at Interest	£41.-7
Sum Total	£123.-9
Taxes 2.5	£1.-5.-6

<u>Sundry Remarks Other Districts not Assessed</u>

John White
Cultivated Lands	3
No. Horses	2
No. Horn Cattle	1
Lotts in Eliza.	3
Money	£100
Money at Interest	£150
Stocks in Trade	£42.-18
Sum Total	£490.-14
Taxes 2.5	£5.-1.-10.25

Edmd. Russ
Bk. Lands Uncult.	200
No. Horses	1
No. Horn Cattle	9
Lotts in Eliza.	2
Money	£40
Poll Taxables	Poll
Taxes 2.5	£0.-1.-10

Saml. Roots
No. Negroes	2
No. Horses	1
Money	£7.-15
Sum Total	£212.-15
Taxes 2.5	£2.-3.-7.25

Willm. McRee
Cultivated Lands	730
Uncultivated Lands	350
Bk. Lands Uncult.	3530
No. Negroes	19
No. Horses	7
No. Horn Cattle	54
Lotts in Eliza.	5
Money	£12
Stocks in Trade	£103.-8
Sum Total	£3731.-15.-5
Taxes 2.5	£38.-18

[Torn] Bryon
Cultivated Lands	[Faded]
No. Negroes	8
No. Horses	2
No. Horn Cattle	48
Money	[Torn]

Sum Total	£1230.-2
Taxes 2.5	£12.-[Faded]

Thos. Hains
Lands in other Districts	500 Hilb. C.T.
No. Negroes	9
No. Horses	4
No. Horn Cattle	26
Lotts in Eliza.	4
Money	£40
Money at Interest	£347.-14
Stocks in Trade	£295
Sum Total	£1481.-14
Taxes 2.5	£15.-8

<u>Sundry Remarks Other Districts not assessed</u>

John Young
Poll Taxables	Poll
Taxes 2.5	£1.-0.-10

Robert Hodge
Poll Taxables	Poll
Taxes 2.5	£1.-0.-10

James Knowls
Poll Taxables	Poll
Taxes 2.5	£1.0-10

David Kid
Poll Taxables	Poll
Taxes 2.5	£1.-0.-10

Willm. Cook
Poll Taxables	Poll
Taxes 2.5	£1.-0.-10

Willm. Singletary
Poll Taxables	Poll
Taxes 2.5	£1.-0.-10

Thos. Hestors Junr.
Poll Taxables	Poll
Taxes 2.5	£1.-0.-10

George Knowls
Poll Taxables	Poll
Taxes 2.5	£1.-0.-10

Benjn. Singletary
Poll Taxes	Poll
Taxes 2.5	£1.-0.-10

Thos McClanon

Chapter 4: Bladen County Tax Lists of 1778

Poll Taxes
Taxes 2.5   Poll £1.-0.-10

John Stone
Poll Taxables
Taxes 2.5   Poll £1.-0.-10

[Faded] Handen Junr.
Poll Taxables
Taxes 2.5   Poll £1.-0.-10

[Torn] Redin
Poll Taxables
Taxes 2.5   Poll £1.-0.-10

****

BLADEN COUNTY TAX LIST OF 1778

The Assessment of Capt Joseph Woods District
[Value given in pounds]

Aaron Strickland	160.-0.-6
Isaac Wilks	126.-3.-8
Danold Campbell	123.-10.-0
John McCrane	324.-15.-6
Danold McLauchlan	107.-0.-0
Edward McFassion	138.-0.-0
John Locklear	163.-5.-0
Jane Watson	124.-0.-0
James Lowary	690.-0.-0
Enoch Hall	177.-18.-4
Lewis Hall	255.-12.-0
Jacob Alford	623.-4.-6
Hector McNeill, Sailor	314.-17.-10

A List of them who pay a pole Tax

Thomas Bud
Abram Strickland
John Butler
Angus Brown
Elexander McArthur
David Beaton
Willm. Samford
Lewis Hall Junr.
Isaac Hall
William Barlow
Malcum Forgason
William Locklear
William Betty
Edmund Revill
Robert Locklear

A List of the names of them that Refused To give in

Neill McFall, Soldier	1100.-0.-0
Malcum Buoie, Soldier	320.-0.-0
Peter McArthur, Soldier	400.-0.-0
John Gilcrease, Soldier	190.-0.-0
Elexander McArthur, Soldier	103.-0.-0
Rodger McGill	110.-0.-0
Malcum McLelan	120.-0.-0
Danold McFater	120.-0.-0
John McNear	117.-0.-0
Archibald Fairly	143.-2.-0
Elexander Grimes	103.-[Torn]
John McBride	112.-0.-0
Lauchlan McNeill	282.-0.-0
Malcum Munrow	180.-0.-0

A list of them Who pay a pole Tax

Elexander Forgason
James Watson
Neill Forgason
Neill McGill
Neill McNeill

Chapter 4: Bladen County Tax Lists of 1778

Angus Wilkinson
Archebald Wilkinson
Neill Wilkinson
Edward Wilkinson
Duncan McMullen
Moses Hodge
[Torn] Hodge
John Fairly
John McAchen
Elexander Love
Danold Smith
John McNeill
Malcum McAlpin
James Forgason
Angus McCollester
John McLocklan
Duncan McCollom
Archelaus Smith
John Gillis

Danold McArthur
Peter McArthur
John McArthur
Neill Brown
Edward Murfy
John McMullen
Neill McNeill, Weavr.

Duly assesed and praised by Us this 26th July 1778

Thomas Ard
Ambrose Powel
Elias Fort
Given in and assesed in the District where they live

***

BLADEN COUNTY TAX LIST OF 1778

Captn. Stephen Anders's district 1778
July 20, 1778
Ordread that the taxabel property be valued in the Behalf of this State by each District South river

600 Akers of Land valued to		200
1 Negro feller	Vd	100
2 Negro wenches	Vd	150
1 Negro Child	Vd	25
71 head of Cattel	Vd	142
2 horses	Vd	20
4 maers & one Cold	Vd	25
Nr. 1 Oathneal Strohon List of Property		662

27 head of Cattel	Vd.	54
2 Mares & Colts	Vd.	20
Cash		63
100 Akers of Land	Vd.	50
Nr. 2 Josiah Sikes his property		187

160 Akers of Land	Vd.	40
4 [Faded]	Vd.	20
2 Cows	Vd.	6
Cash		16-3
Nr. 3 Isaac Hase List of property		82-3

9 head of Cattel	Vd.	18
1 hors & mare & 1 year old	Vd.	20
Cash		13-6
Nr. 4 Jacob Hase List Property		38-13-6

Chapter 4: Bladen County Tax Lists of 1778

1 hors & 1 Mare & 1 too year old	Vd.	30
10 head of Cattel	Vd.	<u>20</u>
Nr. 5 John Wilson Taxebel property		50

200 Akers of Land	Vd.	40
8 head of Cattel	Vd.	16
2 Mares	Vd.	12
Cash		<u>2</u>
Nr. 6 Danel Cooke property		70

1 hors & 1 mare	Vd.	50
5 head of Cattel	Vd.	10
Cash		<u>5-12</u>
Nr. 7 Alex Strohon Sr.		65-12

150 Akers of Land	Vd.	100
23 head of Cattel	Vd.	46
1 hors	Vd.	10
Cash		<u>1-3-2</u>
Nr. 8 John Sikes property		157-3-2

200 Akers of Land	Vd.	50
23 head	Vd.	46
2 Mares	Vd.	20
Cash		<u>30</u>
Nr. 9 Jacob Sikes List property		146

500 Akers of Land	Vd.	150
32 head of Cattel	Vd.	64
1 hors	Vd.	15
Cash		<u>63-6</u>
Nr. 10 Danel Melven List		292-6

1 Negro Man	Vd.	120
1 Negro wench	Vd.	100
1 Negro Garle	Vd.	60
1 Mare & Colt	Vd.	10
7 head of Cattel	Vd.	14
Cash		<u>28</u>
Nr. 11 given by [?] howard for himself & his Nefue		332

400 Akers of Land	Vd.	100
36 head of Cattel	Vd.	72
2 Mares	Vd.	30
Cash		<u>1-13-4</u>
Nr. 12 Samuel Bozeman		230-13-4

150 Akers of Land	Vd.	100
2 Mares & Colts	Vd.	60
Cash		<u>5-12</u>
Nr. 13 Christopher Sutton		165-12

Chapter 4: Bladen County Tax Lists of 1778

150 Akers of Land	Vd.	100
80 head of Cattel	Vd.	160
2 fellers & wench	Vd.	300
3 Negro Children	Vd.	95
4 Mares	Vd.	60
Cash		5-14
Nr. 14 William Crometey		720-14

4 head Cattel	Vd.	8
1 Mair	Vd.	15
Cash		1-2-6
Nr. 15 James Shaw		24-2-6

150 Akers of Land	Vd.	100
24 of Cattel	Vd.	48
1 hors	Vd.	20
Nr. 16 John Fouler		168

19 head of Cattel	Vd.	38
[Torn] Mares	Vd.	25
three year old [Torn]	Vd.	10
1 Negro Wench	Vd.	100
1 Negro Child	Vd.	40
Cash		0-8
Nr. 17 Moses Treadway		218-2

275 Akers of Land	Vd.	250
5 head of Cattel	Vd.	10
1 hors	Vd.	15
1 Mare & Colte	Vd.	25
Nr. 18 Bemen Sutton		300

300 Akers of Land	Vd.	100
30 head of Cattel	Vd.	60
1 hors	Vd.	15
1 mare & Colte	Vd.	20
Nr. 19 John Sutton		195

200 Akers in Cumberland County		
11 head of Cattel	Vd.	22
Cash		1
Nr. 20 John Munroe		23
200 Akers of Land	Vd.	225
200 Akers in Duplin County		
[Torn] Akers in Hanover County		
[Torn] head of Cattel	Vd.	172
1 hors	Vd.	100
1 hors	Vd.	30
1 hors	Vd.	10
1 Mare & Colte	Vd.	40
2 Small mares	Vd.	10
Cash		6-8
Nr. 21 Nathan Meredath		677-8

CHAPTER 5

BLADEN COUNTY TAX LISTS OF 1779

BLADEN COUNTY TAX LIST OF 1779

List of Taxable property Aforsd. as follows by Fras. [?] William Saltar & John Anders for the year 1779

Hudnall Huffam	240 Acres
David Lloyd	940 Acres
Deter Carpenter	
John [?]	570 Acres
James Saltar	150 Acres
John Thomas	71.5 Acres
George Thomas Jr.	
George Thomas Sr.	750 Acres
Ezekiel Davis	982 Acres
Wm Salter for Estate Wilson	611 Acres
David Lock	1400 Acres
Elizabeth Singletary	
Joseph Lock	616 Acres
John Singletary	450 Acres
Richard Lloyd	150 Acres
James Benson	1037 Acres
David Lock Junr.	300 Acres
Ronald McDougall	540 Acres
Samuel Smith	1240 Acres
William Salter }	3910 Acres
} Assrs.	
John Anders }	520 Acres
William Stewart	1200 Acres
William Cromarty	150 Acres
John Mittlester	
Raymond Massie	
Gilbert McKeithan	
Matthew Prigan	37 Acres
John Blyth	
Beamon Sutton	
Eleazer [?]	100 Acres
James Gardner	
Edward Rices[?]	450 Acres
Daniel Melvin	100 Acres
Robert McMullen	300 Acres
John Corry	200 Acres
Daniel [?]	
John Sellars	250 Acres
Sellers Cooper	321 Acres
William Howard	
Stephen Anders [?]	1814 Acres
[?] Sikes	200 Acres
Anguish McAlester	
Anguish McAlester	300 Acres
[?] McAlester	
Josiah Sikes	200 Acres
John Howard	350 Acres
Samuel Bosman	400 Acres
John fowler	150 Acres

No. 2 [?] the fourth & Fourteenth Districts

A List of the Names of those that Neglected to give a list of Taxable property

Benja. Graves
Isaac Hays
Moses Tredaway
Jeremiah Done
John Done
Stephen Scarbrough
Thomas Seamore in the Service on the first of April
Sarah Seamore
Sarah White
Mary McFoster

****

BLADEN COUNTY TAX LIST OF 1779

A List of Taxable property Not Given in, in the Districts of Capt. Yates, Shipman and Clarady's 1779

Thos. Amis, James Shipman and Duncan Morrison Esqrs assessors

Headings for this list include: No. of Acres of Land, No. of Tracts or Ps. of Lands, Slaves, Horses, No. of Cattle, Valuation of Lands, Valuation of Houses

Chapter 5: Bladen County Tax Lists of 1779

[Abreviations will be used for headings.]

Mr. Murray's Land on the Brown Marsh
No. of Tracts   1
Valuation of Lands   £6333.-6.-8
Sum Total   £6333.-6.-8

Wm. Campbell's Brown Marsh
No. of Tracts   2
Valuation of Lands   £2000
Sum Total   £2000

Wm. Norton   Ditto
No. of Tracts   1
Valuation of Lands   £100
Sum Total   £100

Daniel Shaw   Do
No. of Tracts   1
Valuation of Lands   £500
Sum Total   £500

Charles M. Norton   Do
No. of Tracts   1
Valuation of Lands   £100
Sum Total   £100

John Campbell   Do
No. of Tracts   1
Valuation of Lands   £300
Sum Total   £300

George Brown on Bryan Swamp
No. of Tracts   1
Valuation of Lands   £500
Sum Total   £500
Cr. Given Capt. Randols

Andrew Griffin on Drowning Creek
No. of Tracts   1
Valuation of Lands   £150
Sum Total   £150

John Brown   Do
No. of Tracts   1
Valuation of Lands   £60
Sum Total   £60
Cr. Given Capt. Randols

Newat Edwards   Do
No. of Tracts   1
Valuation of Lands   £40
Sum Total   £40

Thos. McGuire   White Marsh
No. of Tracts   1
Valuation of Lands   £400
Sum Total   £400

Jeremiah Vail   Lake
No. of Tracts   1
Valuation of Lands   £1000
Sum Total   £1000

Mortimer's Land   Do
No. of Tracts   1
Valuation of Lands   £400
Sum Total   £400

Rowan's Land   White Marsh
No. of Tracts   1
Valuation of Lands   £1000
Sum Total   £1000

Lewis Taylor   Gape way
No. of Tracts   1
Valuation of Lands   £55
Sum Total   £55

Timothy Hatcher   Do
No. of Tracts   1
Valuation of Lands   £40
Sum Total   £40

Robert Hatcher   Do
No. of Tracts   1
Valuation of Lands   £50
Sum Total   £50

Joshua Stevens   [?]
No. of Tracts   4
Horses   3
No. of Cattle   10
Valuation of Lands   £500
Valuation of Houses   £200
Sum Total   £820

Willm. Sommerset   White Marsh
Slaves   1
Horses   2
Valuation of Houses   £150
Sum Total   £150

Joshua Williams   Do
No. of Tracts   1
Valuation of Lands   £300

Chapter 5: Bladen County Tax Lists of 1779

Sum Total		£300
George Hill	Do	
No. of Tracts		1
Horses		2
No. of Cattle		3
Valuation of Lands		£200
Valuation of Houses		£100
Sum Total		£330
Alexr. Stevenson	Do	
No. of Tracts		1
Valuation of Lands		£400
Sum Total		£400
Rowan Land W: Side W. Marsh		
No. of Tracts		1
Valuation of Lands		£2000
Sum Total		£2000
Genl. Waddells	Do	
No. of Tracts		1
Valuation of Lands		£100
Sum Total		£100
Total for District		£17238.-6.-8

****

BLADEN COUNTY TAX LIST OF 1779

A List of Taxable property Afsd. as follows by Francis Lucas William Saltar & John Anders for the year 1779

Headings for this list include: Bladen Lands, New Hanover Lands, Cumberland Lands, Anson Lands, Rowan Lands, Lots in Bladen Eliza., Lots in Wilmgtn., Lots in Cumb., Lots in Salisbury, Lots in New Bern, Slaves, Money, Horses, Cattle, Total Sum

Genl. Waddell Estate	
Bladen Lands	9025
New Hanover Lands	666 2/3
Cumberland Lands	400
Anson Lands	4490
Rowan Lands	702
Lots in Bladen Eliza.	1
Lots in Wilmgtn.	4
Lots in Salisbury	1
Lots in New Bern	1
Slaves	99
Money	£3783.-13.-4
Horses	4
Cattle	72
Total Sum	£69127.-13.-4
Faithful Graham	
Slaves	1
Money	£71.-0.-7
Horses	5
Cattle	8
Total Sum	£1450.-0.-7
Ann Maultsby	
Bladen Lands	450
Slaves	11
Money	£50.-6.-8
Horses	4
Cattle	30
Total Sum	£6650.-6.-8
John Lucas	
Money	£80
Horses	1
Total Sum	£400
Jacob Mezick	
Money	£4.-8.-0
Horses	2
Cattle	8
Total Sum	£384.-8
Saml. Swindle	
Bladen Lands	250
Slaves	5
Money	£919.-16.-6
Horses	5
Cattle	55
Total Sum	£4469.-16.-6
Turner Davis	
Bladen Lands	200
Money	£100
Horses	3
Cattle	19
Total Sum	£730
James Dowey	
Bladen Lands	805
Money	£8
Horses	3
Cattle	11
Total Sum	£1218
David Thomas	
Bladen Lands	100

Chapter 5: Bladen County Tax Lists of 1779

Money	£20
Horses	1
Total Sum	£220

John O'Dear
Bladen Lands	25
Money	£100.-1.-5
Cattle	3
Total Sum	£230.-1.-5

Jas. Eglison
Money	£50
Horses	9
Cattle	20
Total Sum	£850

James Bland
Money	£0.-4.-0
Horses	1
Total Sum	£50.-4.-0

John Smith for Mary McRee
Slaves	2
Money	£39.-0.-4
Total Sum	£1439.-0.-4

William How
Bladen Lands	150
Money	£15.-16.-0
Horses	4
Cattle	24
Total Sum	£855.-16.-0

Matthew Mesh[?]
Bladen Lands	200
Money	£11
Horses	1
Total Sum	£311

Ralph Miller
Bladen Lands	436
Anson Lands	600
Slaves	10
Money	£219.-11.-6
Horses	5
Cattle	32 1/2
Total Sum	£8275.-11.-6

John Lamb
Money	£33.-16.-0
Horses	1
Total Sum	£133.-16.-0

Malcum McFarter
Money	£25
Horses	1
Cattle	12
Total	£245

John Taylor
Bladen Lands	200
Money	£2
Horses	2
Cattle	18
Total Sum	£532

John Campbell
Bladen Lands	100
Money	£2.-0.-2
Horses	4
Cattle	22
Total Sum	£472.-0.-2

Daniel Robeson
Bladen Lands	100
Money	£0.-0.-9
Horses	1
Cattle	7
Total Sum	£170.-0.-9

James Pemberton
Slaves	2
Horses	1
Total Sum	£900

Margt. Pemberton
Slaves	3
Money	£14
Horses	3
Cattle	7
Total Sum	£1484

John Poynter
Bladen Lands	1200
Money	£29.-9.-0
Horses	6
Cattle	25
Total Sum	£1829.-9.-0

Benoni Claton
Money	£20
Horses	6
Cattle	15
Total Sum	£570

John Pemberton
| Bladen Lands | 120 |

Chapter 5: Bladen County Tax Lists of 1779

Slaves	1
Money	£5
Cattle	4
Total Sum	£295

John Boyd
Bladen Lands	384
Slaves	3
Money	£21.-16.-2
Horses	2
Cattle	13
Total Sum	£2251.-16.-2

Jas. Maultsby
Bladen Lands	200
Money	£4.-1.-0
Horses	2
Cattle	4
Total Sum	£400.-1.-0

John Young
[No listings given]

Thomas Lucas
Bladen Lands	250
Slaves	1
Money	£160.-10.-8
Horses	1
Cattle	20
Total Sum	£1310.-10.-8

Iver McKay
Bladen Lands	1975
Lots in Bladen, Elizabeth Town	1
Lots in Wilmington	1
Lots in Cumberland	1
Slaves	18
Money	£200
Horses	5
Cattle	52
Total Sum	£14285

John Brown
Bladen Lands	1100
Money	£25
Horses	1
Cattle	23
Total Sum	£1155

Joseph White
Bladen Lands	830
Slaves	2
Money	£24
Horses	5
Cattle	10
Total Sum	£4264

George Lucas
Bladen Lands	5060
Slaves	52
Money	£418.-6.-0
Horses	16
Cattle	37
Total Sum	£35793.-6

Thomas Brown
Bladen Lands	2871 & 320 for Motsey Shepherd
Lots in Wilmington	1
Lots in Cumberland	1 1/2
Slaves	26
Money	£505.-15.-0
Horses	22
Cattle	68
Amt. M. Shepherds Land	£100
Total Sum	£21485.-15.-0

Joseph Davis
Money	£188
Horses	1
Total Sum	£288

William Streetey[?]
Money	£8
Horses	1
Total Sum	£208

[Faded] Singletary
Bladen Lands	1140
Lots in Bladen, Elizabeth Town	1
Slaves	5
Money	£20
Horses	5
Cattle	26
Richd. Singletary Land	£1000
Total Sum	£7250

[Faded] [Faded]
Money	£14.-3.-2
Total Sum	£14.-3.-2

John McKinzie
Bladen Lands	375
Slaves	1
Money	£10.-16.-2
Horses	2
Cattle	4

Chapter 5: Bladen County Tax Lists of 1779

Total Sum	£1141.-16.-2

Harbet Taylor
Bladen Lands	150
Slaves	2
Money	£5
Horses	2
Cattle	5
Total Sum	£805

Daniel Bain
Money	£400
Horses	1
Total Sum	£600

John Smith
Bladen Lands	1000
Slaves	18
Money	£314.-11.-0
Horses	4
Cattle	80
Total Sum	£9864.-11

Archd. Taylor
Bladen Lands	1156
Slaves	1
Money	£29
Horses	3
Cattle	22
Total Sum	£1749

Jane Dubois
Bladen Lands	640
Total Sum	£1280

Daniel McFarter
Bladen Lands	400
Horses	2
Cattle	21
Total Sum	£560

Archd. McKeithan
Bladen Lands	100
Money	£14
Horses	6
Cattle	20
Total Sum	£684

John Davis
Bladen Lands	600
Slaves	39
Money	£150
Horses	7
Cattle	5

Total Sum	£18750

Richd. Davidson
Money	£6
Horses	2
Cattle	2
Total Sum	£226

Estate Doctr. Hall
Lands in Brunswick [Faded]
Slaves	6
Total Sum	£2870

James McLartie
Bladen Lands	100
Horses	1
Total Sum	£150

Daniel Downey
Money	£8
Horses	1
Cattle	9
Total Sum	£298

William Jones
Slaves	2
Money	£125.-12
Horses	9
Cattle	22
Old Wench	£150
Total Sum	£1995.-12

Simon Smith
Money	£16
Total Sum	£16

Robert Scott
Bladen Lands	890
Slaves	8
Money	£32
Horses	4
Cattle	21
Total Sum	£4922

Alxr. Graham
Bladen Lands	1000
Bladen Lots, Eliza.	1
Slaves	1
Money	£75.-16.-1
Horses	4
Cattle	35
Total Sum	£2875

Chapter 5: Bladen County Tax Lists of 1779

John Blocker
Bladen Lands	400
Cumberland Lands	640
Bladen Lots, Eliza.	1
Slaves	5
Money	£160.-16.-1
Horses	3
Cattle	22
Total Sum	[Faded]

William Smith
Bladen Lands	299
Slaves	5
Money	£58.-4.-1
Horses	1
Cattle	23
Total Sum	£2481

Daniel McKeithan
Bladen Lands	16
Money	£5.-8.-0
Horses	1
Cattle	6
Total Sum	£140.-8.-0

Benja. Singletary
Bladen Lands	720
Slaves	1
Horses	2
Cattle	3
Total Sum	£2670

Saml. Marshall
Bladen Lands	1460
New Hanover Lands	200
Slaves	2
Money	£24
Horses	6
Cattle	10
Total Sum	£5024

John McFarter
Bladen Lands	200
Horses	2
Cattle	10
Total Sum	£280

Jesse Atkins
Money	£50
Horses	1
Cattle	3
Total Sum	£120

Charles McNaughton
Bladen Lands	200
Money	£30
Horses	3
Cattle	20
Total Sum	£580

John Taylor junr.
Money	£7
Horses	1
Total Sum	£207

Moses Holmes
Bladen Lands	150
Money	£29.-4.-0
Horses	4
Cattle	11
Total Sum	£939.-4.-0

Dugald McKeithan
Money	£4
Horses	1
Cattle	10
Total Sum	£204

Daniel McKeithan
Bladen Lands	150
Horses	1
Cattle	6
Total Sum	£260

Henry Graham
Bladen Lands	640
Slaves	8
Money	£181.-0.-6
Horses	4
Cattle	11
Total Sum	[Faded]

Sarah Bowen
Bladen Lands	1477
Slaves	49
Horses	14
Cattle	67
Total Sum	[Faded]

Thomas Mcgwier
Bladen Lands	3240
New Hanover Lands	1000
Lots Campbleton	2
[?]	100
Slaves	55
Money	£340

Chapter 5: Bladen County Tax Lists of 1779

Horses	9
Cattle	40
Total Sum	[Faded]

Wm. Maultsby
Bladen Lands	1280
Cumberland Lands	675
Lots Campbleton	1
Slaves	1
Money	£5.-8.-0
Horses	3
Cattle	20
Total Sum	[Faded]

Grace Simmonds
Money	£12.-16.-0
Horses	2
Total Sum	[Faded]

Wm. Davis
Bladen Lands	350
Money	£4.-6.-0
Horses	3
Cattle	22
Total Sum	£624

John Connelley
Money	£34
Total Sum	£34

John Poynter Junr.
Money	£6
Horses	2
Cattle	12
Total Sum	£256

John Slingsby
Bladen Lands	982
Lots in Wilmington	1
Slaves	14
Money	£144.-12.-0
Horses	6
Cattle	28
Total Sum	£9678.-12.-0

Isbell McKeithan
Bladen Lands	316
Slaves	1
Money	£12
Horses	2
Cattle	15
Total Sum	£1112

Anguis Taylor
Bladen Lands	100
Money	£2.-8.-0
Horses	1
Cattle	12
Total Sum	£212.-3.-0

James Work
Money	£151.-16.-0
Horses	1
Total Sum	£351.-16.-0

Francis Lucas
Bladen Lands	1020
Slaves	11
Money	£130
Horses	7
Cattle	46
Total Sum	£9710

F. Lucas for the Estate Jas Carver
Bladen Lands	150
Lots in Wilmington	1
Money	£1.-12.-0
Cattle	13
Total Sum	£2201.-12

BLADEN COUNTY TAX LIST OF 1779

A list of the Taxable propertys of Capt. Saml. Smith District. Valued by us Josiah Barnes, Jacob Alford & John Donnelly.

No headings are given for this list. The names are given, and their property is written out, and valued in English Pounds.

John Grantham
200 Acres improved Land	£125
800 Ditto Not improved	£160
2 Negroes over 10 and under 40	£1400
1 Ditto over 5 and under 10	£400
1 Ditto under 5 years old	£150
1 horse	£80
20 head Cattle	£200
Money	£7.-10
Total	£2522.-10

William Caps
300 Acres improved Land	£150
1 horse	£50
11 head Cattle	£110
Total	£310

Chapter 5: Bladen County Tax Lists of 1779

Joseph Page
366 Acres improved Land £150
Total £150

John Starling
200 Acres improved Land £225
1150 Ditto not improved £230
1 Negro over 40 and under 50 £400
16 head Cattle £160
Money £0.-8.-0
Total £1015.-8

Samuel Rowland
300 Acres improved Land £70
1 horse £50
4 head of Cattle £40
Total £160

Samuel Pate
200 Acres of unimproved Land £40
2 horses £100
19 head of Cattle £190
Total £330

Jonathan Taylor
150 Acres of Improved Land £175
1 horse £50
5 head of Cattle £50
Total £275

Nathan Rowland
500 Acres of unimproved Land £100
Money £3.-4.-0
Total £103.-4.-0

Abram Davis
1 horse £50
2 head of Cattle £20
Total £70

Robert Jones
50 Acres of Improved Land £175
150 Do. unimproved £30
3 horses £175
30 head of Cattle £300
Money £5.-12.-6
Total £685

Mathew Jones
100 Acres of Improved Land £50
100 Do. unimproved £25
1 horse £65
10 head of Cattle £100

Total £240

John Smith
3060 Acres of Improved Land £1500
2220 Do. unimproved £440
5 Negroes over forty years old & under 50 £2000
20 Do. over 10 years & under 40 £14000
9 Do. over 5 years & under 10 £3600
19 Do. under 5 years old £2850
17 head of horses £1000
250 head of Cattle £2500
Money £1600
Total £29490

James Risin No Property

The Taxable Property of Josiah Barnes
500 Acres Improved Land £300
200 Acres of unimproved Land £150
Negroes over 10 years & under 40 £700
3 head of horses £400
15 head of Cattle £150
Money £75
Total £1775.-27.-10

The Taxable Property of Jacob Alford
400 Acres of improved Land £500
100 Ditto unimproved £30
2 Negros over 10 & under 40 £1400
15 head Horses £900
72 head Cattle £720
Money £12.-5.-0
Total £3562.-5

The Taxable Property of John Donelley
112 Acres improved Land £150
350 Acres unimproved Land £100
5 head horses £300
100 Acres of Land in Cumberland £100
1 Bool £10
Money £550
Total £1210.-18.-14

Andrew Grifin Refused giving in property
James Grifin hath Refused giving in no property

BLADEN COUNTY TAX LIST OF 1779

A list of the Taxable Properties of Capt. Jacob Alfords District. Valued by us, [?] Barnes, Jacob Alford & John Donelley 1779.

Chapter 5: Bladen County Tax Lists of 1779

No headings are given for this list. The names are given, and their property is written out, and valued in English Pounds.

Neil McGill
100 Acres Land improved £80
1 horse £50
6 head of Cattle £60
Money £15
Total £205

Dunkin McCollome
1 horse £50
4 head Cattle £40
Total £90

John McGlauchlin
1 horse £50
4 head Cattle £40
Total £90

Dunkin McMullin
1 horse £50
6 head Cattle £60
Total £110

Elaxander McCarter
1 horse £35
6 head Cattle £60
Total £95

Elaxander McLoud
1 horse £50
18 head Cattle £180
Money £15
Total £245

Anguish McCallister
1 horse £50
[Faded] Cattle £25
Total £75

James Watson
1 horse £60
6 head Cattle £60
Money £20
Total £140

Archd. Currey
1 horse £50
2 head of Cattle £20
Money £0.-1.-0
Total £70.-1.-0

James Forgason
100 Acres Improved Land £75
200 Do. unimproved £50
4 horses £150
22 head of Cattle £220
Money £6
Total £501

Daniel Smith
3 horses £125
7 head of Cattle £70
Money £3.-4.-0
Total £198.-4.-0

Malcom Munrow
50 Acres of Improved Land £110
400 Do. unimproved £80
2 horses £100
34 head of Cattle £340
Total £620

Neil Brown
500 Acres of improved Land £200
3 horses £150
42 head of Cattle £420
Money £3.-4.-0
Total £773.-4.-0

Peter McCarter Junr.
100 Acres of Improved Land £125
2 Negroes over 10 & under 40 £1400
[Faded] horses £200
35 head of Cattle £350
Money £2
Total 1£2277

Aron Stricklin
250 Acres of Improved Land £175
3 horses £275
17 head of Cattle £170
Money £17.-4.-0
Total £637.-4.-0

Abram Stricklin
5 head of Cattle £50
Total £50

David Beton
1 horse £80
18 head of Cattle £180
Money £3.-6.-0
Total £263.-6.-0

Chapter 5: Bladen County Tax Lists of 1779

Edward Murphey
100 Acres of Improved Land	£100
4 horses	£200
25 head of Cattle	£250
Total	£550

John McNear
150 Acres of Improved Land	£150
1 horse	£50
26 head of Cattle	£260
Money	£8
Total	£468

Hector McClain
100 Acres of Improved Land	£100
3 horses	£150
25 head of Cattle	£250
Total	£500

William McFarter
100 Acres of Improved Land	£100
2 horses	£80
10 head of Cattle	£100
Money	£9
Total	£289

Christan McMullan
100 Acres of Improved Land	£100
4 horses	£200
17 head of Cattle	£170
Money	£4
Total	£474

Edward McFarsion
100 Acres of Improved Land	£100
2 horses	£100
22 head of Cattle	£220
Money	£10
Total	£430

Niel Forgason
1 horse	£40
4 head of Cattle	£40
Money	£2
Total	£82

Malcom McCalpin
2 horses	£100
5 head of Cattle	£50
Money	£7.-9.-0
Total	£157.-9.-0

John McNeil
100 Acres of Improved Land	£100
2 horses	£100
9 head of Cattle	£90
Money	£3.-2.-4
Total	£293.-2.-4

Malcom Forgason
1 horse	£60
6 head of Cattle	£60
Money	£1
Total	£121

James Allen
No Property	......

Archd. Smith
2 horses	£80
2 head of Cattle	£20
Money	£2
Total	£102

John McBride
1 horse	£50
41 head of Cattle	£410
Money	£12
Total	£472

James Lowery
400 Acres of Improved Land	£350
2 Negroes over 10 & under 40 years	£1400
4 horses	£300
100 head of Cattle	£1000
Money	£100
Total	£3150

John McCraney
190 Acres of Improved Land	£200
140 acres Unimproved Land	£25
4 horses	£200
48 head of Cattle	£480
Money	£4
Total	£909

John McCarter
1 horse	£35
3 head of Cattle	£30
Money	£6
Total	£71

Daniel McCarter
50 Acres of Improved Land	£50
6 head of Cattle	£60
Money	£3.-6.-0
Total	£113.-6.-0

Chapter 5: Bladen County Tax Lists of 1779

Peter Smith
1 horse	£60
5 head of Cattle	£50
Money	£10
Total	£120

Archd. Smith
95 Acres of Improved Lands	£125
2 horses	£100
16 head of Cattle	£160
Money	£11.-16.-6
Total	£386.-16.-6

Alexander Forgason
100 Acres of Improved Lands	£50
1 horse	£60
Money	£2.-15.-0
Total	£112.-15.-0

A List of people that Refused giving in ther invitorys

John McFaull
100 Acres of Improved Land	£600
2 Negroes over 10 & under 40	£1400
2 Ditto over 5 & under 10 years	£800
6 head horses	£300
60 head of Cattle	£600
Money	£60
Total	£3760

Nial McFaull
200 Acres of Improved Land	£175
[Torn] head horses	£300
40 head of Cattle	£400
Money	£40
Total	£915

John Gilcrease
200 Acres of Improved Land	£175
3 head horses	£150
50 Head of Cattle	£500
Money	£30
Total	£855

Peter McCarther Senr.
100 Acres Land improved	£125
2 head horses	£120
18 head Cattle	£180
Money	£30
Total	£455

Rodger McGill
150 Acres improved Land	£150
1 horse	£50
18 head of Cattle	£180
Money	£20
Total	£400

James Rowland Junr.
300 Acres of Improved Land	£100
200 Acres unimproved	£40
3 head of horses	£200
19 head of Cattle	£190
Money	£4
Total	1£534

William Tolar
2290 Acres of Improved Land	£400
4 horses	£200
26 head of Cattle	£260
Money	£46
Total	£906

Simon Cox
400 Acres of Improved Land	£160
300 Do. unimproved	£60
3 horses	£200
37 head of Cattle	£370
Money	£9.-10.-0
Total	£799

James Stewart
660 Acres of Improved Land	£350
400 Do. unimproved	£80
1 Negroe over 10 & under 40 Years	£700
1 Do. over 50 & under 60 Years	£150
6 horses	£330
70 head of Cattle	£700
Money	£280
Total	£2590

Hardy Inman
400 Acres of Improved Land	£175
600 Do. unimproved	£120
2 horses	£120
16 head of Cattle	£160
Money	£102.-8.-0
Total	£677.-8.-0

William Barnes
300 Acres of Improved Land	£60
3 horses	£150
Money	£60
Total	£270

Chapter 5: Bladen County Tax Lists of 1779

John Brown
200 Acres of unimproved Land	£40
Money	£102.-8.-0
Total	£142.-8.-0

Tobias Selah
1 horse	£50
Money	£30
Total	£80

Edward Grantham
350 Acres of Improved Land	£200
600 Do. unimproved	£120
4 horses	£230
75 head of Cattle	£750
Money	£80
Total	£1380

Edward Flowers
800 Acres of Improved Land	£400
640 Do. unimproved	£130
1 horse	£10
94 head of Cattle	£940
Money	£1
Total	£1481

Jesse Lee
972 Acres of Improved Land	£500
2 Negroes over 10 & under 40 years	£1400
1 Do. over 5 & under 10 years	£400
5 horses	£375
40 head of Cattle	£400
Money	£117.-4.-0
Total	£3192.-4.-0

Samuel Smith Esqr.
200 of Improved Land	£200
640 Do. in Johnston County	£1200
414 Do. unimproved in Johnston County	£80
4 Negroes over 10 & under 40 Years	£2800
2 Do. over 5 & under 10 years	£800
3 Do. under 5 years old	£450
4 horses	£260
46 head in Cattle	£460
Money	£8
1340 acres of woodland	£260
Total	£6318

Joel Wells
200 Acres of Improved Land	£125
3 horses	£150
3 head of Cattle	£30
Total	£305

Elisabeth Brumble
200 Acres of Improved Land	£100
13 head of Cattle	£130
Money	£8
Total	£238

Gilbert Cox
100 Acres of Improved Land	£120
300 Do. unimproved	£60
2 Negroes over 10 & under forty years	£1400
3 horses	[Torn]
99 head of Cattle	£990
Money	£18
Total	£2738

Andrew Griffin
160 Acres of Improved Land	£150
950 Do. unimproved	£190
4 horses	£220
89 head of Cattle	£890
Money	£4.-10.-0
Total	£1454.-10.-0

Sampson Pope
100 Acres of Improved Land	£125
2 Negroes over 10 & under 40 years	£1400
1 Do. over 5 & under 10	£400
1 Do. over 50 & under 60 years	£150
68 head of Cattle	£680
Money	£21
Total	£2776

Henry Flowers
1 horse	£50
1 cow	£10
Money	£95
Total	£155

Zachariah Hogan
150 Acres Improved Land	£120
1 horse	£20
5 head of Cattle	£50
Total	£190

William Cliburn
100 Acres of Improved Land	£80
1 horse	£50
2 head of Cattle	£20
Money	£40
Total	£190

William Reynalds
100 Acres of Improved Land	£150

Chapter 5: Bladen County Tax Lists of 1779

100 Acres of unimproved Land	£200
2 Negroes over 10 & under 40	£1400
1 Do. over 5 & under 10	£400
2 Do. under 5 years Old	£300
3 horses	£150
3 head of Cattle	£30
Money	£32
Total	£2662

James Inman
200 Acres of Improved Land	£150
450 Do. unimproved	£90
1 Negroe over 10 years & under 40	£700
3 horses	£150
12 head of Cattle	£120
Money	£4
Total	£1214

John Rowland
400 Acres of Improved Land	£360
450 Do. unimproved	£90
2 Negroes over 10 years & under 40	£1400
2 Do. over 5 years & under 10	£800
1 Do. under 5 years Old	£150
6 horses	£200
36 head of Cattle	£360
Money	£734
Total	£4194

Dempsey Barfield
200 Acres of Improved Lands	£125
2 horses	£100
35 head of Cattle	£350
Money	£4
Total	£579

James Rowland Senr.
400 Acres of Improved Land	£200
1 horse	£150
9 head of Cattle	£90
Total	£440

Michael Barnes
100 Acres of Improved Land	£125
850 Acres of unimproved Land	£170
2 horses	[Not given]
32 head of Cattle	£320
Money	£8
Total	£377

Samuel Cane
200 Acres of unimproved Land	£40
2 horses	£75
Money	£20.-10.-6
Total	£135.-10.-6

Charles Barfield
250 Acres of Improved Land	£130
200 Do. unimproved	£40
4 horses	£200
31 head of Cattle	£310
Money	£10.-9.-8
Total	£690.-9.-8

Thomas Rowland
200 Acres of Improved Land	£120
2 horses	£70
17 head of Cattle	£170
Money	£0.-12.-0
Total	£360.-12.-0

Francis Ivey
150 Acres of Improved Land	£75
1 horse	£50
8 head of Cattle	£80
Money	£6
Total	£191

Lewis Ivey
300 Acres of Improved Land	£100
1 horse	£50
9 head of Cattle	£90
Total	£240

Charles Bullock
300 Acres of Improved Land	£200
700 Do. unimproved	£140
4 horses	£200
40 head of Cattle	£400
Money	£136.-2.-4
Total	£976.-2.-4

John Flowers Senr.
300 Acres of Improved Land	£150
1440 Do. unimproved	£250
212 Acres of Improved Land in Edgecomb County	£250
5 horses	£300
50 head of Cattle	£500
Money	£50
Total	£1500

Jacob Pope
100 Acres of Improved Land	£125
4 Negroes over 10 years & under 40	£2800
1 Do. over 5 years and under 10	£400
3 horses	£200

Chapter 5: Bladen County Tax Lists of 1779

100 head of Cattle	£1000
Money	£20
Total	£4545

Joseph Bennet
3 horses	£150
8 head of Cattle	£80
Total	£230

Richard Grantham
700 Acres of Improved Land	£350
300 Do. unimproved	£60
2 horses	£75
47 head of Cattle	£470
Money	£226
Total	£1181

Joel Pitman
100 Acres of Improved Land	£100
500 Do. unimproved	£100
2 horses	£135
15 head of Cattle	£150
Total	£485

David Low
100 Acres of Improved Land	£60
200 Do. unimproved	£40
2 horses	£150
Total	£250

A list of the men that is taking the State o[Torn] in my Company Jacob Alford

John Locklear

Jacob Locklear

William Locklear

John Locklear

Robert Locklear

Edmon Revils

Edmon Revils

[Faded] Loury

William Carter

Abram Hill

James Dunkin

William Landill

Lues Hall

Lues Hall

Isaac Hall

[Faded] Alford

****

BLADEN COUNTY TAX LIST OF 1779

A List of Taxable Property in the 6th or Capt. Shipman's District 1779. Thomas Amis, James Shipman & Duncan Morrison assessors

Headings for this list include: No. of Lotts, No. of Acres of Land, Slaves over 10 and under 40, Slaves between 5 & 10 & between 40 & 50, Slaves under 5 and between 50 & 60, No. of Houses, No. of Cattle, Money, Money at Interest, Stock in Trade, No. of Tracts, Valuation of Lands, Valuation of Houses, & Total.

[Abbreviated terms will be used for headings.]

Maturin Colville
No. of Acres of Land	5180
Slaves over 10 & under 40	21
Slaves between 5 & 10, & 40 & 50	17
Slaves under 5 & between 50 & 60	11
No. of Horses	30
No. of Cattle	80
Money	£40
Valuation of Lands	£10,000
Valuation of Horses	£2550
Total	£35,840

James Shipman Esqr.
No. of Acres of Land	350
Slaves between 5 & 10, & 40 & 50	1
No. of Horses	3
No. of Cattle	13
Money	£6
No. of Tracts	2
Valuation of Lands	£500

Chapter 5: Bladen County Tax Lists of 1779

Valuation of Horses £300
Total £1336

Joseph Powers
No. of Acres of Land 260
No. of Horses 2
No. of Cattle 30
No. of Tracts 2
Valuation of Lands £400
Valuation of Horses £200
Total £900

Matthew Kelly
No. of Acres of Land 1050
Slaves over 10 & under 40 6
Slaves between 5 & 10, & 40 & 50 2
Slaves under 5 & between 50 & 60 6
No. of Horses 10
No. of Cattle 62
Money £181.-0.-5
No. of Tracts 7
Valuation of Lands £890
Valuation of Horses £680
Total £8471

Neil Curry
No. of Acres of Land 100
No. of Horses 1
No. of Cattle 5
No. of Tracts 1
Valuation of Lands £100
Valuation of Horses £80
Total £230

Barnabass Stevens
No. of Acres of Land 1050
Slaves over 10 & under 40 5
Slaves Between 5 & 10, & 40 & 50 2
Slaves under 5 & Between 50 & 60 4
No. of Horses 26
No. of Cattle 178
Money £0.-12.-0
No. of Tracts 6
Valuation of Lands £1260
Valuation of Horses £1800
Total £9740.-12.-0

Daniel Shipman
No. of Acres of Land 1190
Slaves Between 5 & 10, & 40 & 50 1
No. of Horses 7
No. of Cattle 12
Money £20.-8.-0
No. of Tracts 8

Valuation of Lands £730
Valuation of Horses £1155
Total £2425.-8.-0

Cornelius Terrell
No. of Acres of Land 200
No. of Horses 3
No. of Tracts 1
Valuation of Lands £150
Valuation of Horses £330
Total £480

Wm. Ellis
No. of Acres of Land 100
No. of Cattle 7
No. of Tracts 1
Valuation of Lands £40
Total £70

Thos. Browder
No. of Acres of Land 200
No. of Horses 2
No. of Cattle 13
Money £4
No. of Tracts 1
Valuation of Lands £200
Valuation of Horses £50
Total £384

John Kelly
No. of Acres of Land 200
No. of Horses 3
No. of Cattle 22
Money £26.-8.-0
No. of Tracts 1
Valuation of Lands £300
Valuation of Horses £250
Total £796.-8.-0

Joseph Wiggins
No. of Acres of Land 148
Money £40.-16.-0
No. of Tracts 2
Valuation of Lands £150
Total £190.-16.-0

Issum Wiggins
No. of Acres of Land 52
No. of Horses 2
Valuation of Lands £60
Valuation of Horses £140
Total £200

David Marlow

Chapter 5: Bladen County Tax Lists of 1779

No. of Horses	3
Money	£7.-4.-0
No. of Tracts	1
Valuation of Horses	£200
Total	£297.-4.-0

John Roberts

No. of Acres of Land	200
No. of Horses	4
No. of Cattle	8
Money	£24
No. of Tracts	1
Valuation of Lands	£160
Valuation of Horses	£250
Total	£414

John Russ Junr.

No. of Acres of Land	100
No. of Cattle	5
Money	£1.-12.-0
No. of Tracts	1
Valuation of Lands	£150
Total	£201.-12.-0

Joshua Hayes

No. of Acres of Land	683
Slaves over 10 & under 40	2
Slaves under 5 & Between 50 & 60	2
No. of Horses	8
No. of Cattle	60
Money	£19.-4.-0
No. of Tracts	3
Valuation of Lands	£300
Valuation of Horses	£450
Total	£3069.-4.-0

William Brown

No. of Acres of Land	450
No. of Horses	5
No. of Cattle	3
Money	£8
No. of Tracts	3
Valuation of Lands	£300
Valuation of Horses	£350
Total	£688

William McNeil

No. of Acres of Land	540
Slaves over 10 years & under 40	4
Slaves Between 5 & 10, & 40 & 50	4
Slaves under 5 & Between 50 & 60	1
No. of Horses	6
No. of Cattle	36
Money	£1.-12.-0

No. of Tracts	1
Valuation of Lands	£2000
Valuation of Horses	£600
Total	£7511.-12.-0

John McEwin

No. of Acres of Land	100
No. of Horses	4
No. of Cattle	17
No. of Tracts	1
Valuation of Lands	£100
Valuation of Horses	£200
Total	£470

Robert McEwin

No. of Acres of Land	200
No. of Horses	2
No. of Cattle	7
No. of Tracts	2
Valuation of Lands	£100
Valuation of Horses	£130
Total	£300

James Murphey

No. of Cattle	7
Money	£6.-16.-0
Total	£76.-16.-0

John Russ Senr.

No. of Acres of Land	860
Slaves over 10 & under 40	2
Slaves Between 5 & 10, & 40 & 50	1
Slaves under 5 & Between 50 & 60	2
No. of Horses	10
No. of Cattle	46
Money	£8.-10.-0
Money at Interest	£28
No. of Tracts	7
Valuation of Lands	£1070
Valuation of Horses	£500
Total	£3766.-10.-0

Ezekiel Burley [Busby?]

No. of Acres of Land	335
No. of Horses	5
No. of Cattle	15
Money	£1.-14.-0
No. of Tracts	2
Valuation Of Lands	£280
Valuation of Horses	£300
Total	£731.-14.-0

Asbell Bradley

Chapter 5: Bladen County Tax Lists of 1779

No. of Acres of Land	200
No. of Horses	1
No. of Cattle	14
Money	£5
No. of Tracts	1
Valuation of Lands	£100
Valuation of Horses	£80
Total	£325

John McLaran

No. of Acres of Land	160
No. of Horses	4
No. of Cattle	21
Money	£3.-4.-0
No. of Tracts	1
Valuation of Lands	£250
Valuation of Horses	£300
Total	£763.-4.-0

Archd. Shaw

No. of Acres of Land	260
Slaves Between 5 & 10, & 40 & 50	1
No. of Horses	2
No. of Cattle	11
Money	£2.-13.-0
No. of Tracts	1
Valuation of Lands	£300
Valuation of Horses	£200
Total	£1012.-13.-0

Daniel Turner

No. of Acres of Land	650
No. of Horses	3
No. of Cattle	12
Money	£6.-16.-0
No. of Tracts	4
Valuation of Lands	£410
Valuation of Horses	£200
Total	£736.-16.-0

Simon Burney

No. of Acres of Land	300
No. of Horses	6
No. of Cattle	15
Money	£32.-4.-0
Money at Interest	£30
No. of Tracts	3
Valuation of Lands	£500
Valuation of Horses	£500
Total	£1212.-4.-0

Jane Ray

No. of Acres of Land	200
No. of Horses	2

No. of Cattle	15
Money	£7.-4.-0
Stock in Trade	1
No. of Tracts	1
Valuation of Lands	£200
Valuation of Horses	£250
Total	£607.-4.-0

George McGee

No. of Acres of Land	300
No. of Horses	2
No. of Cattle	12
No. of Tracts	1
Valuation of Lands	£120
Valuation of Horses	£150
Total	£390

Neil McCoulskey

No. of Acres of Land	850
Slaves over 10 years & under 40	2
Slaves Between 5 & 10, & 40 & 50	2
Slaves under 5 & Between 50 & 60	2
No. of Horses	6
No. of Cattle	40
Money	£75.-1.-0
No. of Tracts	3
Valuation of Lands	£460
Valuation of Horses	£400
Deduct 150£ for a negroe Given in not Born	
Total	£3835.-1.-0

Thomas Simpson

No. of Acres of Land	900
Slaves over 10 years & under 40	5
Slaves Between 5 & 10, & 40 & 50	2
Slaves under 5 years & Between 50 & 60	1
No. of Horses	5
No. of Cattle	42
Money	£6.-4.-0
No. of Tracts	8
Valuation of Lands	£940
Valuation of Horses	£350
Total	£6166.-4.-0

Benjn. Arrington

No. of Acres of Land	1225
Slaves over 10 years & under 40	1
No. of Horses	7
No. of Cattle	38
Money	£160
No. of Tracts	9
Valuation of Lands	£960
Valuation of Horses	£700
Deduct £700 for negroe and Idiot	

Chapter 5: Bladen County Tax Lists of 1779

Total   £2900

Duncan Henderson
No. of Acres of Land   100
No. of Horses   2
No. of Cattle   12
Money   £4
No. of Tracts   1
Valuation of Lands   £100
Valuation of Horses   £150
Total   £370

Archibald Kelly
No. of Acres of Land   200
No. of Horses   6
No. of Cattle   32
Money   £5.-4.-0
No. of Tracts   1
Valuation of Lands   £200
Valuation of Horses   £330
Total   £855.-4.-0

Francis Lawson
No. of Acres of Land   200
No. of Horses   2
No. of Cattle   6
No. of Tracts   1
Valuation of Lands   £140
Valuation of Horses   £100
Total   £300

Archd. Campbell
No. of Acres of Land   200
No. of Horses   2
No. of Cattle   7
No. of Tracts   1
Valuation of Lands   £290
Valuation of Horses   £200
Total   £560

Daniel Shaw
Slaves over 10 years & under 40   2
Slaves Between 5 & 10, & 40 & 50   2
Slaves under 5 years & Between 50 & 60   1
No. of Horses   3
No. of Cattle   17
Money   £5.-16.-0
Valuation of Horses   £150
Total   £2675.-16.-0

Archd. McBride
No. of Acres of Land   500
No. of Horses   2
No. of Cattle   10
No. of Tracts   3
Valuation of Lands   £250
Valuation of Horses   £200
Total   £550

Archd. Sellers
No. of Acres of Land   200
No. of Horses   3
No. of Cattle   31
No. of Tracts   1
Valuation of Lands   £250
Valuation of Horses   £250
Total   £860

Angus Sellers
No. of Acres of Land   200
No. of Horses   3
No. of Cattle   29
Money   £17.-7.-0
No. of Tracts   2
Valuation of Lands   £300
Valuation of Horses   £250
Total   £857.-7.-0

Solomon Lewis
No. of Acres of Land   250
No. of Horses   3
No. of Cattle   2
Money   £16
No. of Tracts   1
Valuation of Lands   £150
Valuation of Horses   £150
Total   £336

John Campbell
No. of Horses   5
No. of Cattle   25
Money   £112
Valuation of Horses   £350
Total   £712

Dugald McMillan
No. of Acres of Land   400
No. of Horses   4
No. of Cattle   35
Money   £115
No. of Tracts   2
Valuation of Lands   £580
Valuation of Horses   £360
Total   £1405

Daniel McCallum
No. of Acres of Land   300
No. of Horses   1

Chapter 5: Bladen County Tax Lists of 1779

No. of Cattle	11
No. of Tracts	3
Valuation of Lands	£160
Valuation of Horses	£80
Total	£350

Josiah Lewis Senr.
No. of Acres of Land	250
Slaves over 10 years & under 40	4
No. of Horses	34
No. of Cattle	41
Money	£0.-16.-0
No. of Tracts	2
Valuation of Lands	£100
Valuation of Horses	£1880
Total	£4006

Dugald Blew
No. of Acres of Land	406
No. of Horses	4
No. of Cattle	10
Money	£20
No. of Tracts	2
Valuation of Lands	£480
Valuation of Horses	£350
Total	£950

John Blew
No. of Horses	1
No. of Cattle	4
Money	£4
Valuation of Horses	£80
Total	£124

Duncan Lamond
No. of Acres of Land	100
No. of Horses	1
No. of Cattle	8
Money	£27.-16.-0
No. of Tracts	1
Valuation of Lands	£100
Valuation of Horses	£80
Total	£287.-16.-0

Alexander McColl
No. of Horses	1
No. of Cattle	4
Valuation of Horses	£100
Total	£140

Dugald McKay
No. of Acres of Land	330
No. of Horses	2
No. of Cattle	11

Money	£58
No. of Tracts	3
Valuation of Lands	£300
Valuation of Horses	£200
Total	£668

Andrew McLelland
No. of Acres of Land	200
Slaves over 10 years & under 40	1
No. of Horses	1
No. of Cattle	3
Money	£14.-6.-0
No. of Tracts	2
Valuation of Lands	£140
Valuation of Horses	£100
Total	£1074.-16.-0

Mary McLelland
Slaves Between 5 & 10, & 40 & 50	1
Slaves under 5 years & Between 50 & 60	1
No. of Horses	2
No. of Cattle	9
Money	£26.-17.-0
Valuation of Horses	£150
Total	£816.-17.-0

Josiah Lewis Junr.
No. of Acres of Land	500
Slaves Between 5 & 10, & 40 & 50	1
No. of Horses	13
No. of Cattle	39
Money	£6.-8.-0
No. of Tracts	4
Valuation of Lands	£670
Valuation Horses	£770
Total	£2236.-8.-0

John McKay Taylor
No. of Acres of Land	100
No. of Horses	1
No. of Cattle	4
Money	£20.-6.-0
No. of Tracts	1
Valuation of Lands	£60
Valuation of Horses	£100
Total	£220.-6.-0

Dennis Lennon
No. of Acres of Land	550
Slaves over 10 years & under 40	1
No. of Horses	3
No. of Cattle	32
Money	£2.-8.-0
No. of Tracts	3

Chapter 5: Bladen County Tax Lists of 1779

Valuation of Lands	£500
Valuation of Horses	£240
Total	£1862.-8.-0

John Lennon
No. of Acres of Land	420
Slaves over 10 years & under 40	2
Slaves Between 5 & 10, & 40 & 50	2
No. of Horses	4
No. of Cattle	16
Money	£12
No. of Tracts	2
Valuation of Lands	£900
Valuation of Horses	£250
Total	£3522

James Lewis
No. of Horses	1
No. of Cattle	1
Valuation of Horses	£80
Total	£90

John Robeson
No. of Horses	1
No. of Cattle	2
Valuation of Horses	£80
Total	£100

Angus McKay
No. of Acres of Land	240
No. of Horses	2
No. of Cattle	14
Money	£200.-8.-0
No. of Tracts	1
Valuation of Lands	£500
Valuation of Horses	£200
Total	£1040.-8.-0

John McKay
No. of Acres of Land	300
No. of Cattle	5
Money	£2.-8.-0
No. of Tracts	2
Valuation of Lands	£120
Total	£172.-8.-0

Wm. Starkey
No. of Acres of Land	520
No. of Horses	2
No. of Cattle	8
Money	£50
No. of Tracts	2
Valuation of Lands	£580
Valuation of Horses	£100

Total	£710

Duncan Shaw
No. of Horses	1
No. of Cattle	2
Money	£3.-5.-0
Valuation of Horses	£130
Total	£153

William Bryan Junr.
No. of Acres of Land	150
No. of Horses	5
No. of Cattle	2
Money	£22.-7.-0
No. of Tracts	1
Valuation of Lands	£60
Valuation of Horses	£330
Total	£432.-7.-0

John Bryan
No. of Acres of Land	100
No. of Horses	3
No. of Cattle	7
Money	£4.-12.-0
No. of Tracts	1
Valuation of Lands	£100
Valuation of Horses	£250
Total	£424.-12.-0

Wm. Bryan Senr.
No. of Acres of Land	660
Slaves over 10 years & under 40	2
Slaves under 5 years & between 50 & 60	1
No. of Horses	3
No. of Cattle	8
Money	£10.-7.-0
No. of Tracts	4
Valuation of Lands	£660
Valuation of Horses	£200
Total	£1900.-7.-0

John Shaw
Slaves under 5 years & Between 50 & 60	1
No. of Horses	2
No. of Cattle	5
Money	£2.-8.-0
Valuation of Horses	£200
Total	£402.-6.-0

Wm. Bigford
No. of Acres of Land	440
Slaves over 10 years & under 40	2
Slaves Between 5 & 10, & 40 & 50	1
No. of Horses	1

Chapter 5: Bladen County Tax Lists of 1779

No. of Cattle	7
Money	£1.-12.-0
No. of Tracts	1
Valuation of Lands	£500
Valuation of Horses	£80
Total	£2451.-12.-0

John Purkepine

No. of Acres of Land	238
No. of Horses	2
No. of Cattle	5
Valuation of Horses	£180
Total	£130

[The last two figures are given as stated in the tax list]

John McViccar

No. of Acres of Land	200
No. of Horses	5
No. of Cattle	8
Money	£9.-11.-0
No. of Tracts	1
Valuation of Lands	£100
Valuation of Horses	£300
Total	£489.-11.-0

Margaret McMillan

No. of Cattle	18
Money	£13.-8.-0
Total	£193.-8.-0

****

BLADEN COUNTY TAX LIST OF 1779

A List of Taxable Property in Capt. Yates District 1779. Thos. Amis, James Shipman, & Duncan Morrison Assessors

The headings for this list are the same as those in the preceding list.

David Godwin

No. of Acres of Land	1438
Slaves over 10 & under 40	9
Slaves Between 5 & 10, & 40 & 50	3
Slaves under 5 & Between 50 & 60	1
No. of Horses	15
No. of Cattle	100
Money	£126.-3.-0
Money at Interest	£249.-5.-0
No. of Tracts of Land	10
Valuation of Lands	[Torn]
Valuation of Horses	£1315
Total	£13020.-8.-0

Dempsey Dawson

No. of Acres of Land	820
Slaves over 10 & under 40	3
Slaves Between 5 & 10, & 40 & 50	2
No. of Horses	4
No. of Cattle	29
Money	£36.-16.-0
No. of Tracts	7
Valuation of Lands	£645
Valuation of Horses	£740
Total	£4571.-16.-0

Moses Coleman

No. of Acres of Land	700
No. of Horses	4
No. of Cattle	65
Money	£59.-7.-0
No. of Tracts	4
Valuation of Lands	£800
Valuation of Horses	£550
Total	£1759.-7.-0

Willm. Strickland

No. of Acres of Land	340
No. of Horses	3
No. of Cattle	10
Money	£2
No. of Tracts	3
Valuation of Lands	£300
Valuation of Horses	£400
Total	£952

Coleman Nickols

No. of Acres of Land	833
No. of Horses	5
No. of Cattle	79
Money	£28
No. of Tracts	5
Valuation of Lands	£980
Valuation of Horses	£400
Total	£952

Alexr. Godwin

No. of Acres of Land	250
No. of Horses	1
No. of Cattle	17
Money	£2
No. of Tracts	1
Valuation of Lands	£500
Valuation of Horses	£100
Total	£772

Chapter 5: Bladen County Tax Lists of 1779

Ezekiel Bryant
No. of Acres of Land	200
No. of Horses	4
No. of Cattle	14
Money	£47.-5.-0
No. of Tracts	2
Valuation of Lands	£80
Valuation of Horses	£500
Total	£767.-5.-0

David Duncan
No. of Acres of Land	250
Slaves over 10 & under 40	1
Slaves Between 5 & 10, & 40 & 50	1
No. of Horses	10
No. of Cattle	34
Money	£6
No. of Tracts	2
Valuation of Lands	£170
Valuation of Horses	£500
Total	£2110

Simon Smith
No. of Horses	3
No. of Cattle	50
Money	£2
Valuation of Horses	£150
Total	£652

Joel Hill
No. of Acres of Land	250
No. of Horses	6
No. of Cattle	8
Money	£16
No. of Tracts	2
Valuation of Lands	£400
Valuation of Horses	£400
Total	£896

John Sojourner
No. of Horses	2
No. of Cattle	8
Valuation of Horses	£100
Total	£180

Shadrach Harper
No. of Acres of Land	200
Slaves over 10 & under 40	2
No. of Horses	2
No. of Cattle	8
Valuation of Horses	£200
Total	£1680

William Oliphant
No. of Acres of Land	200
Slaves over 10 & under 40	1
Slaves under 5 & Between 50 & 60	2
No. of Horses	3
No. of Cattle	16
Money	£4
No. of Tracts	1
Valuation of Lands	£100
Valuation of Horses	£350
Total	£1614

John Coleman
No. of Acres of Land	1240
No. of Horses	6
No. of Cattle	25
Money	£91.-4.-0
No. of Tracts	8
Valuation of Lands	£550
Valuation of Horses	£366.-13.-4
Total	£1257.-17.-4

Daniel Flinn
No. of Acres of Land	360
No. of Horses	8
No. of Cattle	58
Money	£10
No. of Tracts	2
Valuation of Lands	£880
Valuation of Horses	£450
Total	£1920

Thos. Hardwick Junr.
No. of Acres of Land	50
Money	£0.-16.-0
Valuation of Land	£50
Total	£50.-16.-0

John Kennedy
No. of Acres of Land	100
No. of Horses	2
No. of Cattle	9
Money	£16.-8.-0
No. of Tracts	1
Valuation of Horses	£50
Total	£156.-8.-0

Thos. Robeson
No. of Horses	2
Valuation of Horses	£130
Total	£130

Thos. Hardwick Senr.
[No taxable property listed]

Chapter 5: Bladen County Tax Lists of 1779

John Johnston Junr.
No. of Acres of Land	150
No. of Horses	4
No. of Cattle	8
Money	£1.-4.-0
No. of Tracts	2
Valuation of Lands	[Faded]
Valuation of Horses	£250
Total	£471.-4.-0

Saml. Hardwick
No. of Acres of Land	100
No. of Horses	1
No. of Cattle	2
Money	£6.-16.-0
No. of Tracts	1
Valuation of Lands	[Torn]
Valuation of Horses	£80
Total	£146.-16.-0

Aaron Tomlinson
No. of Acres of Land	150
No. of Horses	5
No. of Cattle	14
No. of Tracts	1
Valuation of Lands	[Torn]
Valuation of Horses	£350
Total	£690

James Wilson
No. of Acres of Land	200
No. of Horses	2
No. of Cattle	20
No. of Tracts	2
Valuation of Lands	[Torn]
Valuation of Horses	£200
Total	£600

John Branton Junr.
No. of Acres of Land	100
No. of Cattle	10
Money	£2.-16.-0
Stock in Trade	1
No. of Tracts	1
Valuation of Lands	£60
Total	£162.-16.-0

Joel Sellers
No. of Acres of Land	450
No. of Horses	4
No. of Cattle	26
Money	£42.-2.-0
Valuation of Lands	£320
Valuation of Horses	£340
Total	£862.-2.-0

William Johnston
No. of Acres of Land	100
No. of Horses	5
No. of Cattle	21
Money	£6.-8.-0
No. of Tracts	1
Valuation of Lands	£120
Valuation of Horses	£300
Total	£606.-8.-0

Thos. Sessione
No. of Acres of Land	400
Slaves over 10 years & under 40	3
No. of Horses	12
No. of Cattle	29
Money	£229.-19.-0
No. of Tracts	2
Valuation of Lands	£310
Valuation of Horses	£750
Total	£2619.-19.-0

William Stevens
No. of Acres of Land	250
Slaves Between 5 & 10, & 40 & 50	1
No. of Horses	8
No. of Cattle	22
No. of Tracts	2
Valuation of Lands	£250
Valuation of Horses	£550
Total	£1420

Stephen Barefield
No. of Acres of Land	700
No. of Horses	2
No. of Cattle	9
No. of Tracts	3
Valuation of Lands	£360
Valuation of Horses	£200
Total	£650

John Andrews
No. of Acres of Land	100
No. of Horses	3
No. of Cattle	28
Money	£41.-12.-0
No. of Tracts	1
Valuation of Lands	£150
Valuation of Horses	£300
Total	£771.-12.-0

Chapter 5: Bladen County Tax Lists of 1779

Lucke Barefield
Slaves over 10 years & under 40   5
Slaves Between 5 & 10, & 40 & 50   3
Slaves under 5 years & Between 50 & 60 5
No. of Horses   1
No. of Cattle   9
Valuation of Horses   £100
Total Valuation   £5140

Edward Wall
No. of Acres of Land   200
No. of Horses   3
No. of Cattle   17
No. of Tracts   1
Valuation of Lands   [Torn]
Valuation of Horses   £210
Total   £530

Michael Whiteman
No. of Horses   1
No. of Cattle   5
Money   £0.-16.-0
Total   £50.-16.-0

George Harper
No. of Horses   2
No. of Cattle   14
Money   £0.-10.-0
Valuation of Horses   £160
Total   £330.-10.-0

William Flanagan
No. of Horses   1
No. of Cattle   7
Money   £5.-4.-0
Valuation of Horses   £80
Total   £135.-4.-0

Benjn. Tredwell
No. of Acres of Land   100
No. of Horses   7
No. of Cattle   15
Money   £35.-17.-0
No. of Tracts   1
Valuation of Lands   £100
Valuation of Horses   £400
Total   £985.-17.-0

John Johnston Senr.
No. of Acres of Land   100
No. of Horses   2
No. of Cattle   5
Money   £1.-12.-0

No. of Tracts   1
Valuation of Lands   £180
Valuation of Horses   £180
Total   £411.-12.-0

Thos. Dyson
No. of Acres of Land   200
No. of Horses   11
No. of Cattle   10
Money   £40.-12.-0
No. of Tracts   3
Valuation of Lands   [Torn]
Valuation of Horses   £650
Total   £990.-12.-0

John Branton Senr.
No. of Acres of Land   100
No. of Horses   5
No. of Cattle   4
Money   £69.-17.-0
No. of Tracts   1
Valuation of Lands   £100
Valuation of Horses   £350
Total   £559.-17.-0

John Money
No. of Acres of Land   100
No. of Horses   3
No. of Cattle   3
No. of Tracts   1
Valuation of Lands   [Torn]
Valuation of Horses   £200
Total   £350

Phillip Strickland
No. of Acres of Land   200
No. of Horses   1
No. of Cattle   10
Money   £2.-8.-0
No. of Lots   2
Valuation of Lands   £120
Valuation of Horses   £100
Total   £322.-8.-0

Richd. Bright
No. of Horses   1
No. of Cattle   5
Valuation of Horses   £150
Total   £200

Ezekiel Hill
No. of Acres of Land   500
No. of Horses   7

Chapter 5: Bladen County Tax Lists of 1779

No. of Cattle	27
No. of Tracts	3
Valuation of Lands	£450
Valuation of Horses	£450
Total	£1190

Edward Willson
No. of Acres of Land	200
No. of Horses	1
No. of Cattle	10
Money	£0.-12.-0
No. of Tracts	1
Valuation of Lands	£80
Valuation of Horses	£50
Total	£230.-12.-0

Suthey Hayes
No. of Acres of Land	400
Slaves Between 5 & 10, & 40 & 50	1
No. of Horses	3
No. of Cattle	23
Money	£48
No. of Tracts	3
Valuation of Lands	£240
Valuation of Horses	£180
Total	£1198

Absalom Powell
No. of Acres of Land	500
No. of Horses	9
No. of Cattle	47
Money	£14.-8.-0
No. of Tracts	3
Valuation of Lands	£520
Valuation of Horses	£680
Total	£1684.-8.-0

Israel Tomlinson
No. of Horses	1
No. of Cattle	8
Money	£0.-10.-0
Valuation of Horses	£50
Total	£130.-10.-0

John Wingate Senr.
No. of Acres of Land	900
Slaves over 10 years & under 40	13
Slaves Between 5 & 10, & 40 & 50	3
Slaves under 5 years & Between 50 & 60	4
No. of Horses	29
No. of Cattle	70
Money	£571.-12.-0
Money at Interest	£72
No. of Tracts	4
Valuation of Lands	£1800
Valuation of Horses	£1700
Total	£11645.-12.-0

Ann Gallaway
No. of Acres of Land	200
No. of Horses	2
No. of Cattle	12
Money	£12
No. of Tracts	2
Valuation of Lands	£200
Valuation of Horses	£140
Total	£472

John Fokes
No. of Acres of Land	200
No. of Horses	1
No. of Cattle	13
Money	£18
No. of Tracts	1
Valuation of Lands	£400
Valuation of Horses	£200
Total	£748

Jacob Hanchey
No. of Acres of Land	100
No. of Horses	1
No. of Cattle	2
Money	£10.-4.-0
No. of Tracts	1
Valuation of Lands	£40
Valuation of Horses	£50
Total	£120.-4.-0

Hardy Horn
No. of Acres of Land	100
No. of Horses	2
No. of Cattle	20
Valuation of Lands	£400
Valuation of Horses	£350
Total	£950

Linvill Hardwick
No. of Acres of Land	400
No. of Horses	3
No. of Cattle	27
Money	£34
No. of Tracts	2
Valuation of Lands	£480
Valuation of Horses	£240
Total	£1024

David Clark
No. of Acres of Land	150

Chapter 5: Bladen County Tax Lists of 1779

No. of Horses	2
No. of Cattle	28
No. of Tracts	1
Valuation of Lands	**[Torn]**
Valuation of Horses	£250
Total	£730

John Willson
No. of Acres of Land	200
No. of Horses	1
No. of Cattle	19
Money	£1.-12.-0
No. of Tracts	1
Valuation of Lands	£200
Valuation of Horses	£100
Total	£791.-12.-0

Abraham Stevens
No. of Acres of Land	200
No. of Horses	3
No. of Cattle	5
Money	£2.-12.-0
No. of Tracts	1
Valuation of Lands	£200
Valuation of Horses	£250
Total	£502.-12.-0

Allen Hardwick
No. of Acres of Land	150
No. of Cattle	3
Valuation of Lands	£60
Total	£90

Jacob Fokes
No. of Horses	2
No. of Cattle	16
Money	£2.-8.-0
Valuation of Horses	£200
Total	£362.-8.-0

William Fokes
No. of Horses	2
No. of Cattle	2
Money	£1.-16.-0
Valuation of Horses	£150
Total	£171.-16.-0

Thomas Johnston
No. of Acres of Land	100
No. of Horses	4
No. of Cattle	29
Money	£1.-12.-0
Valuation of Lands	£110

Valuation of Horses	£250
Total	£581.-12.-0

John Green
No. of Acres of Land	740
Slaves over 10 years & under 40	1
Slaves Under 5 & Between 50 & 60	1
No. of Horses	7
No. of Cattle	27
Money	£30
Valuation of Lands	**[Torn]**
Valuation of Horses	£350
Total	£2520

Simon Bright
No. of Acres of Land	750
No. of Horses	13
No. of Cattle	41
Money	£8.-16.-0
Valuation of Lands	£630
Valuation of Horses	£780
Cr. for £700 for his negroe	
Total	£1828.-16.-0

William Boice
No. of Acres of Land	350
No. of Horses	3
No. of Cattle	24
Money	£51
Valuation of Lands	**[Torn]**
Valuation of Horses	£200
Total	£701

William Sibbet
No. of Acres of Land	100
No. of Horses	3
No. of Cattle	2
Valuation of Lands	£120
Valuation of Horses	£150
Total	£190

John Badget
No. of Acres of Land	250
No. of Cattle	4
Money	£2
No. of Tracts	1
Valuation of Lands	**[Torn]**
Total	£100

James Bright
No. of Horses	1
Money	£6.-8.-0
Valuation of Horses	£60

Chapter 5: Bladen County Tax Lists of 1779

Total	£66.-18.-0

Stephen Godwin
No. of Acres of Land	300
No. of Horses	1
No. of Cattle	8
Money	£6
No. of Tracts	2
Valuations of Lands	£200
Valuation of Horses	£130
Total	£416

James Money
No. of Acres of Land	650
Slaves under 5 & Between 50 & 60	1
No. of Horses	14
No. of Cattle	34
Money	£2.-16.-0
No. of Tracts	5
Valuation of Lands	£540.-9.-0
Valuation of Horses	£920
Cr. £400 for Infirm negro	
Total	£2602.-16.-0

Benjamin Money
No. of Acres of Land	100
No. of Horses	1
No. of Cattle	3
No. of Tracts	1
Valuation of Lands	£40
Valuation of Horses	£100
Total	£170

Thos. Sanders
No. of Acres of Land	200
Slaves Between 5 & 10, & 40 & 50	2
No. of Horses	2
No. of Cattle	30
Money	£200
No. of Tracts	1
Valuation of Lands	£500
Valuation of Horses	£108
Total	£1908

William Long
Money	£35
Total	£35

John Baldwin Junr.
No. of Acres of Land	200
Slaves over 10 years & under 40	1
Slaves Between 5 & 10, & 40 & 50	3
Slaves under 5 & Between 50 & 60	3
No. of Horses	9
No. of Cattle	7
No. of Tracts	1
Valuation of Lands	£300
Valuation of Horses	£700
Total	£4357

John Flinn
No. of Horses	3
No. of Cattle	6
Valuation of Horses	£340
Total	£400

John Yates
No. of Acres of Land	900
No. of Horses	2
No. of Cattle	25
Money	£137
No. of Tracts	6
Valuation of Lands	£200
Valuation of Horses	£250
Total	£1157

Simon Green
No. of Acres of Land	200
Slaves over 10 years & under 40	1
Slaves Between 5 & 10, & 40 & 50	1
No. of Horses	4
No. of Cattle	21
Money	£2
No. of Tracts	2
Valuation of Lands	£200
Valuation of Horses	£270
Total	£1682

Solomon Dyson
No. of Acres of Land	250
No. of Horses	10
No. of Cattle	34
No. of Tracts	3
Valuation of Lands	£160
Valuation of Horses	£200
Total	£1100

Ignatious Flowers
No. of Acres of Land	350
No. of Horses	2
No. of Cattle	38
No. of Tracts	3
Valuation of Lands	£700
Valuation of Horses	£250
Total	£1330

Pierce Godwin
No. of Acres of Land	160

Chapter 5: Bladen County Tax Lists of 1779

No. of Horses	1
No. of Cattle	5
Money	£4
No. of Tracts	1
Valuation of Lands	£160
Valuation of Horses	£200
Total	£414

Thos. Amis Esqr.
No. of Acres of Land	3777
Slaves over 10 & under 40	19
Slaves Between 5 & 10, & 40 & 50	4
Slaves under 5 & Between 50 & 60	2
No. of Horses	20
No. of Cattle	160
Money	£1072.-1.-0
Money at Interest	£395.-8.-0
Valuation of Lands	£2650
Valuation of Horses	£3000
Cr. by one Infirm negroe £700	
Total	£19017.-8

Mary Amis
Slaves over 5 years & under 40	11
Slaves Between 5 & 10, & 40 & 50	2
Slaves under 5 & Between 50 & 60	2
No. of Horses	5
Money	£4.-8.-0
Valuation of Horses	£530
Total	£9034.-8.-0

William Buffalow
No. of Horses	1
Money	£157.-12.-0
Valuation of Horses	£100
Total	£257.-12.-0

Joseph Noble
No. of Acres of Land	1000
No. of Horses	1
No. of Cattle	14
Money	£11.-7.-0
No. of Tracts	3
Valuation of Lands	£840
Valuation of Horses	£100
Total	£1091.-7.-0

Elias Strickland
No. of Acres of Land	100
No. of Horses	3
No. of Cattle	8
Money	£8.-16.-0
No. of Tracts	1
Valuation of Lands	£20

Valuation of Horses	£310
Total	£418.-16.-0

Stephen Glear
No. of Acres of Land	1200
Slaves Between 5 & 10, & 40 & 50	1
Slaves under 5 & Between 50 & 60	2
No. of Horses	3
No. of Cattle	17
No. of Tracts	5
Valuation of Lands	£500
Valuation of Horses	£200
Total	£1370

Jas. & Archd. McColskey
No. of Acres of Land	1020
No. of Horses	8
No. of Cattle	50
Money	£24.-4.-0
No. of Tracts	5
Valuation of Lands	£400
Valuation of Horses	£400
Total	£1320

Henry Bosswell
No. of Acres of Land	400
No. of Horses	3
No. of Cattle	1
Money	£33.-12.-0
No. of Tracts	1
Valuation of Lands	£160
Valuation of Horses	£100
Total	£303.-12.-0

John Bargwin[?] Esqr.
No. of Lotts	8
No. of Acres of Land	4850
Slaves over 5 & under 40	31
Slaves Between 5 & 10, & 40 & 50	23
Slaves under 5 & Between 50 & 60	11
No. of Horses	9
No. of Cattle	56
Money	£40
Money at Interest	£6282.-8.-2
No. of Tracts	10
Valuation of Lands	£24038.-6.-8
Valuation of Horses	£800
Total	£64270.-14.-10

****

BLADEN COUNTY TAX LIST OF 1779

Chapter 5: Bladen County Tax Lists of 1779

A List of Taxable Property in the 5th or Capt. Clardy's District 1779. Thos. Amis, James Shipman & Duncan Morrison assessors

The headings in this list are the same as those in the preceding list.

John Richardson
No. of Acres of Land	100
No. of Horses	2
No. of Cattle	9
Money	£10.-8.-0
No. of Tracts	1
Valuation of Lands	£50
Valuation of Horses	£100
Total	£250.-8.-0

Hardy Hobbs
No. of Acres of Land	200
No. of Horses	2
No. of Tracts of Land	1
Valuation of Lands	£80
Valuation of Horses	£100
Total	£240

Grace Smith
No. of Acres of Land	50
Slaves Between 5 & 10, & 40 & 50	1
No. of Horses	5
No. of Cattle	20
Money	£9.-4.-0
No. of Tracts	1
Valuation of Lands	£20
Valuation of Horses	£250
Total	£879.-4.-0

Thomas Jones
No. of Acres of Land	50
No. of Horses	1
No. of Cattle	3
Money	£24.-9.-0
No. of Tracts	1
Valuation of Lands	£40
Valuation of Horses	£100
Total	£194.-9.-0

Margaret Kerr
No. of Acres of Land	100
No. of Horses	1
No. of Cattle	5
Money	£5.-12.-0
No. of Tracts	1
Valuation of Lands	£500
Valuation of Horses	£100
Total	£655.-12.-0

James Smith
No. of Acres of Land	400
No. of Horses	1
No. of Tracts	2
Valuation of Lands	£540
Valuation of Horses	£60
Total	£600

Leonard Lock
No. of Acres of Land	350
Slaves over 10 & under 40	2
Slaves Between 5 & 10, & 40 & 50	2
Slaves under 5 & Between 50 & 60	2
No. of Horses	5
No. of Cattle	18
Money	£1.-10.-0
No. of Tracts	2
Valuation of Lands	£1040
Valuation of Horses	£300
Total	£4221.-10.-0

Richard Small
No. of Acres of Land	200
No. of Horses	2
No. of Cattle	18
No. of Tracts	1
Valuation of Lands	£100
Valuation of Horses	£100
Total	£380

Benjn. Beesley
No. of Acres of Land	650
Slaves over 10 & under 40	2
Slaves Between 5 & 10, & 40 & 50	1
No. of Horses	4
No. of Cattle	26
Money	£61.-15.-0
No. of Tracts	5
Valuation of Lands	£370
Valuation of Horses	£300
Total	£2791.-15.-0

James Dupre
No. of Acres of Land	1336
Slaves over 10 & under 40	9
Slaves Between 5 & 10, & 40 & 50	2
Slaves under 5 & Between 50 & 60	7
No. of Horses	14
No. of Cattle	35
Money	£14.-8.-0
No. of Tracts	4

Chapter 5: Bladen County Tax Lists of 1779

Valuation of Lands	£3615
Valuation of Horses	£2425
Total	£15254.-8.-0

Lewis Dupre
No. of Acres of Land	820
Slaves over 10 & under 40	5
Slaves Between 5 & 10, & 40 & 50	1
No. of Horses	5
No. of Cattle	10
Money	£50
No. of Tracts	2
Valuation of Lands	£1280
Valuation of Horses	£300
Total	£5630

John Clark
No. of Acres of Land	200
No. of Horses	3
No. of Cattle	8
Money	£0.-1.-18
No. of Tracts	1
Valuation of Lands	£100
Valuation of Horses	£200
Total	£381.-18.-0

Samuel McRee
No. of Acres of Land	300
Slaves Between 5 & 10, & 40 & 50	1
No. of Horses	5
No. of Cattle	24
Money	£108.-12.-0
No. of Tracts	4
Valuation of Lands	£205
Valuation of Horses	£350
Total	£1303.-12.-0

Iver McCallum
No. of Acres of Land	100
No. of Horses	2
No. of Cattle	14
Money	£2.-16.-0
No. of Tracts	1
Valuation of Lands	£100
Valuation of Horses	£200
Total	£442.-16.-0

Arthur Smith
No. of Acres of Land	500
No. of Horses	3
No. of Cattle	19
Money	£6
No. of Tracts	2
Valuation of Lands	£766.-13.-4

Valuation of Horses	£200
Total	£1102.-13.-4

John Turner Esqr.
No. of Acres of Land	1040
Slaves over 10 & under 40	10
Slaves Between 5 & 10, & 40 & 50	8
Slaves under 5 & Between 50 & 60	1
No. of Horses	16
No. of Cattle	49
Money	£1682.-12.-0
No. of Tracts	4
Valuation of Lands	£2660
Valuation of Horses	£1400
Total	£16682.-12.-0

James Ellis
No. of Acres of Land	100
Slaves over 10 & under 40	3
Slaves under 5 & Between 50 & 60	1
No. of Horses	2
No. of Cattle	13
No. of Tracts	1
Valuation of Lands	£300
Valuation of Horses	£150
Total	£2830

Morris Biven
No. of Acres of Land	100
No. of Horses	2
No. of Cattle	5
Money	£24.-10.-0
No. of Tracts	1
Valuation of Lands	£40
Valuation of Horses	£150
Total	£264.-10.-0

William Burney Senr.
No. of Acres of Land	900
Slaves over 10 & under 40	1
Slaves Between 5 & 10, & 40 & 50	2
Slaves Under 5 & Between 50 & 60	2
No. of Horses	8
No. of Cattle	29
Money	£121
No. of Tracts	2
Valuation of Lands	£3000
Valuation of Horses	£550
Total	£5961

Duncan Morrison Esqr.
No. of Acres of Land	1510
Slaves over 10 & under 40	14
Slaves Between 5 & 10, & 40 & 50	7

Chapter 5: Bladen County Tax Lists of 1779

Slaves under 5 & Between 50 & 60	6
No. of Horses	8
No. of Cattle	34
Money	£75
Valuation of Lands	£1310
Valuation of Horses	£500
Total	£15725

James Green
No. of Acres of Land	450
Slaves under 5 & Between 50 & 60	1
No. of Horses	2
No. of Cattle	2
Money	£2
No. of Tracts	2
Valuation of Lands	£540
Valuation of Horses	£200
Total	£1012

Simon Simpson
No. of Acres of Land	250
No. of Horses	1
No. of Cattle	1
Money	£6.-10.-0
No. of Tracts	1
Valuation of Lands	£100
Valuation of Horses	£20
Total	£136

Thos. Ellis
No. of Acres of Land	200
Slaves over 10 & under 40	1
No. of Horses	1
No. of Tracts	2
Valuation of Lands	£276.-6.-8
Valuation of Horses	£50
Total	£1026.-6.-8

John Chancey
No. of Acres of Land	500
No. of Horses	6
No. of Cattle	9
Money	£6.-8.-0
No. of Tracts	3
Valuation of Lands	£340
Valuation of Horses	£350
Total	£786.-8.-0

Nickson Chester
No. of Acres of Land	640
Slaves Between 5 & 10, & 40 & 50	1
No. of Horses	3
Money	£100
Money At Interest	£20

Valuation of Lands	£300
Valuation of Horses	£200
Total	£1020

Thomas Richison
No. of Acres of Land	625
No. of Horses	1
No. of Cattle	29
Money	£2.-10.-0
No. of Tracts	5
Valuation of Lands	£910
Valuation of Horses	£17.-13.-4
Total	£1220.-3.-4

Peter Meshaw
No. of Acres of Land	200
No. of Horses	3
No. of Cattle	7
Money	£2
No. of Tracts	1
Valuation of Lands	£120
Valuation of Horses	£200
Total	£392

John Ellis
No. of Acres of Land	250
Slaves Between 5 & 10, & 40 & 50	1
No. of Horses	2
No. of Cattle	8
No. of Tracts	2
Valuation of Lands	£540
Valuation of Horses	£200
Total	£1220

Charles Baldwin
No. of Acres of Land	600
Slaves over 10 & under 40	4
Slaves Between 5 & 10, & 40 & 50	2
Slaves under 5 & Between 50 & 60	1
No. of Horses	6
No. of Cattle	26
No. of Tracts	3
Valuation of Lands	£1140
Valuation of Horses	£700
Total	£6020

John Baldwin Senr.
No. of Acres of Land	450
Slaves over 10 & under 40	6
Slaves Between 5 & 10, & 40 & 50	3
Slaves under 5 & Between 50 & 60	6
No. of Horses	11
No. of Cattle	41
Money	£41

Chapter 5: Bladen County Tax Lists of 1779

Money At Interest	£100
No. of Tracts	3
Valuation of Lands	£1080
Valuation of Horses	£1160
Total	£9690
John Dores	
No. of Horses	3
No. of Cattle	4
Valuation of Horses	£150
Total	£190
Stephen Smith	
No. of Acres of Land	1390
No. of Horses	2
No. of Cattle	14
No. of Tracts	11
Valuation of Lands	£1730
Valuation of Horses	£100
Total	£1970
Thomas Davis	
No. of Acres of Land	650
No. of Horses	5
Money	£48
No. of Tracts	4
Valuation of Lands	£260
Valuation of Horses	£450
Total	£750
Nathl. Baldwin	
No. of Acres of Land	250
No. of Cattle	15
No. of Tracts	1
Valuation of Lands	£250
Total	£400
Robert [Torn]llis	
No. of Acres of Land	100
Slaves over 10 & under 40	1
No. of Horses	1
No. of Cattle	2
No. of Tracts	1
Valuation of Lands	£40
Valuation of Horses	£100
Total	£860
Joseph Mersingale	
No. of Acres of Land	100
No. of Horses	2
No. of Cattle	1
Money	£17.-13.-0
No. of Tracts	1

Valuation of Lands	£60
Valuation of Horses	£500
Total	£587.-13.-0
Jacob Simpson	
No. of Horses	2
Valuation of Horses	£300
Total	£300
William Wilkinson	
No. of Acres of Land	370
Slaves under 5 & Between 50 & 60	1
No. of Horses	5
No. of Cattle	19
Money	£13.-4.-0
No. of Tracts	3
Valuation of Lands	£600
Valuation of Horses	£450
Total	£1503.-4.-0
William White	
No. of Acres of Land	300
Slaves over 10 & under 40	1
Slaves Between 5 & 10, & 40 & 50	1
Slaves under 5 & Between 50 & 60	2
No. of Horses	7
No. of Cattle	55
Money	£14.-13.-0
No. of Tracts	2
Valuation of Lands	£360
Valuation of Horses	£540
Total	£2764.-13.-0
Thos. Mims Senr.	
No. of Acres of Land	550
Slaves over 10 & under 40	1
Slaves Between 5 & 10, & 40 & 50	2
No. of Horses	19
No. of Cattle	40
Money	£2
No. of Tracts	3
Valuation of Lands	£1190
Valuation of Horses	£1050
Total	£4142
Duncan King	
No. of Acres of Land	250
No. of Horses	5
No. of Cattle	18
Money	£1
Money at Interest	£105
Valuation of Lands	£200
Valuation of Horses	£600
Total	£1086

Chapter 5: Bladen County Tax Lists of 1779

Joseph Ray
No. of Acres of Land	150
No. of Horses	1
No. of Cattle	5
Money	£35
No. of Tracts	1
Valuation of Lands	£100
Valuation of Horses	£80
Total	£205

John Cohoon
No. of Acres of Land	300
No. of Horses	1
No. of Cattle	28
Money	£28
No. of Tracts	2
Valuation of Lands	£300
Valuation of Horses	£80
Total	£688

Britton Jones
No. of Acres of Land	450
No. of Horses	2
No. of Cattle	2
Money	£29.-3.-0
Money at Interest	£5.-6.-0
No. of Tracts	2
Valuation of Lands	£500
Valuation of Horses	£150
Total	£704

Semore Simpson
No. of Horses	2
Valuation of Horses	£150
Total	£104

John Powell Senr.
No. of Acres of Land	460
Slaves over 10 & under 40	5
Slaves under 5 years & Between 50 & 60	1
No. of Horses	12
No. of Cattle	60
Money	£43.-7.-0
Stocks in Trade	2
No. of Tracts	2
Valuation of Lands	£2500
Valuation of Horses	£850
Total	£8243.-7.-0

Thos. Mims Junr.
No. of Acres of Land	200
No. of Horses	9
No. of Cattle	16
Money	£2.-7.-0
No. of Tracts	2
Valuation of Lands	£240
Valuation of Horses	£500
Total	£902.-7.-0

William Cohoon
No. of Acres of Land	200
No. of Horses	1
Money	£39.-4.-0
No. of Tracts	1
Valuation of Lands	£80
Valuation of Horses	£150
Total	£269.-4.-0

Richard Ronalds Senr.
No. of Horses	1
No. of Cattle	11
Valuation of Horses	£100
Total	£210

Robt. Richardson
No. of Acres of Land	50
No. of Cattle	3
No. of Tracts	1
Valuation of Lands	£50
Total	£80

Richd. Ronalds Junr.
No. of Acres of Land	250
No. of Horses	1
No. of Cattle	1
Money	£3.-4.-0
No. of Tracts	1
Valuation of Lands	£200
Valuation of Horses	£100
Total	£333.-4.-0

Benjn. Woodard
No. of Acres of Land	100
No. of Horses	3
No. of Tracts	1
Valuation of Lands	£40
Valuation of Horses	£200
Total	£240

Stephen Daniel
No. of Acres of Land	230
Slaves over 10 & under 40	4
Slaves Between 5 & 10, & 40 & 50	3
Slaves under 5 years & Between 50 & 60	2
No. of Horses	2
No. of Cattle	8
Money	£5

Chapter 5: Bladen County Tax Lists of 1779

Money at Interest	£200
No. of Tracts	1
Valuation of Lands	£1000
Valuation of Horses	£300
Total	£6085

Elisha Smith
No. of Acres of Land	150
No. of Horses	3
No. of Cattle	3
No. of Tracts	1
Valuation of Lands	£60
Valuation of Horses	£150
Total	£240

James Fokes
No. of Acres of Land	200
No. of Horses	2
No. of Cattle	7
Money	£0.-8.-0
No. of Tracts	1
Valuation of Lands	£300
Valuation of Horses	£200
Total	£570.-8.-0

Richd. Stubbs
No. of Acres of Land	100
No. of Horses	3
No. of Cattle	7
Money	£0.-4.-0
No. of Tracts	1
Valuation of Lands	£40
Valuation of Horses	£100
Total	£180.-4.-0

Dempsey Ronalds
No. of Acres of Land	100
No. of Horses	1
No. of Tracts	1
Valuation of Lands	£40
Valuation of Horses	£50
Total	£90

Zachariah Chancey
No. of Acres of Land	100
No. of Horses	4
No. of Cattle	5
Money	£2.-8.-0
No. of Tracts	1
Valuation of Lands	£60
Valuation of Horses	£250
Total	£362

John Stubbs Junr.
No. of Acres of Land	100
No. of Horses	2
No. of Cattle	9
Money	£2.-8.-0
No. of Tracts	1
Valuation of Lands	£40
Valuation of Horses	£140
Total	£272

John Stubbs Senr.
No. of Acres of Land	200
No. of Horses	1
No. of Tracts	1
Valuation of Lands	£200
Valuation of Horses	£100
Total	£300

William Parker
No. of Acres of Land	150
No. of Horses	1
No. of Cattle	2
No. of Tracts	1
Valuation of Lands	£100
Valuation of Horses	£200
Total	£320

Benjn. Lambethson
No. of Acres of Land	520
Slaves over 10 & under 40	7
Slaves under 5 & Between 50 & 60	5
No. of Horses	5
No. of Cattle	10
Money	£14
No. of Tracts	2
Valuation of Lands	£1400
Valuation of Horses	£600
Total	£9164

Warren Baldwin
No. of Horses	2
No. of Cattle	7
Valuation of Horses	£200
Total	£270

Sarah Daniel
No. of Acres of Land	330
Slaves over 10 & under 40	3
Slaves Between 5 & 10, & 40 & 50	2
Slaves under 5 & Between 50 & 60	2
No. of Horses	1
No. of Cattle	13
Money at Interest	£1000
No. of Tracts	1
Valuation of Lands	£500

Chapter 5: Bladen County Tax Lists of 1779

Valuation of Horses	£150
Total	£5164

Robert Daniel
No. of Acres of Land	850
Slaves over 10 & under 40	6
Slaves under 5 & Between 50 & 60	2
No. of Horses	10
No. of Cattle	9
Money at Interest	£120
No. of Tracts	3
Valuation of Lands	£1240
Valuation of Horses	£650
Total	£10000

James Clardy
No. of Acres of Land	840
Slaves over 10 & under 40	6
Slaves under 5 & Between 50 & 60	3
No. of Horses	5
No. of Cattle	12
Money	£115.-4.-0
No. of Tracts	3
Valuation of Lands	£2080
Valuation of Horses	£540
Total	£7805.-4.-0

Richd. Lambethson
No. of Acres of Land	100
Slaves over 10 & under 40	1
Slaves Between 5 & 10, & 40 & 50	1
No. of Horses	1
No. of Cattle	11
No. of Tracts	1
Valuation of Lands	£100
Valuation of Horses	£50
Total	£1360

John Folk
No. of Acres of Land	650
No. of Horses	3
No. of Cattle	8
Money	£0.-8.-0
No. of Tracts	4
Valuation of Lands	£260
Valuation of Horses	£350
Total	£690.-8.-0

Britain Hargrove
No. of Acres of Land	300
Slaves over 10 & under 40	1
Slaves under 5 & Between 50 & 60	1
No. of Horses	6
No. of Cattle	7
Money	£211.-16.-0
No. of Tracts	3
Valuation of Lands	£300
Valuation of Horses	£400
Total	£1931.-16.-0

William Burney Junr.
No. of Acres of Land	300
No. of Horses	10
No. of Cattle	50
Money	£273.-6.-0
No. of Tracts	4
Valuation of Lands	£400
Valuation of Horses	£650
Total	£1823.-6.-0

[Name Torn]
No. of Horses	2
No. of Cattle	31
Money	£10
Valuation of Horses	£160
Total	£480

Handson Lewis Senr.
No. of Acres of Land	440
Slaves Between 5 & 10, & 40 & 50	1
Slaves under 5 & Between %0 & 60	1
No. of Horses	7
No. of Cattle	27
Money	£20.-16.-0
No. of Tracts	3
Valuation of Lands	£700
Valuation of Horses	£500
Total	£2040.-16.-0

Handson Lewis Junr.
No. of Horses	1
Money	£8.-16.-0
Valuation of Horses	£200
Total	£208.-16.-0

David Mims
No. of Acres of Land	550
Slaves Between 5 & 10, & 40 & 50	1
No. of Horses	7
No. of Cattle	26
Money	£4.-12.-0
No. of Tracts	4
Valuation of Lands	£620
Valuation of Horses	£450
Total	£1734.-12.-0

John Smith Junr.
No. of Acres of Land	100

Chapter 5: Bladen County Tax Lists of 1779

Money	£2.-8.-0
No. of Tracts	1
Valuation of Lands	£40
Total	£42.-8.-0

James Mims
No. of Horses	3
Money	£7.-4.-0
Valuation of Horses	£200
Total	£207.-4.-0

Alexr. McGillip
No. of Horses	1
No. of Cattle	13
Valuation of Horses	£100
Total	£230

Micajah Cohoon
No. of Acres of Land	200
No. of Tracts	1
Valuation of Lands	£100
Total	£100

John Powell Junr.
No. of Acres of Land	500
No. of Horses	11
No. of Cattle	8
Money	£6
No. of Tracts	4
Valuation of Lands	£300
Valuation of Horses	£900
Total	£1226

Abraham Freeman
No. of Acres of Land	300
No. of Horses	5
No. of Cattle	15
Money	£4.-18.-0
No. of Tracts	3
Valuation of Lands	£400
Valuation of Horses	£300
Total	£854.-18.-0

Willm. Freeman
No. of Acres of Land	100
No. of Horses	2
No. of Cattle	3
Money	£7.-12.-0
No. of Tracts of Land	1
Valuation of Land	£40
Valuation of Horses	£130
Total	£207.-12.-0

John Webb
No. of Acres of Land	100
No. of Horses	4
No. of Cattle	3
Money	£3.-12.-0
No. of Tracts of Land	1
Valuation of Lands	£40
Valuation of Horses	£300
Total	£373.-12.-0

Saml. Freeman
No. of Horses	1
Money	£0.-12.-0
Valuation of Horses	£80
Total	£80.-12.-0

Roger Freeman
No. of Acres of Land	50
No. of Horses	1
No. of Cattle	3
Money	£4
No. of Tracts of Land	1
Valuation of Lands	£50
Valuation of Horses	£80
Total	£164.-4.-0

Willm. Webb
No. of Horses	1
No. of Cattle	1
Money	£0.-4.-0
Valuation of Horses	£100
Total	£110.-4.-0

John Smith Sr.
No. of Acres of Land	100
No. of Horses	2
No. of Cattle	5
Money	£2
No. of Tracts of Land	1
Valuation of Lands	£60
Valuation of Horses	£150
Total	£262

Joseph Baldwin
No. of Acres of Lands	500
Slaves under 5 & Between 50 & 60	1
No. of Horses	8
No. of Cattle	26
Money	£70
No. of Tracts of Land	3
Valuation of Lands	£1060
Valuation of Horses	£552
Total	£2092

Howell Aitkins

Chapter 5: Bladen County Tax Lists of 1779

No. of Horses	2
Valuation of Horses	£250
Total	£250

John Atkins
No. of Acres of Land	260
No. of Horses	2
Money	£6.-10.-0
No. of Tracts of Land	2
Valuation of Lands	£540
Valuation of Horses	£200
Total	£746

John Blanks
No. of Acres of Land	100
No. of Horses	3
No. of Cattle	5
No. of Tracts of Land	1
Valuation of Lands	£150
Valuation of Horses	£200
Total	£400

Seth Due
No. of Acres of Land	100
No. of Horses	2
No. of Cattle	2
Money	£10
No. of Tracts of Land	1
Valuation of Lands	£40
Valuation of Horses	£150
Total	£220

Saml. Russell
Money	£300
Total	£300

Willm. Baldwin
No. of Acres of Land	400
No. of Tracts of Land	1
Valuation of Lands	£40
Total	£40

[Torn] Moore
No. of Acres of Land	1520
Slaves over 10 & under 40	14
Slaves Between 5 & 10, & 40 & 50	4
Slaves under 5 Between 50 & 60	10
No. of Horses	13
No. of Cattle	19
Money	£100
Money at Interest	£19
No. of Tracts 0f Land	5
Valuation of Lands	£2180
Valuation of Horses	£700
Total	£17089

[Name Torn]
Slaves Between 5 & 10, & 40 & 50	1
Slaves under 5 & Between 50 & 60	1
No. of Horses	5
No. of Cattle	22
Money	£15.-13.-0
Valuation of Horses	£350
Total	£1235.-13.-0

Saml. Carman
No. of Acres of Land	660
No. of Horses	1
No. of Cattle	6
Money	£31.-8.-0
No. of Tracts of Land	4
Valuation of Lands	£100
Valuation of Horses	£410
Total	£601.-8.-0

William Green
Slaves over 10 & under 40	1
No. of Horses	4
Valuation of Horses	£250
Total	£250

William Dubois
No. of Horses	3
No. of Cattle	7
Money	£1.-12.-0
Valuation of Horses	£240
Total	£311.-12.-0

John Demery
No. of Acres of Land	550
No. of Horses	2
No. of Cattle	3
No. of Tracts	2
Valuation of Lands	£200
Valuation of Horses	£150
Total	£280

Jas. Baldwin's Estate
No. of Acres of Land	1040
Slaves over 10 & under 40	4
Slaves under 5 & Between 50 & 60	1
No. of Horses	12
No. of Cattle	82
Money	£4
No. of Tracts of Land	5
Valuation of Lands	£2840
Valuation of Horses	£600

Chapter 5: Bladen County Tax Lists of 1779

Total	£7314

Jas. Council
No. of Acres of Land	250
No. of Horses	4
Money	£4.-17.-0
No. of Tracts of Land	1
Valuation of Lands	£100
Valuation of Horses	£200
Total	£304.-17.-0

Drury Haddock
No. of Acres of Land	100
No. of Horses	2
Money	£0.-12.-0
No. of Tracts of Land	1
Valuation of Lands	£40
Valuation of Horses	£50
Total	£90.-12.-0

Jeremiah Bigford
No. of Horses	2
Valuation of Horses	£200
Total	£200

Burrell Hargrove
No. of Acres of Land	250
No. of Horses	2
No. of Cattle	6
Money	£4.-12.-0
No. of Tracts of Land	1
Valuation of Lands	£200
Valuation of Horses	£180
Total	£444.-12.-0

Samuel Rourk
No. of Acres of Land	450
Slaves over 10 & under 40	1
No. of Horses	9
No. of Cattle	5
Money	£318
No. of Tracts of Land	5
Valuation of Lands	£1120
Valuation of Horses	£800
Total	£2548

****

BLADEN COUNTY TAX LIST OF 1779

We the Subscribers agreeable to an order of [Torn] to us Directed to assess the Taxable Property [Torn] Captains Robison, Ellis & Harrisons Districts, In Obedience to said Order we have Assessed the said Districts, and has made Due Particular and faithfull Return of the Same. Saml. Cain, John King, David White

Headings for this list include: Polls, Bladen Lands, Lots, Slaves, Horses, Cattle, [Four columns for land in other counties], & Total.

Capt. Peter Robeson
Bladen Lands	1030
Slaves	11
Horses	7
Cattle	47
Total	£7168.-4.-0

John DuCamp
	Poll
Bladen Lands	100
Total	[None]

Judith Eustace
Bladen Lands	200
Horses	1
Cattle	11
Total	£325

Laurance Byrne
Bladen Lands	50
Horses	2
Cattle	10
Total	£190

Jeremiah Plummer
Bladen Lands	71
Cattle	6
Total	£67.-2.-0

John Smith Siegnr.
Bladen Lands	100
Horses	2
Cattle	11
Total	£170

Thos. Lock
Bladen Lands	460
Slaves	3
Horses	4
Cattle	18
Total	£3130

John Plummer
Bladen Lands	130
Horses	1

Chapter 5: Bladen County Tax Lists of 1779

Cattle 2
Total £380

Peter Byrne
Bladen Lands 150
Slaves 1
Horses 4
Cattle 15
Total £940.-4.-0

Elipha [Elisha] Plummer
Bladen Lands 150
Slaves 1
Horses 4
Cattle 17
Total £1155

David Lenze White
Bladen Lands 2340
Lots 1
Slaves 5
Horses 7
Cattle 23
Tryon County Lands 376
Total £5400

Lazarus Johnston Poll
Horses 1
Cattle 4
Total [None]

John Moor
Bladen Lands 850
Slaves 1
Horses 7
Cattle 52
Total £2546

Gidian Prick
Bladen Lands 100
Cattle 18
Total £210

James Beard
Bladen Lands 647
Slaves 3
Horses 3
Cattle 55
Total £2443.-10.-0

John Beard
Bladen Lands 670
Slaves 1

Horses 4
Cattle 30
Total £2119

John Smith Junr.
Bladen Lands 100
Horses 1
Cattle 12
Total £160

William Smith Poll
Bladen Lands 100
Horses 1
Cattle 6
Total £116

David Legett
Bladen Lands 600
Slaves 1
Horses 2
Total £515

Elias Stone Poll
Horses 1
Cattle 2
Total [None]

John Murphey
Bladen Lands 700
Slaves 1
Horses 5
Cattle 57
Cumberland County Lands 300
Total £2130

Able Corbet
Bladen Lands 350
Horses 3
Cattle 10
Total £245

Elizth. Newberry
Bladen Lands 200
Slaves 1
Cattle 5
Total £954

Joseph Thime
Bladen Lands 1040
Slaves 6
Horses 4
Cattle 39
Total £5883

Chapter 5: Bladen County Tax Lists of 1779

Richd. Plummer — Poll
Horses — 1
Total — £140

Matthew Byrne — Poll
Lots — 1
Total — £70

John Lock Junr.
Bladen Lands — 300
Slaves — 1
Horses — 3
Cattle — 6
Total — £1125.-15.-0

Willm. Kirk Patrick
Bladen Lands — 1273
Slaves — 7
Horses — 3
Cattle — 22
Total — £4529.-1.-6

Benjamin Clark
Bladen Lands — 2446
Slaves — 5
Horses — 7
Cattle — 18
Total — £6571.-8.-0

Daniel Beard
Bladen Lands — 550
Horses — 3
Cattle — 16
Total — £1430

William Champin
Bladen Lands — 500
Horses — 3
Cattle — 2
Total — £1744.-17.-9

Isaac Jessop
Bladen Lands — 300
Horses — 2
Cattle — 24
Total — £322.-16.-0

Nathaniel Reaves
Bladen Lands — 750
Slaves — 4
Horses — 4
Cattle — 15
Total — £4520.-4.-0

John Hollingsworth
Bladen Lands — 570
Horses — 3
Cattle — 17
Total — £497

Jesse Newberry
Bladen Lands — 2809
Slaves — 10
Horses — 8
Cattle — 45
Total — £10101

John Storm
Bladen Lands — 300
Horses — 2
Cattle — 9
Total — £240.-13.-0

Robt. Edwards
Bladen Lands — 3000
Lots — 4
Slaves — 8
Horses — 1
Cattle — 16
Cumberland County Lands — 800
Anson County Lands — 900
Total — £6327.-11.-8

James Moor Junr.
Bladen Lands — 200
Slaves — 2
Horses — 3
Cattle — 13
Total — £1392

Rachel Graham
Bladen Lands — 74
Horses — 1
Cattle — 8
Total — £329

David Halloway
Bladen Lands — 760
Slaves — 5
Horses — 5
Cattle — 5
Total — £4913.-10.-0

Saml. Maultsby
Lots — 1
Total — £308.-8.-0

Chapter 5: Bladen County Tax Lists of 1779

Mary Storm
Horses 2
Cattle 8
Total £210.-18.-0

Thos. Kervin
Bladen Lands 150
Horses 1
Cattle 12
Total £207

Henry Ivey
Horses 1
Cattle 9
Total £490

James McDonnel
Bladen Lands 650
Slaves 1
Horses 7
Cattle 18
Total £2625

Silvanus Wilson
Bladen Lands 7299
Slaves 14
Horses 8
Cattle 31
Total £10095.-14.-0

Benjamin Willis Junr. Poll
Horses 1
Total [None]

John Councill
Bladen Lands 525
Slaves 4
Horses 3
Cattle 30
Total £2918.-6.-0

Agerton Willis Poll
Bladen Lands 100
Total £24

Benjamin Willis Snr.
Bladen Lands 1500
Slaves 4
Horses 3
Cattle 30
Total £3615

Malica Burges Poll

Horses 1
Total £332

Absolam Cordel Poll
Horses 3
Total £140

Solomon Wilson
Bladen Lands 150
Horses 3
Cattle 19
Total £585

Peter Lord
Bladen Lands 1190
Lots 2
Slaves 5
Horses 4
Cattle 15
Cumberland County Lands 169
Total £4511.-18.-0

Richd. Wilkinson
Bladen Lands 500
Horses 2
Cattle 15
Total £371.-2.-0

Zacariah Reaves
Bladen Lands 150
Horses 1
Total £750

William Bradford Poll
Total [None]

Benjamin Branty
Bladen Lands 629
Slaves 3
Horses 4
Cattle 9
Total £2017.-8.-0

Benjamin Sims
Bladen Lands 1220
Horses 3
Cattle 18
Total £463.-16.-0

Titus Overton
Bladen Lands 500
Horses 3
Cattle 3

Chapter 5: Bladen County Tax Lists of 1779

Total	£237
Sampson Carver	
Bladen Lands	1340
Slaves	7
Horses	2
Cattle	11
Total	£3818.-10.-0
James Jackson	
Bladen Lands	1220
Slaves	1
Cattle	27
Total	£1380.-10.-0
Isaac Sims	
Bladen Lands	1430
Slaves	1
Horses	4
Cattle	30
Total	£1792.-12.-0
John Carter	Poll
Bladen Lands	200
Cattle	3
Total	£58
Jesse Thims	
Bladen Lands	900
Slaves	2
Horses	3
Cattle	14
Total	£3115
John Purnell	
Bladen Lands	200
Horses	2
Cattle	10
Total	£185.-17.-0
James Moorhead	Poll
Horses	1
Total	£150
Benjamin Cooper	
Slaves	[Torn]
Horses	[Torn]
Cumberland County Lands	62 1/2
Total	£193.-8.-0
Mary Cooper	
Bladen Lands	480
Slaves	2

Horses	3
Cattle	10
Total	£2284
John Lock Seignr.	
Bladen Lands	840
Slaves	8
Horses	5
Cattle	40
Cumberland County Lands	160
Total	£4910.-11.-0
Danl. Willis Junr.	
Bladen Lands	400
Horses	1
Cattle	8
Total	£1032.-3.-0
Danl. Willis Seignr. Trustee	
Bladen Lands	2360
Slaves	21
Horses	6
Cattle	59
Total	£14994
Danl. Willis pr. Selfe	
Bladen Lands	1000
Slaves	4
Horses	5
Total	£3152
James Moor Seignr.	Poll
Total	**[None]**
Jas. Council Trustee for Fred. Grage	
Total	£153.-9.-10
James Council - Self	
Bladen Lands	930
Slaves	21
Horses	11
Cattle	40
Cumberland County Lands	1527
Total	£17278.-7.-0
James Council trustee for Jas. Brumlow	
Lots	8
Slaves	3
Cumberland County Lands	861
Anson County Lands	75
Meclinburgh County Lands	230
Total	£3031

Chapter 5: Bladen County Tax Lists of 1779

William Sims
Slaves	10
Horses	5
Total	£4295

Zacriah Plummer
Bladen Lands	200
Horses	2
Total	£443

Jas. Singletary Junr.
Bladen Lands	248
Slaves	2
Horses	2
Cattle	11
Total	£1483

Joseph Mott
	Poll
Horses	1
Total	£280

Richd. Singletary Snr.
Bladen Lands	640
Slaves	5
Horses	6
Cattle	13
Total	£4829

Joseph Butler
Bladen Lands	220
Slaves	2
Horses	3
Cattle	18
Total	£2174

James Stone
Bladen Lands	100
Horses	1
Cattle	2
Total	£354.-8.-0

Jas. Singletary Seignr.
Bladen Lands	1200
Lots	1
Slaves	1
Horses	6
Cattle	12
Total	£3392

Steaphen Freeman
	Poll
Horses	2
Total	£100

Elizth. Evins
Bladen Lands	100
Horses	1
Cattle	16
Total	£191.-16.-0

Benjn. Lansdell
Horses	1
Total	£834

Thos. Scriving
	Poll
Bladen Lands	200
Horses	1
Cattle	3
Total	£165.-10.-0

Richd. Singletary Junr.
Bladen Lands	200
Horses	4
Cattle	19
Total	£682

Peter Simpson
	Poll
Bladen Lands	50
Horses	1
Total	£125

Philip Wood
Bladen Lands	350
Slaves	1
Horses	3
Cattle	24
Total	£1850

Joseph Wood
Bladen Lands	620
Slaves	1
Horses	5
Cattle	42
Total	£2515

Saml. Hollingsworth
Bladen Lands	3050
Slaves	7
Horses	11
Cattle	34
Total	£7359.-4.-0

Saml. Hollingsworth is listed as Guardian of the next five names. The names are Saml. Carver, Jesse Carver, James Carver, John Carver, & Mary Carver.

Saml. Carver
Bladen Lands	600
Horses	5

Chapter 5: Bladen County Tax Lists of 1779

Total	£595

Jesse Carver
Bladen Lands	200
Slaves	2
Horses	1
Total	£1500

James Carver
Bladen Lands	100
Slaves	3
Total	£2110

John Carver
Bladen Lands	100
Slaves	2
Total	£1410

Mary Carver
Slaves	2
Horses	1
Total	£1450

William Cain
Bladen Lands	1290
Slaves	14
Horses	7
Cattle	39
Cumberland County Lands	100
Total	£9762

John Newberry
Bladen Lands	970
Slaves	5
Horses	6
Cattle	8
Total	£4529

Janet Gates
Bladen Lands	100
Horses	1
Cattle	8
Total	£110

James Ellis
Bladen Lands	2146
Slaves	4
Horses	5
Cattle	35
Total	£4349.-17.-10

Isaac Ray
Bladen Lands	840
Lots	1

Slaves	14
Horses	4
Cattle	23
Total	£8453.-5.-8

Leavy Young
Bladen Lands	990
Slaves	7
Horses	3
Cattle	17
Total	£4340

John Rogerson
Bladen Lands	600
Slaves	5
Horses	3
Cattle	13
Total	£3170

Rachel McMaster
Bladen Lands	200
Horses	2
Cattle	15
Total	£290

John McDonnel
Bladen Lands	450
Slaves	1
Horses	2
Cattle	9
Total	£996

Margaret Byrne
Bladen Lands	1280
Slaves	[Torn]
Horses	6
Cattle	24
Total	£13529

Colo. Thos. Robeson
Bladen Lands	8783
Slaves	30
Horses	21
Cattle	140
Total	£23754

Robt. Sims
Bladen Lands	1520
Horses	3
Cattle	18
Total	£482

Saml. Richardson

Chapter 5: Bladen County Tax Lists of 1779

Bladen Lands	3400
Slaves	15
Horses	5
Cattle	26
Mecklenburgh County Lands	400
Total	£8712

Joseph Cain
Bladen Lands	1050
Lots	2
Slaves	4
Horses	9
Cattle	28
Duplin County Lands	200
Total	£4756.-6.-4

Saml. Butler
Bladen Lands	645
Slaves	5
Horses	6
Cattle	17
Total	£3892.-10.-0

Richd. Elwell
Bladen Lands	200
Horses	3
Cattle	12
Total	£490

George Willis
Bladen Lands	570
Slaves	4
Horses	3
Cattle	27
Total	£3936.-16.-6

Agerton Willis Junr. — Poll
Total	[None]

John Wilson
Bladen Lands	350
Slaves	6
Horses	7
Total	£3778.-15.-6

William Anderson
Bladen Lands	260
Horses	3
CattleCattle	40
Total	£980

William Wilkinson — Poll
Horses	1
Total	£100

William McRee
Bladen Lands	4550
Lots	5
Slaves	16
Horses	7
Cattle	33
Total	£13542.-14.-0

Steaphen Hester
Bladen Lands	600
Horses	3
Cattle	26
Total	£642

Saml. Curry — Poll
Cattle	6
Total	£62.-10.-0

Robt. Baker
Bladen Lands	640
Horses	3
Cattle	18
Total	£1954.-16.-0

William Dowles — Poll
Bladen Lands	100
Horses	1
Cattle	7
Total	£130

Argules Pointer
Bladen Lands	100
Lots	1
Horses	4
Cattle	5
Total	£699

Benjn. Fitz. Randolph
Bladen Lands	740
Slaves	6
Horses	4
Cattle	17
Total	£3820

Abraham Gray
Bladen Lands	100
Slaves	1
Horses	2
Cattle	19
Total	£1610

Benjamin Humphrey

Chapter 5: Bladen County Tax Lists of 1779

Lots	4
Cattle	3
Total	£468

Robt. Hodge
Bladen Lands	750
Slaves	1
Horses	1
Cattle	8
Total	£979.-16.-0

Joseph Camp
Bladen Lands	1003 ½
Lots	2
Slaves	3
Horses	2
Cattle	30
Anson County Lands	500
Total	£1793.-10.-0

Thos. Kinlaw
Bladen Lands	350
Horses	3
Cattle	25
Total	£524

Dennis Collom
Bladen Lands	320
Horses	4
Cattle	11
Total	£815

John Maultsby
Bladen Lands	220
Lots	1
Horses	1
Total	£589.-6.-0

David Russ
Bladen Lands	740
Lots	3
Slaves	1
Horses	3
Cattle	15
Total	£1207.-12.-0

William Russ
Bladen Lands	1130
Horses	2
Cattle	15
Total	£374.-12.-0

George Wier
Bladen Lands	170

Lots	2
Horses	1
Cattle	13
Total	£536.-13.-3

John McMullen
	Poll
Cattle	4
Total	£70

Steaphen Bryon
Bladen Lands	100
Slaves	1
Horses	3
Cattle	16
Total	£1276

Alexr. Harvey
Bladen Lands	200
Lots	2
Slaves	1
Cattle	5
Total	£1233

Rikam Reding
	Poll
Bladen Lands	400
Total	£41.-12.-0

Alexr. Schaw
	Poll
Horses	1
Total	£100

Niel Schaw Junr.
	Poll
Cattle	3
Total	£30

William Bryon
	Poll
Bladen Lands	100
Horses	1
Total	£134.-16.-0

Edward Davis
Bladen Lands	2000
Lots	2
Slaves	5
Horses	4
Cattle	38
Total	£4729

Mary Singletary
Slaves	4
Horses	3
Cattle	18
Total	£3081.-4.-0

Chapter 5: Bladen County Tax Lists of 1779

Josiah Hendon
Bladen Lands	625
Lots	2
Slaves	6
Horses	3
Cattle	12
Anson County Lands	400
Total	£3586.-4.-0

John Harrison
Bladen Lands	744
Slaves	1
Horses	2
Cattle	19
Total	£2364.-9.-0

John Stone
	Poll
Horses	1
Total	£251.-8.-0

William Chisher
	Poll
Horses	1
Total	£100

Eithamon Singletary
	Poll
Bladen Lands	160
Horses	4
Cattle	7
Total	£330

Richard Chesher
Bladen Lands	[Torn]
Slaves	[Torn]
Horses	[Torn]
Cattle	18
Total	[Torn]

James Washbyrne
Bladen Lands	160
Slaves	[Torn]
Cattle	2
Total	£463

Benjn. Thomas
	Poll
Cattle	2
Total	£20.-10.-0

James Cain
Bladen Lands	400
Horses	3
Cattle	23
Total	£492.-9.-0

John White
Bladen Lands	2
Lots	3
Horses	2
Cattle	4
Total	£840

Richd. Salter
Bladen Lands	1060
Slaves	2
Horses	3
Cattle	56
Total	£3344.-8.-0

James Isham
Bladen Lands	350
Slaves	1
Horses	4
Cattle	24
Total	£825

Elizth. Bryon
Horses	2
Cattle	23
Total	£306

John Bryon Estate
Bladen Lands	412
Slaves	4
Horses	2
Cattle	10

William Harrison
Bladen Lands	350
Lots	1
Slaves	1
Horses	4
Cattle	45
Total	£1435

John Harrison Junr.
Bladen Lands	1850
Slaves	2
Horses	4
Cattle	35
Total	£2515

Edward Fowler
Bladen Lands	300
Horses	3
Cattle	8
Total	£601

George Lyon

Chapter 5: Bladen County Tax Lists of 1779

Bladen Lands	1020
Slaves	7
Horses	5
Cattle	20
Total	£5990

Evin Ellis
Bladen Lands	650
Horses	6
Cattle	45
Total	£2187.-9.-0

George Nowls	Poll
Bladen Lands	50
Horses	1
Cattle	4
Total	£160

Jaret Ervin
Horses	3
Cattle	3
Total	£752

John Allen	Poll
Bladen Lands	60
Horses	3
Cattle	2
Total	£96

Robt. McRee
Bladen Lands	500
Horses	5
Cattle	18
Total	£550

Robt. Wells
Bladen Lands	444
Lots	2
Slaves	4
Horses	1
Cattle	12
Total	£3884

Thos. White	Poll
Bladen Lands	150
Horses	3
Total	£320

William Griffin	Poll
Total	[None]

Willis Barfil	Poll
Horses	1

Total	£100.-4.-0

Saml. Porter
Bladen Lands	320
Lots	1
Slaves	1
Total	£892

Mary Correnton
Slaves	4
Horses	1
Cattle	6
Total	£2810

John Hilliard Poll	Delinquent
Total	[None]

Major Thos. Owen
Bladen Lands	7165
Lots	4
Slaves	22
Horses	10
Cattle	45
Brunswick County Lands	385
Total	£14842.-11.-2

Robt. McConky
Bladen Lands	562
Slaves	2
Horses	3
Cattle	26
Total	£2260

Catheron Owen
Bladen Lands	2400
Lots	1
Slaves	14
Horses	7
Cattle	20
Total	£9810.-9.-0

Isaac Jones Esqr.
Bladen Lands	1417
Lots	5
Slaves	9
Horses	11
Cattle	76
Total	£6521.-16.-0

Richd. Smith Esqr.
Bladen Lands	698
Slaves	2
Horses	8

Chapter 5: Bladen County Tax Lists of 1779

Cattle 70
Total £4341

William Kook Poll
Total £98

Matthew Rone White
Bladen Lands 340
Horses 2
Total £392.-8.-0

Thos. Hains
Bladen Lands 350
Lots 5
Slaves 11
Horses 3
Cattle 24
Total £8150.-9.-2

George Brown Esqr.
Bladen Lands 1180
Slaves 9
Horses 17
Cattle 32
Total £7083

William McRee Junr.
Lots 1
Horses 1
Total £359.-12.-0

John Hester
Bladen Lands 224
Horses 1
Cattle 8
Total £271

Archd. Darrah
Bladen Lands 100
Lots 1
Slaves 1
Horses 1
Cattle 13
Total £1026.-7.-0

John Darrah Poll
Horses 1
Cattle 6
Total £260

Thos. Hester
Bladen Lands 300
Horses 4
Cattle 11

Total £388.-9.-0

Alexr. McLarty
Horses 2
Cattle 6
Total £310

James Nowls Poll
Horses 1
Total [None]

Steaphen Hester
Bladen Lands 350
Slaves 1
Horses 3
Cattle 34
Total £1695.-11.-0

Edward Jones
Bladen Lands 190
Horses 5
Total £870

Jacob Guiton
Cattle 15
Total [Torn]

John Hill
Bladen Lands 50
Horses 3
Cattle 7
Total £230

James Evers
Bladen Lands 600
Horses 3
Cattle 14
Total £430

Thos. Howard
Bladen Lands 80
Horses 2
Cattle 10
Total £276.-8.-0

William White
Bladen Lands 910
Slaves 2
Horses 4
Cattle 13
Total £1967

Thos. Hester Junr.

Chapter 5: Bladen County Tax Lists of 1779

Bladen Lands	500
Horses	2
Cattle	2
Total	£205

Joseph Singletary
Bladen Lands	450
Lots	2
Slaves	7
Horses	5
Cattle	27
Total	£4070

Mathew Monthe Poll
Bladen Lands	50
Horses	1
Cattle	2
Total	£55.-16.-0

James Ervin
Lots	1
Horses	1
Cattle	5
Total	£430

Griffith Jones White
Bladen Lands	883
Horses	4
Cattle	7
Total	£963.-6.-0

William Hendon
Bladen Lands	1160
Lots	1
Slaves	4
Horses	6
Cattle	19
Total	£3541.-10.-0

John Schaw
Bladen Lands	300
Horses	2
Cattle	22
Total	£301.-10.-0

Mary White
Bladen Lands	300
Slaves	6
Horses	2
Cattle	17
Total	£3752.-9.-3

Benjamin Stone
Bladen Lands	1184

Lots	1
Slaves	4
Horses	4
Cattle	17
Hanover County Land	900
Total	£6850

John Dridin
Bladen Lands	640
Horses	2
Cattle	22
Total	£419

Jacob Months
Bladen Lands	88
Horses	1
Cattle	12
Total	£316

Thos. McLenon
Bladen Lands	200
Horses	6
Cattle	6
Total	£113.-12.-0

Saml. Guiton Poll
Horses	1
Cattle	4
Total	£90

Neil Schaw
Bladen Lands	150
Slaves	5
Horses	2
Cattle	11
Total	£2827

Edward Harrison
Bladen Lands	850
Lots	2
Slaves	2
Horses	6
Cattle	37
Total	£2079

Edward Bryon
Bladen Lands	562
Slaves	7
Horses	3
Cattle	40
Total	£5309.-4.-0

Richd. Harrison
Bladen Lands	790

Chapter 5: Bladen County Tax Lists of 1779

Slaves	1
Horses	2
Cattle	26
Total	£1327

David Bryon
Bladen Lands	500
Horses	3
Cattle	19
Total	£316.-15.-0

John Lasly
Bladen Lands	60
Horses	1
Cattle	2
Total	£136

Philemon Bryon
Bladen Lands	210
Horses	1
Cattle	17
Total	£492

Majr. Jas. Richardson
Bladen Lands	1030
Slaves	12
Horses	3
Cattle	13
Total	£6083

Capt. William Ellis
Bladen Lands	850
Horses	4
Cattle	24
Total	£650

William Cain
	Poll
Total	[None]

James Cain
	Poll
Total	[None]

William Smith
	Poll
Total	[None]

Saml. Rowan
Cattle	30
Total	£300

John Suggs
Horses	1
Cattle	19
Total	£246

Wm. Johnston
Bladen Lands	1070
Horses	3
Cattle	16
Total	£757

William Owens
Bladen Lands	800
Slaves	7
Horses	3
Cattle	50
Total	£3804

John Cashwell
Bladen Lands	400
Horses	3
Cattle	35
Total	£640

John Smith Junr.
Bladen Lands	100
Horses	1
Cattle	7
Total	£110

Archd. McDonnel
Bladen Lands	100
Horses	2
Cattle	15
Total	£342

Thos. Suggs
Bladen Lands	200
Horses	6
Cattle	24
Total	£580

Francis Davis
Bladen Lands	200
Cattle	15
Total	£180.-1.-6

Sampson Davis
Horses	1
Cattle	13
Total	£188

Thos. Cessome
Horses	1
Cattle	17
Total	£220

Thos. Avent

Chapter 5: Bladen County Tax Lists of 1779

Bladen Lands	100			
Horses	1	Cade Weathersby		
Cattle	12	Bladen Lands	350	
Duplin County Land	100	Slaves	6	
Total	£170	Horses	6	
		Cattle	88	
Jonathan Sikes		Total	£5590.-16	
Bladen Lands	75			
Horses	1	James Weathersby		
Cattle	11	Cattle	17	
Total	£168	Total	£104.-16	

Jonathan Sikes
Bladen Lands   75
Horses   1
Cattle   11
Total   £168

John Mains   Poll
Bladen Lands   100
Total   [None]

Thos. Cashwell
Bladen Lands   100
Horses   4
Cattle   12
Total   £485

John Pharis
Bladen Lands   400
Cattle   61
Total   £980

John Davis
Bladen Lands   200
Horses   1
Cattle   8
Total   £150

William Moorhead
Bladen Lands   350
Slaves   2
Horses   4
Total   £1400

Isaac Hollingsworth
Bladen Lands   150
Horses   3
Cattle   40
Total   £582

James Johnston   Poll
Bladen Lands   640
Total   £96

David McDonnol
Horses   1
Cattle   6
Total   £112.-12.-3

Cade Weathersby
Bladen Lands   350
Slaves   6
Horses   6
Cattle   88
Total   £5590.-16

James Weathersby
Cattle   17
Total   £104.-16

John Suggs
Bladen Lands   100
Cattle   27
Total   £271.-4

Joseph Carter
Bladen Lands   200
Horses   2
Cattle   23
Total   £406

John Parker
Bladen Lands   150
Horses   3
Cattle   16
Total   £338.-4

Saml. Hails[?]
Bladen Lands   100
Horses   2
Cattle   6
Total   £240

Thos. Bedsoal
Bladen Lands   200
Horses   2
Cattle   6
Total   £190

Saml. Johnston
Bladen Lands   640
Total   £64

Charles Johnston
Bladen Lands   400
Total   £46.-16

Baxter Davis
Bladen Lands   100
Cattle   17
Total   £185

Chapter 5: Bladen County Tax Lists of 1779

John McCollom
Bladen Lands   100
Horses   1
Cattle   12
Total   £192.-18.-2

John Bedsoal   Poll
Bladen Lands   200
Total   £21.-12

Jno. Smith Seignr.
Bladen Lands   200
Horses   6
Cattle   78
Duplin County Lands   150
Total   £1591.-10

Robt. Grist
Bladen Lands   100
Cattle   24
Total   £265

Mical Thomas
Bladen Lands   300
Horses   5
Cattle   57
Total   £893.-4

Jeremiah Simmons
Bladen Lands   100
Horses   1
Cattle   15
Total   £323.-14

Lewes Averit
Bladen Lands   640
Horses   2
Cattle   9
Total   £217.-4

James West
Bladen Lands   150
Horses   5
Cattle   16
Total   £542.-10

Thos. Alford
Bladen Lands   300
Horses   1
Cattle   5
Total   £200

Benjn. Clark
Bladen Lands   100
Horses   1
Cattle   23
Total   £295

Charles Clark
Horses   3
Total   £466

Henry Clark
Bladen Lands   100
Horses   3
Total   £165

William Cain
Bladen Lands   100
Cattle   27
Total   £185

John Edge
Bladen Lands   100
Horses   1
Cattle   12
Total   £235

Benjamin Clark Jnr.   Poll
Bladen Lands   100
Total   £15

Ezekiah Jones
Bladen Lands   250
Horses   3
Cattle   16
Total   £367

Drury Maclimore
Bladen Lands   100
Horses   1
Cattle   9
Total   £155

Drury Maclimore Jnr.   Poll
Horses   1
Total   £50

Jesse Carter
Bladen Lands   300
Horses   2
Cattle   36
Total   £517

Apollo Rowan
Horses   1
Cattle   20

Chapter 5: Bladen County Tax Lists of 1779

Total	£250.-8
John Cain	Poll
Cattle	1
Total	£14
William [Faded]	
Bladen Lands	650
Total	£62.-5
Joel Allen	
Bladen Lands	300
Slaves	1
Horses	4
Cattle	9
Total	£1200
David White (Sessor)	
Bladen Lands	1450
Lots	1
Slaves	2
Horses	4
Cattle	32
Total	£3140
Saml. Cain (Sessor)	
Bladen Lands	600
Slaves	3
Horses	3
Cattle	42
Total	£2829.-13.-4
John King (Sessor)	
Bladen Lands	1470
Lots	2
Slaves	6
Horses	5
Cattle	14
Total	£3847.-10

We the Subscribers agreeable to an order of the court to us Directed, to Assess the Taxable Property of Captains Robison, Ellis and Harrisons Districts

In Obedience to said order we have Assesd. the said Districts, and has made Due Particular and Faithfull return of the same.
Saml. Cain
John King
David   White

CHAPTER 6

BLADEN COUNTY TAX LISTS OF 1786

BLADEN COUNTY TAX LIST OF 1786

Headings for this list include: Persons names & head of Family, White Males from twenty one years old to Sixty, White Males under twenty one years & above Sixty, White females of every Age, Blacks of each Sex from Twelve to Fifty Years, Blacks Above Fifty & under Twelve.

[Abbreviations will be used for headings.]

A list of the black & White Inhabitants in Captain Ards District of Every age & sex Taken 15th April Agreeable to Courts Order, February Term 1786   John Willis

Heads of Family	Mark Broom
White Males from 21 to 60	1
White Females	6

Heads of Family	Charles Oxendine
White Males from 21 to 60	1
White Males under 21 & over 60	6
White Females	5

Heads of Family	John Little
White Males under 21 & over 60	3
White Females	3

Heads of Family	Archd. Smith
White Males from 21 to 60	1
White Males under 21 & over 60	2
White Females	3

Heads of Family	John Best
White Males from 21 to 60	1
White Females	3

Heads of Family	Hannah Pitman
White Males under 21 & over 60	1
White Females	1

Heads of Family	John Buie
White Males from 21 to 60	1
White Males under 21 & over 60	2
White Females	5

Heads of Family	Alex Carlile
White Males from 21 to 60	1
White Males under 21 & over 60	1
White Females	3

Heads of Family	Robert Carslile
White Males from 21 to 60	1
White Males under 21 & over 60	3
White Females	2

Heads of Family	Chambers Humphrey
White Males from 21 to 60	2
White Males under 21 & over 60	5
White Females	3

Heads of Family	Isaac kenedy
White Males from 21 to 60	1
White Males under 21 & over 60	2
White Females	4

Heads of Family	Wm. Mo[?]
White Males from 21 to 60	1
White Males under 21 & over 60	2
White Females	7

Heads of Family	Green Bodiford
White Males under 21 & over 60	4
White Females	4

Heads of Family	Dugald McLaughlin
White Males from 21 to 60	1
White Males under 21 & over 60	2
White Females	5

Heads of Family	Da[?] Crawford
White Males from 21 to 60	1
White Males under 21 & over 60	1
White Females	2

Heads of Family	Daniel Rozar
White Males from 21 to 60	1

Chapter 6: Bladen County Tax Lists of 1786

Heads of Family	John McDaniel
White Males from 21 to 60	1
White Males under 21 & over 60	5
White Females	2

Heads of Family	Cannon Cumbo
White Males under 21 & over 60	8
White Females	4
Blacks from 12 to 50	1

Heads of Family	Gibeon Cumbo
White Males from 21 to 60	1
White Females	3

Heads of Family	Jesse Harrell
White Males from 21 to 60	1
White Males under 21 & over 60	4
White Females	3
Blacks from 12 to 50	1

Heads of Family	Neill Brown
White Males from 21 to 60	1
White Males under 21 & over 60	1
White Females	4
Blacks from 12 to 50	1
Blacks under 12 & over 50	2

Heads of Family	Peter McAtter[?]
White Males from 21 to 60	1
White Males under 21 & over 50	4
White Females	3

Heads of Family	Duncan Grimes
White Males from 21 to 60	1
White Males under 21 & over 60	1
White Females	3

Heads of Family	Robert McEahan
White Males from 21 to 60	1
White Males under 21 & over 60	3
White Females	7

Heads of Family	Ambrouse Powell
White Males from 21 to 60	1
White Males under 21 & over 60	4
White Females	4

Heads of Family	Alexander Little
White Males from 21 to 60	2
White Males under 21 & over 60	1
White Females	3

Heads of Family	Angus Brown

White Males from 21 to 60	1
White Males under 21 & over 60	3
White Females	1

Heads of Family	Daniel Campbell
White Males from 21 to 60	1
White Males under 21 & over 60	4
White Females	4
Blacks from 12 to 50	2

Heads of Family	Joseph Fort
White Males from 21 to 60	1
White Males under 21 & over 60	2
White Females	1
Blacks from 12 to 50	9
Blacks under 12 & over 50	8

Heads of Family	John Fort
White Males from 21 to 60	1
White Males under 21 & over 60	1
White Females	1
Blacks from 12 to 50	5
Blacks under 12 & over 50	7

Heads of Family	George Stener[?]
White Males from 21 to 60	1
White Males under 21 & over 60	1
White Females	1

Heads of Family	Tarlor Oquinn Junr.
White Males from 21 to 60	1
White Males under 21 & over 60	7
White Females	2

Heads of Family	Mary Young Wid.
White Males under 21 & over 60	2
White Females	4

Heads of Family	Thomas Ard
White Males from 21 to 60	1
White Males under 21 & over 60	4
White Females	3
Blacks from 12 to 50	2
Blacks under 12 & over 50	1

Heads of Family	John Scot
White Males under 21 & over 60	2
White Females	2

Heads of Family	Tarlor Oquinn Senr.
White Males under 21 & over 60	4
White Females	2

Chapter 6: Bladen County Tax Lists of 1786

Heads of Family	Neill McArvie
White Males from 21 to 60	1
White Males under 21 & over 60	4
White Females	5

Heads of Family	Wm. Young
White Males under 21 & over 60	1
White Females	1

Heads of Family	John Buie
White Males from 21 to 60	1
White Males under 21 & over 60	2
White Females	3

Heads of Family	Wm. Brown
White Males from 21 to 60	1
White Females	4

Heads of Family	Arch. Little
White Males from 21 to 60	1
White Females	3

Heads of Family	Archd. McGill
White Males from 21 to 60	1
White Males under 21 & over 60	2
White Females	3

Heads of Family	Angus Ray
White Males from 21 to 60	1
White Males under 21 & over 60	7
White Females	1

Heads of Family	Bryan Best
White Males from 21 to 60	1
White Males under 21 & over 60	1
White Females	7

Heads of Family	Hugh Brown Junr.
White Males from 21 to 60	1

Heads of Family	Elisha Harrell
White Males from 21 to 60	1
White Females	4
Blacks of each Sex from 12 to 50	2
Blacks above 50 & under 12	1

Heads of Family	Hugh McCraney
White Males from 21 to 60	1
White Males under 21 & over 60	4
White Females	2
Blacks of each Sex from 12 to 50	3
Blacks above 50 & under 12	6

Heads of Family	Alexr. McDugal
White Males from 21 to 60	3
White Males under 21 & over 60	1
White Females	2

Heads of Family	Charles Powell
White Males from 21 to 60	1
White Males under 21 & over 60	2
White Females	4

Heads of Family	Duncan Kelley
White Males from 21 to 60	2
White Males under 21 & over 60	4
White Females	2

Heads of Family	James Biggs
White Males from 21 to 60	1
White Males under 21 & over 60	4
White Females	3

Heads of Family	Lewis Jenkins
White Males from 21 to 60	2
White Males under 21 & over 60	2
White Females	2

Heads of Family	Pharibe Edwards
White Males under 21 & over 60	3
White Females	3

Heads of Family	George Williams
White Males from 21 to 60	1
White Males under 21 & over 60	1
White Females	1

****

BLADEN COUNTY TAX LIST OF 1786

Headings for this list include: The Head Familys, White Males from twenty one years old to sixty, White Males under twenty one years old and above sixty, White Females of every age, Blacks of each Sex from twelve to fifty, Blacks upwards fifty and under twelve years old.

[Abbreviations will be used for headings.]

List of all the Inhabetants of Capt. Whites District Taken the 27th Apr 1786.

Head of Family	Kei[?] Douglass
White Males from 21 to 60	1

Chapter 6: Bladen County Tax Lists of 1786

White Males under 21 & over 60	1
White Females	7

Head of Family	Andr. Puff
White Males from 21 to 60	1
White Males under 21 & over 60	3
White Females	3

Head of Family	Reff[?] Barlow
White Males from 21 to 60	1
White Males under 21 & over 60	3
White Females	2

Head of Family	Jno. Buchar
White Males from 21 to 60	1

Head of Family	Felix Eknar
White Males from 21 to 60	1
White Males under 21 & over 60	3

Head of Family	Jas Earrd
White Males from 21 to 60	1
White Males under 21 & over 60	8
White Females	1
Blacks from 12 to 50	1
Blacks over 50 & under 12	1

Head of Family	Lewes Munrow
White Males from 21 to 60	1
White Males under 21 & over 60	1
White Females	9

Head of Family	Wm. Barlow
White Males from 21 to 60	1
White Males under 21 & over 60	3
White Females	1

Head of Family	Jno. Barlow
White Males under 21 & over 60	1

Head of Family	Godr. McNeill
White Males from 21 to 60	2
White Males under 21 & over 60	6
White Females	4

Head of Family	Neil McNeil
White Males from 21 to 60	3
White Males undr 21 & over 60	2
White Females	2

Head of Family	Dan. Mathies
White Males from 21 to 60	1
White Males under 21 & over 60	3

White Females	5

Head of Family	Jacob Apley
White Males from 21 to 60	1
White Males under 21 & over 60	1
White Females	4

Head of Family	Alexr. McKorter
White Males from 21 to 60	1
White Males under 21 & over 60	4
White Females	4

Head of Family	Jno. Mcswain
White Males from 21 to 60	3
White Males under 21 & over 60	2
White Females	2

Head of Family	Alexr Curry
White Males from 21 to 60	2
White Males under 21 & over 60	2
White Females	4

Head of Family	Henr. Messer
White Males from 21 to 60	1
White Males under 21 & over 60	2
White Females	3
Blacks from 12 to 50	1

Head of Family	Dun. McMillan
White Males from 21 to 60	1
White Males under 21 & over 60	2
White Females	8

Head of Family	Saggy[?] McDonald
White Males under 21 & over 60	2
White Females	3

head of Family	Hugh Brown
White Males from 21 to 60	1
White Males under 21 & over 60	1
White Females	3
Blacks from 12 to 50	2
Blacks under 12 & over 50	3

Head of Family	Neil Morison
White Males from 21 to 60	1

Head of Family	Malc. Withers
White Males from 21 to 60	1

Head of Family	Petter Smith
White Males from 21 to 60	2
White Females	3

Chapter 6: Bladen County Tax Lists of 1786

Head of Family	Dand. McSwain
White Males from 21 to 60	2
White Females	2

Head of Family	Neil MacMillan
White Males from 21 to 60	1
White Males under 21 & over 60	2
White Females	2

Head of Family	Mal. McSwain
White Males from 21 to 60	1
White Females	1

Head of Family	Jno. McMillan
White Males from 21 to 60	1
White Males under 21 & over 60	3
White Females	5

Head of Family	Jas. McNeil
White Males from 21 to 60	1
White Males under 21 & over 60	3
White Females	8
Blacks from 12 to 50	3
Blacks under 12 & over 50	6

Head of Family	David Buchan
White Males from 21 to 60	1
White Males under 21 & over 60	1
White Females	2

Head of Family	Jno. Johnston
White Males from 21 to 60	2
White Males under 21 & over 60	2
White Females	4
Blacks from 12 to 50	1

Head of Family	Mal. Shaw
White Males from 21 to 60	2
White Males under 21 & over 60	1
White Females	1

Head of Family	Dun. Paterson
White Males from 21 to 60	1
White Males under 21 & over 60	4
White Females	2

Head of Family	Gilbart McKinzie
White Males from 21 to 60	1
White Males under 21 & over 60	2
White Females	3

Head of Family	Malcolm McMillan
White Males from 21 to 60	2
White Females	1

Head of Family	Petter Messar
White Males under 21 & over 60	1
White Females	1

Head of Family	Murdock McLoud
White Males from 21 to 60	1
White Males under 21 & over 60	3
White Females	4

Head of Family	Alexr. Johnston
White Males from 21 to 60	1
White Males under 21 & over 60	5
White Females	4

Head of Family	Jas Black
White Males from 21 to 60	1
White Males under 21 & over 60	1
White Females	5

Head of Family	Alexr Paterson
White Males under 21 & over 60	1
White Females	1

Head of Family	Archd. McLean
White Males from 21 to 60	1
White Males under 21 & over 60	1
White Females	1

Head of Family	Dand. MacKeacharn
White Males from 21 to 60	1
White Males under 21 & over 60	5
White Females	2

Head of Family	Lach Cameron
White Males from 21 to 60	1
White Males under 21 & over 60	2
White Females	5

Head of Family	Geo. Torry
White Males from 21 to 60	1
White Males under 21 & over 60	3
White Females	1

Head of Family	Jno. Johnston
White Males from 21 to 60	1
White Males under 21 & over 60	6
White Females	1

Head of Family	Dond. Paterson
White Males from 21 to 60	1

Chapter 6: Bladen County Tax Lists of 1786

White Males under 21 & over 60	1
White Females	6
Blacks under 12 & over 50	1

Head of Family   Angus McDonald
White Males from 21 to 60	1
White Males under 12 & over 60	1
White Females	3

Head of Family   Jno. McLachlen
White Males from 21 to 60	1
White Females	2

Head of Family   Roger McKree
White Males from 21 to 60	1
White Males under 21 & over 60	2
White Females	1

Head of Family   John McAulay
White Males from 21 to 60	1
White Females	2

Head of Family   Archd. McMillan
White Males from 21 to 60	1
White Females	1

Head of Family   Kenneth McKinzie
White Males from 21 to 60	2
White Males under 21 & over 60	4
White Females	4

Head of Family   Jno. MacCallum
White Males from 21 to 60	1
White Males under 21 & over 60	2
White Females	3

Head of Family   Jno. Patterson
White Males from 21 to 60	1
White Males under 21 & over 60	1
White Females	2

Head of Family   Archd Johnston
White Males from 21 to 60	1

Head of Family   Angus Johnston
White Males from 21 to 60	1
White Males under 21 & over 60	1
White Females	3

Head of Family   Jas Black
White Males from 21 to 60	1
White Males under 21 & over 60	3
White Females	3

Head of Family   Dond. Johnston
White Males from 21 to 60	1
White Females	5

Head of Family   Donald McDuffie
White Males from 21 to 60	1
White Males under 21 & over 60	3
White Females	7

Head of Family   Jas. Craft
White Males from 21 to 60	1
White Males under 21 & over 60	4
White Females	2

Head of Family   Thos. White
White Males from 21 to 60	1
White Males under 21 & over 60	2
White Females	3
Blacks from 12 to 50	2
Blacks over 50 & under 12	2

Head of Family   Michel Fiels
White Males from 21 to 60	1
White Males under 21 & over 60	2
White Females	2

Head of Family   Dun. Henderson
White Males from 21 to 60	1
White Females	3

Head of Family   Archd. Buie
White Males from 21 to 60	1
White Males under 21 & over 60	5
White Females	1

Head of Family   Jno. Smart
White Males from 21 to 60	2
White Males under 21 & over 60	1
White Females	2

Head of Family   Dond. McDonald
White Males from 21 to 60	1
White Males under 21 & over 60	2
White Females	3

Head of Family   Chas. Walker
White Males from 21 to 60	1
White Females	3

Head of Family   Neil Smith
White Males from 21 to 60	1
White Males under 21 & over 60	2

Chapter 6: Bladen County Tax Lists of 1786

White Females	4

Head of Family	Jno. Smith
White Males from 21 to 60	1
White Males under 21 & over 60	2
White Females	5

Head of Family	Jas. Smith
White Males from 21 to 60	1
White Males under 21 & over 60	2
White Females	4

Head of Family	Gilbart McKay
White Males from 21 to 60	2
White Males under 21 & over 60	6
White Females	3

Head of Family	Neil Murphy
White Males from 21 to 60	1
White Males under 21 & over 60	4
White Females	3

Head of Family	Dond. McNeil
White Males from 21 to 60	2
White Males under 21 & over 60	5
White Females	3
Blacks from 12 to 50	1

Head of Family	Damse[?] Taylor
White Males under 21 & over 60	5
White Females	1
Blacks over 50 & under 12	1

Head of Family	Dun. Buie
White Males from 21 to 60	3
White Males under 21 & over 60	2
White Females	5
Blacks over 50 & under 12	1

Head of Family	M[?] Campbell
White Males from 21 to 60	3
White Males under 21 & over 60	3
White Females	1

Head of Family	Dun. Campbell
White Males from 21 to 60	1
White Males under 21 & over 60	1
White Females	2

Head of Family	Annie Meason
White Males under 21 & over 60	2
White Females	2

Head of Family	Neil McMillan
White Males from 21 to 60	1
White Males under 21 & over 60	5
White Females	4

Head of Family	Wm. Blew
White Males from 21 to 60	2
White Females	1

Head of Family	Wm McMillan
White Males from 21 to 60	1
White Males under 21 & over 60	6
White Females	4

Head of Family	Dond. McKinley
White Males from 21 to 60	1
White Females	3

Head of Family	Neil Thomson
White Males from 21 to 60	1
White Males under 21 & over 60	3
White Females	7

Head of Family	Archd. Little
White Males from 21 to 60	1
White Males under 21 & over 60	2
White Females	4

Head of Family	Jno. Councill
White Males from 21 to 60	1
White Males under 21 & over 60	1
White Females	5
Blacks from 12 to 50	2
Blacks over 50 & under 12	3

Head of Family	Chas. Councill
White Males from 21 to 60	1
White Males under 21 & over 60	3
White Females	4

Head of Family	Samson Baker
White Males under 21 & over 60	1
White Females	1

Head of Family	Jno. Sinkelton
White Males from 21 to 60	1
White Males under 21 & over 60	1
White Females	4

Head of Family	Jno. McFall
White Males from 21 to 60	1
White Males under 21 & over 60	2
White Females	2

Chapter 6: Bladen County Tax Lists of 1786

Head of Family	Dond. McFall
White Males under 21 & over 60	1
White Females	1

Head of Family	Alexr. McAlpin
White Males from 21 to 60	1
White Males under 21 & over 60	2
White Females	2

Head of Family	Robt. Semes[?]
White Males from 21 to 60	1
White Males under 21 & over 60	1
White Females	7
Blacks from 12 to 50	1

Head of Family	Jno. McMillan
White Males from 21 to 60	1
White Males under 21 & over 60	2
White Females	2

Head of Family	Sam. Kenedy
White Males from 21 to 60	1
White Females	1
Blacks over 50 & under 12	1

Head of Family	Evie Drurie
White Males under 21 & over 60	3
White Females	3

Head of Family	Dond. McDonald
White Males from 21 to 60	1
White Males under 21 & over 60	2
White Females	3

Head of Family	Jno. McDond.
White Males from 21 to 60	1
White Males under 21 & over 60	2
White Females	3

Head of Family	Malcom McNeill
White Males from 21 to 60	1
White Males under 21 & over 60	3
White Females	3
Blacks from 12 to 50	1
Blacks over 50 & under 12	3

Head of Family	Wm. Smith
White Males from 21 to 60	1
White Males under 21 & over 60	1
White Females	4

Head of Family	Uriah Lambert

White Males from 21 to 60	1
White Males under 21 & over 60	1
White Females	3

Head of Family	David Smith
White Males from 21 to 60	1
White Males under 21 & over 60	1
White Females	1

Head of Family	John McBride
White Males from 21 to 60	1
White Males under 21 & over 60	1
White Females	3

Head of Family	Jno. Smith
White Males from 21 to 60	2
White Males under 21 & over 60	3
White Females	3

Head of Family	Benjamin Brassel[?]
White Males from 21 to 60	1
White Females	1

Head of Family	Samuel Smith
White Males from 21 to 60	1
White Males under 21 & over 60	1
White Females	1

Head of Family	Lazerous Johnston
White Males from 21 to 60	3
White Females	3

Head of Family	Nathan Brassel
White Males from 21 to 60	1
White Males under 21 & over 60	1
White Females	1

Head of Family	James Smith
White Males from 21 to 60	1
White Males under 21 & over 60	4
White Females	1

Head of Family	John McPherson
White Males from 21 to 60	1
White Males under 21 & over 60	1
White Females	3
Blacks from 12 to 50	6
Blacks over 50 & under 12	9

Taken Agreeable to Order Court the list of Capt Whites District P me Hugh Brown.

Chapter 6: Bladen County Tax Lists of 1786

John Turners List of his Family given in Agreeable to Law Apr the 29 1786
White Males under 21 & over 60	2
White Females	3
Blacks from 12 to 50	15
Blacks over 50 & under 12	15

Thos. Richardsons List of soles for the year 1786
White Males from 21 to 60	1
White Males under 21 & over 60	4
White Females	2

William Trumans List of Soles for the year 1786
Blacks from 12 to 50	2
Blacks over 50 & under 12	2

Wm. Wilearson[?] List of Soles for the year 1786
White Males from 21 to 60	1
White Females	6

John Blanks List of Soles for the year 1786
Blacks from 12 to 50	2
Blacks over 50 & under 12	4

Ann Locklear her List of Soles for the year 1786
Blacks from 12 to 50	1
Blacks over 50 & under 12	6

John Webb List of Soles for the year 1786
Blacks from 12 to 50	4
Blacks over 50 & under 12	5

Roger Fremans List of Soles for the Year 1786
Blacks from 12 to 50	2
Blacks over 50 & under 12	6

James Parkers list of Soles for the year 1786
White Males from 21 to 60	1

Margaret Daniel List
Blacks from 12 to 50	2
Blacks over 50 & under 12	3

****

BLADEN COUNTY LIST OF 1786

A List of all the Persons of Every Age Sex & Condition in Capt. Shipmans District   April 29th 1786

Headings for this list include: Names, White Males from 21 years to 60, White Males under 21 years & above 60, White Females of Every Age, Blacks of Each Sex from 12 to 50, Blacks upward 50 & under 12 years, & Total Amt.

[Abbreviations will be used for this list.]

Names	Wm Cohoon
White Males from 21 to 60	1
White Males under 21 & over 60	3
White Females	4
Total Amt.	8

Names	Wm Green
White Males from 21 to 60	1
Blacks from 12 to 50	1
Total Amt.	2

Names	Jacob Simpson
White Males from 21 to 60	1
White Females	3
Total Amt.	4

Names	Hanson Lewis
White Males from 21 to 60	1
White Males under 21 & over 60	5
White Females	7
Blacks from 12 to 50	2
Total Amt.	15

Names	Peter Port[Post?]
White Males from 21 to 60	1
White Females	2
Blacks from 12 to 50	2
Total Amt.	5

Names	James Folk
White Males from 21 to 60	1
White Females	2
Blacks over 50 & under 12	2
Total Amt.	5

Names	James Fokes
White Males from 21 to 60	1
White Males under 21 & over 60	1
White Females	2
Total Amt.	4

Chapter 6: Bladen County Tax Lists of 1786

Names	Nathaniel Baldwin
White Males from 21 to 60	1
White Females	6
Blacks over 50 & under 12	1
Total Amt.	8

Names	Robert Simpson
White Males from 21 to 60	1
White Males under 21 & over 60	1
White Females	4
Total Amt.	6

Names	Arthur Smith
White Males from 21 to 60	1
White Males under 21 & over 60	3
White Females	2
Total Amt.	6

Names	Micajah Cohoon
White Males from 21 to 60	1
White Males under 21 & over 60	5
White Females	3
Total Amt.	9

Names	Zachariah Smith
White Males from 21 to 60	1
White Males under 21 & over 60	1
White Females	1
Total Amt.	3

Names	John Simpson
White Males from 21 to 60	1
White Males under 21 & over 60	1
White Females	3
Blacks from 12 to 50	1
Total Amt.	6

Names	John Bryant
White Males from 21 to 60	1
White Males under 21 & over 60	2
White Females	1
Total Amt.	4

Names	John Stubbs
White Males from 21 to 60	1
White Females	1
Total Amt.	2

Names	George Stubbs
White Males from 21 to 60	1
White Females	3
Total Amt.	4

Names	Caleb Green
White Males from 21 to 60	1
White Males under 21 & over 60	1
White Females	1
Blacks over 50 & under 12	4
Total Amt.	7

Names	Richard Reonalds
White Males from 21 to 60	1
White Females	2
Total Amt.	3

Names	Elijah Reonalds
White Males from 21 to 60	1
White Females	1
Blacks over 50 & under 12	2
Total Amt.	4

Names	Robert Elless
White Males from 21 to 60	1
White Males under 21 & over 60	2
White Females	3
Blacks from 12 to 50	1
Total Amt.	6

Names	Cortney Lambethson
White Females	1
Blacks from 12 to 50	2
Blacks over 50 & under 12	2
Total Amt.	5

Names	James Green
White Males from 21 to 60	1
Blacks over 50 & under 12	1
Total Amt.	2

Names	Eley Smith
White Males from 21 to 60	1
White Males under 21 & over 60	1
White Females	1
Total Amt.	3

Names	Joseph Massengale
White Males from 21 to 60	1
White Females	1
Total Amt.	2

Names	James Mims
White Males from 21 to 60	1
White Males under 21 & over 60	2
White Females	2
Blacks over 50 & under 12	1

Chapter 6: Bladen County Tax Lists of 1786

Total Amt.	6

Names	James Council
White Males from 21 to 60	1
White Males under 21 & over 60	2
White Females	2
Total Amt.	5

Names	Davd. Council
White Males from 21 to 60	1
White Males under 21 & over 60	1
White Females	3
Total Amt.	5

Names	John Cohoon
White Males from 21 to 60	1
Total Amt.	1

Names	Chloe Jones
White Males from 21 to 60	1
White Males under 21 & over 60	4
White Females	4
Total Amt.	9

Names	Simon Simpson
White Males from 21 to 60	1
White Males under 21 & over 60	3
White Females	1
Total Amt.	5

Names	Melea Bearfoot
White Males under 21 & over 60	2
White Females	6
Total Amt.	8

Names	Isaac Hobbs
White Males from 21 to 60	1
White Males under 21 & over 60	3
White Females	3
Total Amt.	7

Names	Christan Fitchet
White Males under 21 & over 60	2
White Females	3
Total Amt.	5

Names	John Folk
White Males from 21 to 60	1
White Males under 21 & over 60	2
White Females	4
Total Amt.	7

Names	Thos Penny
White Males from 21 to 60	1
White Males under 21 & over 60	4
White Females	3
Total Amt.	8

Names	Richd. Stubbs
White Males from 21 to 60	1
White Males under 21 & over 60	2
White Females	3
Total Amt.	6

Names	Joseph Baldwin
White Males from 21 to 60	1
White Males under 21 & over 60	3
White Females	4
Blacks from 12 to 50	3
Total Amt.	9

Names	John Clark
White Males from 21 to 60	1
White Males under 21 & over 60	5
White Females	2
Blacks over 50 & under 12	1
Total Amt.	9

Names	Isaac Woolf
White Males from 21 to 60	1
White Males under 21 & over 60	1
White Females	1
Total Amt.	3

Names	John Richardson
White Males from 21 to 60	1
White Females	1
Total Amt.	2

Names	Jemima Ray
White Males under 21 & over 60	4
White Females	2
Total Amt.	6

Names	Seth Dula[?]
White Males from 21 to 60	1
White Males under 21 & over 60	2
White Females	4
Total Amt.	7

Names	John Demry
White Males from 21 to 60	1
White Males under 21 & over 60	6
White Females	1
Total Amt.	8

Chapter 6: Bladen County Tax Lists of 1786

Names	William Barnes Senr.
White Males under 21 & over 60	1
Blacks from 12 to 50	1
Blacks over 50 & under 12	6
Total Amt.	8

Names	William Burney
White Males from 21 to 60	1
White Males under 21 & over 60	2
White Females	2
Total Amt.	5

Names	James Clardy
White Males from 21 to 60	3
White Males under 21 & over 60	3
White Females	4
Blacks from 12 to 50	6
Blacks over 50 & under 12	7
Total Amt.	23

Names	Duncan King
White Males from 21 to 60	1
White Males under 21 & over 60	6
White Females	3
Total Amt.	10

Names	Marah White
White Males under 21 & over 60	3
White Females	5
Blacks from 12 to 50	2
Blacks over 50 & under 12	6
Total Amt.	16

Names	James Dupre
White Males from 21 to 60	2
White Males under 21 & over 60	1
White Females	2
Blacks from 12 to 50	10
Blacks over 50 & under 12	12
Total Amt.	27

Names	Margaret Morison
White Males from 21 to 60	1
White Males under 21 & over 60	3
White Females	2
Blacks from 12 to 50	16
Blacks over 50 & under 12	16
Total Amt.	38

Names	Zachariah Chancey
White Males from 21 to 60	1
White Males under 21 & over 60	1
White Females	1
Total Amt.	3

Names	Miriam Chancey
White Males under 21 & over 60	3
White Females	2
Total Amt.	5

Names	Jeremiah Bigford
White Males from 21 to 60	1
White Males under 21 & over 60	2
White Females	5
Total Amt.	8

Names	Reuben Corbins
White Males under 21 & over 60	1
Total Amt.	1

Names	Burwell Hargrove
White Males from 21 to 60	1
White Males under 21 & over 60	1
White Females	2
Total Amt.	5

****

BLADEN COUNTY TAX LIST OF 1786

John Turners List for John Turner Esqr.

Headings for this list are the same as the previous list.

Names	John Dore
White Males from 21 to 60	1
White Females	2
Blacks from 12 to 50	1
Blacks over 50 & under 12	1
Total Amt.	5

Names	Thos Jones
White Males from 21 to 60	1
Total Amt.	1

Names	Mary Beaven
White Females	4
Total Amt.	4

Names	Wm. Smith
White Males from 21 to 60	1
Total Amt.	1

Names	Isom Beaven
White Males from 21 to 60	1

Chapter 6: Bladen County Tax Lists of 1786

Total Amt	1

Names: Joseph Davis
White Males from 21 to 60	1
Total Amt.	1

Names: Wm. Webb
Blacks from 12 to 50	1
Total Amt.	1

Names: Burrel Hargrove
White Males from 21 to 60	1
White Males under 21 & over 60	4
White Females	5
Total Amt.	10

Names: David Mims
White Males from 21 to 60	1
White Males under 21 & over 60	4
White Females	5
Blacks from 12 to 50	2
Blacks over 50 & under 12	3
Total Amt.	15

Names: Wm. Parker
White Males from 21 to 60	1
White Males under 21 & over 60	3
White Females	4
Total Amt.	8

Names: Drury Haddick
White Males from 21 to 60	1
White Males under 21 & over 60	1
White Females	1
Total Amt.	3

Names: Aquilla Green
White Males from 21 to 60	1
White Females	1
Total Amt.	2

Names: James Ellis
White Males from 21 to 60	1
White Males under 21 & over 60	1
White Females	3
Blacks from 12 to 50	3
Blacks over 50 & under 12	4
Total Amt.	12

Names: Wm. Dubois
White Males from 21 to 60	1
White Females	2
Total Amt.	3

Names: Richard Runolds Senr.
White Males from 21 to 60	1
White Males under 21 & over 60	1
White Females	2
Total Amt.	4

Names: John Ellis
White Males from 21 to 60	1
White Males under 21 & over 60	1
White Females	9
Blacks from 12 to 50	1
Blacks over 50 & under 12	1
Total Amt.	13

Names: Charles Baldwin
White Males from 21 to 60	1
White Males under 21 & over 60	1
White Females	4
Blacks from 12 to 50	3
Blacks over 50 & under 12	6
Total Amt.	15

Names: John Baldwin
White Males from 21 to 60	1
White Males under 21 & over 60	1
White Females	5
Blacks from 12 to 50	10
Blacks over 50 & under 12	15
Total Amt.	32

Names: Warren Baldwin
White Males from 21 to 60	1
White Males under 21 & over 60	1
White Females	2
Total Amt.	4

Names: Abraham Runolds
White Males from 21 to 60	1
White Males under 21 & over 60	1
White Females	3
Total Amt.	5

Names: Dempsy Runolds
White Males from 21 to 60	1
White Males under 21 & over 60	1
White Females	1
Blacks from 12 to 50	2
Blacks over 50 & under 12	1
Total Amt.	6

Names: John Smith
White Males from 21 to 60	1

Chapter 6: Bladen County Tax Lists of 1786

White Females	7
Total Amt.	8

Names	Josiah Ray
White Males from 21 to 60	1
White Females	2
Total Amt	3

Names	Mary[?] Cohoon
White Males under 21 & over 60	3
White Females	3
Total Amt.	6

Names	Willis Hull
White Males from 21 to 60	1
White Females	1
Total Amt.	2

Names	Allen Demery
White Males from 21 to 60	1
White Males under 21 & over 60	2
White Females	3
Total Amt.	6

Names	John Powel
White Males from 21 to 60	1
White Males under 21 & over 60	1
White Females	3
Blacks from 12 to 50	5
Total Amt.	10

Names	Barney Powel
White Males from 21 to 60	1
White Males under 21 & over 60	1
Total Amt.	2

Names	Lucrecia Fair Cloth
White Males from 21 to 60	1
White Females	3
Total Amt.	4

Names	Robert Richeson
White Males from 21 to 60	2
White Females	1
Total Amt.	3

Names	Stephen Jones
White Males from 21 to 60	1
White Males under 21 & over 60	1
White Females	1
Total Amt.	3

Names	Britton Hairgrove

White Males from 21 to 60	2
White Males under 21 & over 60	2
White Females	4
Blacks from 12 to 50	2
Blacks over 50 & under 12	2
Total Amt.	12

Names	James Shipman
White Males from 21 to 60	1
White Males under 21 & over 60	1
White Females	4
Blacks from 12 to 50	2
Blacks over 50 & under 12	1

Names	John McCoya
White Males from 21 to 60	1
White Males under 21 & over 60	1
White Females	3
Total Amt.	5

****

BLADEN COUNTY TAX LIST OF 1786

Return of the No. of Souls in Capt. Byrns District taken pr Saml. Cain

Headings for this list are the same as the previous list.

Names	Saml. Cain
White Males from 21 to 60	1
White Males under 21 & over 60	1
White Females	2
Blacks from 12 to 50	3
Blacks over 50 & under12	8
Total Amt.	15

Names	Joseph Butler
White Males from 21 to 60	1
White Males under 21 & over 60	1
White Females	5
Blacks from 12 to 50	2
Total Amt.	9

Names	Barnaby Murrel
White Males from 21 to 60	1
Total Amt.	1

Names	Richd. Singletary Senr.
White Males from 21 to 60	1
White Males under 21 & over 60	2
White Females	4

Chapter 6: Bladen County Tax Lists of 1786

Blacks from 12 to 50   2
Blacks over 50 & under 12   2
Total Amt.   11

Names   James Singletary Junr.
White Males from 21 to 60   1
White Males under 21 & over 60   1
White Females   3
Blacks from 12 to 50   1
Blacks over 50 & under 12   3
Total Amt.   9

Names   John Bennet
White Males from 21 to 60   1
White Females   3
Blacks over 50 & under 12   1
Total Amt.   5

Names   Joseph Singletary
White Males from 21 to 60   1
White Females   2
Blacks from 12 to 50   2
Total Amt.   5

Names   *Mary Walker free Negro*
Blacks from 12 to 50   1
Blacks over 50 & under 12   1
Total Amt.   2

Names   William Lansdell
White Males from 21 to 60   1
White Females   1
Total Amt.   2

Names   Tarrance Conner
White Males from 21 to 60   1
White Males under 21 & over 60   2
White Females   1
Total Amt.   4

Names   Elizth. Prickett
White Males from 21 to 60   2
White Males under 21 & over 60   1
White Females   2
Total Amt.   5

Names   Elipha Fowler
White Males under 21 & over 60   2
White Females   1
Total Amt.   3

Names   James Saml. Purdie
White Males from 21 to 60   1

Blacks from 12 to 50   3
Blacks over 50 & under 12   3
Total Amt.   7

Names   William McRee
White Males from 21 to 60   1
White Males under 21 & over 60   1
White Females   4
Blacks from 12 to 50   5
Blacks over 50 & under 12   6
Total Amt.   17

Names   Aaron Plummer
White Males from 21 to 60   1
White Males under 21 & over 60   2
White Females   1
Blacks from 12 to 50   1
Total Amt.   5

Names   E. Lalleestedt
White Males from 21 to 60   1
Blacks from 12 to 50   9
Blacks over 50 & under 12   2
Total Amt.   12

Names   James Council
White Males from 21 to 60   1
White Males under 21 & over 60   3
White Females   5
Blacks from 12 to 50   14
Blacks over 50 & under 12   9
Total Amt.   32

Names   Peter Robeson
White Males from 21 to 60   1
White Males under 21 & over 60   2
White Females   2
Blacks from 12 to 50   4
Blacks over 50 & under 21   7
Total Amt.   16

Names   Mary Storm
White Females   2
Total Amt.   2

Names   James Cain
White Males from 21 to 60   1
White Males under 21 & over 60   2
White Females   5
Blacks from 12 to 50   3
Blacks over 50 & under 12   1
Total Amt.   12

Chapter 6: Bladen County Tax Lists of 1786

Names	Olive Cain
White Females	2
Blacks from 12 to 50	3
Total Amt.	5

Names	John Rogerson
White Males under 21 & over 60	1
White Females	1
Blacks from 12 to 50	3
Blacks over 50 & under 12	3
Total Amt.	8

Names	John Oviter
White Males from 21 to 60	1
White Females	3
Blacks from 12 to 50	10
Blacks over 50 & under 12	9
Total Amt.	23

Names	Peter Lord
White Males from 21 to 60	4
White Females	2
Blacks from 12 to 50	2
Blacks over 50 & under 12	4
Total Amt.	12

Names	Thos. Scriving
White Males from 21 to 60	1
White Females	3
Total Amt.	4

Names	Peter Gates
White Males from 21 to 60	1
White Females	3
Total Amt.	4

Names	John Gates
White Males from 21 to 60	1
White Males under 21 & over 60	2
White Females	4
Total Amt.	7

Names	Edward Gates
White Males from 21 to 60	1
White Females	2
Total Amt.	3

Names	Joseph Plummer
White Males from 21 to 60	1
White Females	1
Total Amt.	2

Names	Malaciah Burges
White Males from 21 to 60	1
White Males under 21 & over 60	1
White Females	2
Blacks from 12 to 50	1
Blacks over 50 & under 12	1
Total Amt.	6

Names	William Kirby
White Males from 21 to 60	1
White Males under 21 & over 60	4
White Females	4
Total Amt.	9

Names	Mary Wilson
White Males under 21 & over 60	1
White Females	1
Blacks from 12 to 50	1
Total Amt.	3

Names	John Beard
White Males from 21 to 60	1
White Males under 21 & over 60	4
White Females	2
Blacks from 12 to 50	3
Blacks over 50 & under 12	1
Total Amt.	11

Names	Agerton Willis
White Males from 21 to 60	1
White Females	4
Total Amt.	5

Names	Joseph Willis
White Males from 21 to 60	2
Blacks from 12 to 50	2
Blacks over 50 & under 12	1
Total Amt.	5

Names	John Moor
White Males from 21 to 60	2
White Males under 21 & over 60	2
White Females	5
Blacks from 12 to 50	1
Total Amt.	10

Names	Benjamin Willis
White Males from 21 to 60	2
White Females	2
Blacks from 12 to 50	2
Blacks over 50 & under 12	3
Total Amt.	9

Names	Benjamin Lansdell

Chapter 6: Bladen County Tax Lists of 1786

White Males from 21 to 60	1
White Males under 21 & over 60	2
White Females	1
Total Amt.	4

Names	Margaret Byrn
White Males from 21 to 60	1
White Males under 21 & over 60	1
White Females	1
Blacks from 12 to 50	14
Blacks over 50 & under 12	11
Total Amt.	28

Names	John Hilliard
White Males from 21 to 60	1
White Females	3
Total Amt.	4

Names	Jeremiah Willis
White Males from 21 to 60	2
White Males under 21 & over 60	1
White Females	4
Total Amt.	7

Names	William Godfrey
White Males from 21 to 60	1
White Males under 21 & over 60	2
White Females	2
Total Amt.	5

Names	Morris Richards
White Males from 21 to 60	1
White Males under 21 & over 60	1
White Females	4
Blacks from 12 to 50	1
Blacks over 50 & under 12	1
Total Amt.	8

Names	Joseph Thims
White Males from 21 to 60	1
White Males under 21 & over 60	2
White Females	2
Blacks from 12 to 50	10
Blacks over 50 & under 12	10
Total Amt.	25

Names	John Newberry
White Males from 21 to 60	1
White Males under 21 & over 60	3
White Females	4
Total Amt.	8

Names	Martha Thims
White Males under 21 & over 60	2
White Females	3
Blacks from 12 to 50	3
Blacks over 50 & under 12	1
Total Amt.	9

Names	James Jackson
White Males from 21 to 60	1
White Males under 21 & over 60	4
White Females	4
Blacks from 12 to 50	8
Blacks over 50 & under 12	2
Total Amt.	19

Names	James Ellis
White Males under 21 & over 60	4
White Females	5
Blacks from 12 to 50	2
Blacks over 50 & under 12	3
Total Amt.	14

Names	Jesse Thims
White Males from 21 to 60	1
White Males under 21 & over 60	3
White Females	4
Blacks over 50 & under 12	1
Total Amt.	9

Names	Robert Edwards
White Males from 21 to 60	1
White Males under 21 & over 60	2
White Females	3
Blacks from 12 to 50	4
Blacks over 50 & under 12	7
Total Amt.	17

Names	Abel Corbet
White Males from 21 to 60	1
White Females	1
Total Amt.	2

Names	Samuel Hollingsworth
White Males from 21 to 60	2
White Males under 21 & over 60	3
White Females	3
Blacks from 12 to 50	5
Blacks over 50 & under 12	3
Total Amt.	16

Names	John Lock
White Males from 21 to 60	1
White Males under 21 & over 60	1
White Females	5

Chapter 6: Bladen County Tax Lists of 1786

Blacks from 12 to 50	1
Blacks over 50 & under 12	1
Total Amt.	9

Names	Thos. Lock
White Males from 21 to 60	1
White Males under 21 & over 60	1
White Females	5
Blacks from 12 to 50	5
Blacks over 50 & under 12	4
Total Amt.	16

Names	Robt. McKonkey
White Males under 21 & over 60	4
White Females	2
Blacks over 50 & under 12	2
Total Amt.	8

Names	Elizth. Lock
White Females	4
Blacks from 12 to 50	4
Blacks over 50 & under 12	4
Total Amt.	12

Names	Joseph Lock
White Males from 21 to 60	1
Total Amt.	1

Names	James Mash
White Males from 21 to 60	1
White Males under 21 & over 60	5
White Females	3
Total Amt.	9

Names	Elizth. Willis
White Males from 21 to 60	1
White Males under 21 & over 60	1
White Females	2
Blacks from 12 to 50	2
Blacks over 50 & under 12	4
Total Amt.	10

Names	Joseph Willis
White Males from 21 to 60	1
White Males under 21 & over 60	1
White Females	1
Blacks from 12 to 50	2
Total Amt.	5

Names	William Clark
White Males from 21 to 60	1
White Females	1
Blacks from 12 to 50	1

Blacks over 50 & under 12	1
Total Amt.	4

Names	Cielia Laurance
White Females	2
Total Amt.	2

Names	Daniel Willis
White Males from 21 to 60	1
White Males under 21 & over 60	3
White Females	1
Blacks from 12 to 50	2
Total Amt.	7

Names	John Small
White Males	1
Total Amt.	1

Names	William Elmore
White Males from 21 to 60	1
White Males under 21 & over 60	1
White Females	2
Total Amt.	4

Names	Mary White
White Males from 21 to 60	3
White Males under 21 & over 60	5
White Females	3
Blacks from 12 to 50	6
Blacks over 50 & under 12	2
Total Amt.	19

Names	Garat Woodward
White Males under 21 & over 60	2
White Females	2
Total Amt.	4

Names	Rebeckah Lock
White Males under 21 & over 60	4
White Females	5
Blacks from 12 to 50	2
Blacks over 50 & under 12	5
Total Amt.	16

Names	Sarah Willis
White Males under 21 & over 60	2
White Females	8
Blacks from 12 to 50	2
Blacks over 50 & under 12	2
Total Amt.	14

Names	Rebekah Wilson
White Males under 21 & over 60	2

Chapter 6: Bladen County Tax Lists of 1786

White Females	4
Blacks from 12 to 50	10
Blacks over 50 & under 12	3
Total Amt.	19

Names	Robert Wilson
White Males from 21 to 60	1
White Males under 21 & over 60	1
White Females	2
Blacks from 12 to 50	1
Total Amt.	5

Names	Isaac Sims
White Males from 21 to 60	1
White Males under 21 & over 60	3
White Females	3
Blacks from 12 to 50	2
Total Amt.	9

Names	Benjn. Sims
White Males from 21 to 60	1
White Males under 21 & over 60	3
White Females	5
Blacks from 12 to 50	1
Total Amt.	10

Names	David Dannel
White Males from 21 to 60	1
White Males under 21 & over 60	5
White Females	1
Total Amt.	7

Names	William Thims
White Males from 21 to 60	1
White Males under 21 & over 60	2
White Females	3
Total Amt.	6

Names	William Howard
White Males from 21 to 60	1
White Females	3
Total Amt.	4

Names	James Stone
White Males from 21 to 60	1
White Females	3
Total Amt.	4

Names	Arthur Graham
White Males from 21 to 60	2
White Males under 21 & over 60	4
White Females	2
Total Amt.	8

Names	Thomas Thims
White Males from 21 to 60	1
White Males under 21 & over 60	1
White Females	1
Total Amt.	3

Names	Joseph Chason
White Males from 21 to 60	1
White Males under 21 & over 60	4
White Females	5
Total Amt.	10

Names	Avery Dye
White Males from 21 to 60	1
White Females	3
Total Amt.	4

Names	Stephen Hollingsworth
White Males from 21 to 60	1
White Males under 21 & over 60	1
White Females	2
Total Amt.	4

Names	John McDannel
White Males from 21 to 60	1
White Males under 21 & over 60	1
White Females	2
Blacks from 12 to 50	1
Total Amt.	5

Names	Mary Clark
White Males under 21 & over 60	1
White Females	1
Blacks from 12 to 50	3
Total Amt.	5

Names	Thomas Stepto
White Males from 21 to 60	1
White Females	2
Total Amt.	3

Names	David Holloway
White Males from 21 to 60	1
White Females	5
Blacks from 12 to 50	3
Blacks over 50 & under 12	3
Total Amt.	12

Names	Jesse Newbery
White Males from 21 to 60	3
White Males under 21 & over 60	4
White Females	1

Chapter 6: Bladen County Tax Lists of 1786

Blacks from 12 to 50	8
Blacks over 50 & under 12	2
Total Amt.	18

Names	John Newbery
White Males from 21 to 60	1
White females	2
Blacks from 12 to 50	2
Blacks over 50 & under 12	2
Total Amt.	7

Names	Isaac Jesup
White Males from 21 to 60	1
White Males under 21 & over 60	5
White Females	5
Total Amt.	11

Names	George Thygert
White Males from 21 to 60	1
White Females	2
Total Amt.	3

Names	Archd. Bone
White Males from 21 to 60	1
White Males under 21 & over 60	3
White Females	4
Total Amt.	8

Names	Daniel Beard
White Males from 21 to 60	1
White Males under 21 & over 60	3
White Females	3
Blacks from 12 to 50	2
Total Amt.	9

Names	Elizth. Hollingsworth
White Males under 21 & over 60	3
White Females	4
Total Amt.	7

Names	Benjn. Atkinson
White Males under 21 & over 60	5
White Females	2
Total Amt.	7

Names	Wm. Gray McDaniel
White Males from 21 to 60	2
White Males under 21 & over 60	3
White Females	2
Blacks from 12 to 50	3
Blacks over 50 & under 12	1
Total Amt.	11

Names	Nathaniel Reaves
White Males from 21 to 60	2
White Males under 21 & over 60	1
White Females	5
Blacks from 12 to 50	5
Blacks over 50 & under 12	3
Total Amt.	16

Names	John Stepto
White Males from 21 to 60	1
White Females	2
Blacks from 12 to 50	4
Total Amt.	7

Names	William Brafford
White Males from 21 to 60	1
White Males under 21 & over 60	4
White Females	5
Total Amt.	10

Names	Robt. Council
White Males from 21 to 60	1
White Males under 21 & over 60	1
White Females	3
Blacks from 12 to 50	1
Total Amt.	6

Names	Jeremiah Plummer
White Males from 21 to 60	1
White Males under 21 & over 60	1
White Females	2
Total Amt.	4

Names	Joel Pitman
White Males from 21 to 60	1
White Males under 21 & over 60	1
White Females	5
Blacks from 12 to 50	1
Total Amt.	8

Names	Peter Byrne
White Males from 21 to 60	1
White Males under 21 & over 60	1
White Females	3
Blacks from 12 to 50	2
Total Amt.	7

Names	Mathew Byrne
White Males from 21 to 60	1
White Females	2
Blacks from 12 to 50	1
Total Amt.	4

Chapter 6: Bladen County Tax Lists of 1786

Names	Jesse Carver
White Males from 21 to 60	2
White Males under 21 & over 60	2
Blacks from 12 to 50	2
Total Amt.	6

Names	James Beard
White Males from 21 to 60	1
White Males under 21 & over 60	2
White Females	5
Blacks from 12 to 50	2
Blacks over 50 & under 12	2
Total Amt.	12

Names	William Anderson
White Males from 21 to 60	2
White Males under 21 & over 60	4
White Females	6
Total Amt.	12

Names	William Sims
White Males from 21 to 60	1
White Males under 21 & over 60	2
White Females	3
Blacks from 12 to 50	5
Blacks over 50 & under 12	7
Total Amt.	17

Names	John Lansdell
White Males from 21 to 60	1
White Males under 21 & over 60	2
White Females	2
Total Amt.	5

Names	Joseph Cain
White Males from 21 to 60	1
White Females	1
Blacks from 12 to 50	4
Blacks over 50 & under 12	2
Total Amt.	8

Names	John Singletary
White Males from 21 to 60	1
White Females	1
Blacks from 12 to 50	2
Blacks over 50 & under 12	4
Total Amt.	8

Names	James Singletary Senr.
White Males from 21 to 60	1
White Males under 21 & over 60	6
White Females	5
Total Amt.	12

Names	Elipha Plummer
White Males from 21 to 60	1
White Males under 21 & over 60	1
Total Amt.	2

Names	William Plummer
White Males from 21 to 60	1
Total Amt.	1

Names	Zacariah Plummer
White Males from 21 to 60	1
Total Amt	1

Names	John Plummer
White Males from 21 to 60	1
White Males under 21 & over 60	3
White Females	1
Total Amt.	5

Names	Rachel Johnson
White Males under 21 & over 60	1
White Females	2
Total Amt.	3

Names	Nathaniel Plummer
White Males from 21 to 60	1
Total Amt.	1

Names	Mary Robeson
White Males from 21 to 60	1
White Males under 21 & over 60	2
White Females	4
Blacks from 12 to 50	11
Blacks over 50 & under 12	10
Total Amt.	28

Names	Saml Butlar
White Males from 21 to 60	4
White Males under 21 & over 60	3
White Females	5
Blacks from 12 to 50	2
Blacks over 50 & under 12	4
Total Amt.	18

Names	Sampson Carver
White Males from 21 to 60	1
White Males under 21 & over 60	2
White Females	3
Blacks from 12 to 50	5
Blacks over 50 & under 12	3
Total Amt.	14

Chapter 6: Bladen County Tax Lists of 1786

Names	John Parnal
White Males from 21 to 60	1
White Males under 21 & over 60	2
White Females	5
Total Amt.	8

Names	Saml Carver Wilson
White Males from 21 to 60	1
Total Amt.	1

Return of the No. of Souls in Capt. Burns District Pr Saml Cain, May 1st 1786, Total Amount 1041.

****

BLADEN COUNTY TAX LIST OF 1786

Headings for this list include: Heads of Families, White Males from 21 years old to 60, White Males under 21 years & above 60, Females of every age, Blacks upwards 12 & under 50, Blacks upwards of 50 & under 12.

[Abbreviations will be used for headings.]

Heads	Mark Carter
White Males from 21 to 60	1
White Females	2

Heads	Nathaniel Hawthorn
White Males under 21 & over 60	2
White Females	1

Heads	Lewis Ivey
White Males from 21 to 60	1
White Males under 21 & over 60	1
White Females	4

Heads	Joel Pitman
White Males from 21 to 60	1
White Males under 21 & over 60	5
White Females	3

Heads	Francis Ivey
White Males from 21 to 60	2
White Males under 21 & over 60	3
White Females	5

Heads	Joseph Atkinson
White Males from 21 to 60	1
White Males under 21 & over 60	2

Heads	John Bell
White Males from 21 to 60	1
White Females	2

Heads	Arthur Lamb
White Males from 21 to 60	1
White Males under 21 & over 60	2
White Females	7

Heads	Luke Carter
White Males from 21 to 60	1
White Males under 21 & over 60	1
White Females	1

Heads	Campbell Lamb
White Males from 21 to 60	1
White Males under 21 & over 60	1
White Females	1

Heads	James Moore Junr.
White Males from 21 to 60	1
White Females	2

Heads	Daniel Drinkwater
White Males from 21 to 60	1
White Females	4

Heads	Thomas Rowland
Males from 21 to 60	1
White Males under 21 & over 60	5
White Females	4

Heads	John Roziar
White Males from 21 to 60	1
White Females	1

Heads	Charles Thompson
White Males from 21 to 60	1
White Males under 21 & over 60	1
White Females	2
Blacks from 12 to 50	2
Blacks over 50 & under 12	4

Heads	Hardy Pitman
White Males from 21 to 60	1
White Females	4

Heads	Lucy Lee Widow
White Males under 21 & over 60	4
White Females	3

Heads	Isam Pitman
White Males from 21 to 60	2

Chapter 6: Bladen County Tax Lists of 1786

White Females	1

Heads	Thomas Little
White Males from 21 to 60	1
White Males under 21 & over 60	4
White Females	1

Heads	Newat Pitman
White Males from 21 to 60	1
White Males under 21 & over 60	3
White Females	2

Heads	James Phillips
White Males from 21 to 60	1
White Males under 21 & over 60	3
White Females	3

Heads	Moore Spear
White Males from 21 to 60	1
White Females	1

Heads	Elijah Powell
White Males from 21 to 60	1
White Males under 21 & over 60	3
White Females	1

Heads	Elisha Brown
White Males from 21 to 60	1
White Males under 21 & over 60	1
White Females	2

Heads	Wm. Thompson
White Males from 21 to 60	1
White Males under 21 & over 60	2
White Females	2

Heads	Soloman James
White Males from 21 to 60	2
White Males under 21 & over 60	2
White Females	5

Heads	Soloman James Sr.
White Males under 21 & over 60	1

Heads	Richd. Hammon
White Males from 21 to 60	1
White Females	7

Heads	Wm. Thompson
White Males from 21 to 60	1
White Males under 21 & over 60	5
White Females	1
Blacks over 50 & under 12	1

Heads	James Carter Junr.
White Males from 21 to 60	1
White Males under 21 & over 60	1
White Females	5

Heads	Thomas White
White Males from 21 to 60	1
White Females	2

Heads	Eliza Willson
White Females	2

Heads	Henry Pope
White Males from 21 to 60	1
White Males under 21 & over 60	3
White Females	5
Blacks from 12 to 50	3
Blacks over 50 & under 12	7

Heads	Sampson Pope
White Males under 21 & over 60	1
White Females	1
Blacks from 12 to 50	3
Blacks over 50 & under 12	1

Heads	Gilbert Cox
White Males from 21 to 60	1
White Males under 21 & over 60	1
White Females	4
Blacks from 12 to 50	2
Blacks over 50 & under 12	3

Heads	Charles Barker
White Males from 21 to 60	1
White Males under 21 & over 60	3
White Females	4
Blacks from 12 to 50	1

Heads	James Carter Senr.
White Males from 21 to 60	1
White Males under 21 & over 60	4
White Females	6

Heads	John Cox
White Males from 21 to 60	1
White Males under 21 & over 60	1
White Females	1

Heads	Eliza. Brumble
White Males under 21 & over 60	2
White Females	3

Chapter 6: Bladen County Tax Lists of 1786

Heads	Simon Cox
White Males from 21 to 60	1
White Males under 21 & over 60	3
White Females	4

Heads	Lamuel Britt
White Males from 21 to 60	2
White Males under 21 & over 60	2
White Females	6

Heads	Solomn. Whitley
White Males from 21 to 60	1
White Females	4

Heads	Adam Ivey
White Males from 21 to 60	1
White Males under 21 & over 60	2
White Females	8

Heads	Joseph Ratley
White Males from 21 to 60	1
White Males under 21 & over 60	1
White Females	2

Heads	John Little
White Males from 21 to 60	2
White Females	1

Heads	Benja. Britt
White Males from 21 to 60	2
White Males under 21 & over 60	3
White Females	5

Heads	David Barefield
White Males from 21 to 60	1
White Males under 21 & over 60	1
White Females	3

Heads	James Rowland
White Males from 21 to 60	1
White Males under 21 & over 60	2
White Females	1

Heads	Jesse Lee Senr.
White Males from 21 to 60	2
White Males under 21 & over 60	4
White Females	4
Blacks from 12 to 50	2

Heads	Isaac Carter
White Males from 21 to 60	1
White Males under 21 & over 60	2
White Females	3

Heads	Mary Kersey
White Males under 21 & over 60	1
White Females	2

Heads	John Rowland
White Males from 21 to 60	1
White Males under 21 & over 60	3
White Females	5
Blacks from 12 to 50	4
Blacks over 50 & under 12	2

Heads	Samuel Porter
White Males from 21 to 60	1
White Males under 21 & over 60	1
White Females	4
Blacks from 12 to 50	1

Heads	Thomas Pitman Senr.
White Males from 21 to 60	1
White Males under 21 & over 60	8
White Females	8

Heads	Eliza. Rowland Widow
White Males from 21 to 60	1
White Males under 21 & over 60	4
White Females	3

Heads	Harriss Spear
White Males from 21 to 60	1
White Males under 21 & over 60	1
White Females	3

Heads	Isaac Bird
White Males from 21 to 60	1
White Males under 21 & over 60	1
White Females	1

Heads	David Roziar
White Males from 21 to 60	1
White Males under 21 & over 60	6
White Females	2

Names	James Moore Senr.
White Males from 21 to 60	1
White Males under 21 & over 60	3
White Females	3

Names	Jesse Pitman
White Males from 21 to 60	1
White Males under 21 & over 60	2
White Females	6

Chapter 6: Bladen County Tax Lists of 1786

Names	Jesse Lee Junr.
White Males from 21 to 60	1
White Males under 21 & over 60	3
White Females	3

Names	David Law
White Males from 21 to 60	2
White Males under 21 & over 60	4
White Females	4

Names	Michael Barnes
White Males from 21 to 60	2
White Males under 21 & over 60	3
White Females	6

Names	Mearddy[?] Lamb
White Males from 21 to 60	1
White Males under 21 & over 60	2
White Females	5

Names	Charles Bullock
White Males from 21 to 60	1
White Males under 21 & over 60	6
White Females	6

Names	Abram Barnes
White Males from 21 to 60	1
Blacks from 12 to 50	3
Blacks over 50 & under 12	3

Names	Jacob Odom
White Males from 21 to 60	1

Names	Hardy Inman
White Males from 21 to 60	1
White Males under 21 & over 60	5
White Females	4

****

BLADEN COUNTY TAX LIST OF 1786

A List of the Inhabitants of Eavery age in Capt. Mulfords District May 1786

Headings for this list are the same as the previous list.

Names	Hudnall Huffham
White Males from 21 to 60	1
White Males under 21 & over 60	2
White Females	5
Blacks over 50 & under 12	2

Names	James Benson
White Males from 21 to 60	2
White Males under 21 & over 60	5
White Females	3

Names	Turner Davis
White Males from 21 to 60	1
White Males under 21 & over 60	3
White Females	4

Names	James Larkins
White Males from 21 to 60	3
White Males under 21 & over 60	5
White Females	6
Blacks from 12 to 50	5
Blacks over 50 & under 12	7

Names	Brayton Singletary
White Males from 21 to 60	1
White Males under 21 & over 60	1
White Females	3
Blacks from 12 to 50	1
Blacks over 50 & under 12	1

Names	Peter Burdox
White Males from 21 to 60	1
White Males under 21 & over 60	1
White Females	3

Names	Benjamin Elwell
White Males from 21 to 60	1
White Males under 21 & over 60	2
White Females	3
Blacks over 50 & under 12	2

Names	Hezakiah Davis
White Males from 21 to 60	2
Blacks from 12 to 50	6
Blacks over 50 & under 12	8

Names	David Lloyd
White Males from 21 to 60	2
White Males under 21 & over 60	2
White Females	3
Blacks from 12 to 50	2

Names	Do. Richd. Lloyd's Estate
Blacks over 50 & under 12	2

Names	John Russ
White Males from 21 to 60	1
White Males under 21 & over 60	1

Chapter 6: Bladen County Tax Lists of 1786

Blacks over 50 & under 12	1

Names	George Thomas
White Males from 21 to 60	1
White Males under 21 & over 60	2
White Females	3
Blacks from 12 to 50	3
Blacks over 50 & under 12	1

Names	John Thomas
White Males from 21 to 60	2
White Males under 21 & over 60	1
White Females	2
Blacks over 50 & under 12	1

Names	Hugh Murpha
White Males from 21 to 60	1
White Females	3
Blacks over 50 & under 12	1

Names	William White
White Males from 21 to 60	1
White Males under 21 & over 60	2
White Females	2
Blacks from 12 to 50	1
Blacks over 50 & under 12	1

Names	Mathew White
White Males from 21 to 60	1
White Females	1
Blacks from 12 to 50	2

Names	James Saltar
White Males from 21 to 60	1
White Females	2
Blacks from 12 to 50	5
Blacks over 50 & under 12	4

Names	William Saltar
White Males from 21 to 60	1
White Males under 21 & over 60	2
White Females	6
Blacks from 12 to 50	17
Blacks over 50 & under 12	13

Names	Do. G. Waddell Estate
Blacks from 12 to 50	17
Blacks over 50 & under 12	20

Names	George Wilson
White Males from 21 to 60	1
White Males under 21 & over 60	2
White Females	8

Blacks from 12 to 50	1
Blacks over 50 & under 12	1

Names	John Pointer
White Males from 21 to 60	1
White Males under 21 & over 60	3
White Females	3

Names	George Melvin
White Males from 21 to 60	2
White Males under 21 & over 60	1
White Females	1
Blacks over 50 & under 12	1

Names	Daniel Turner
White Males from 21 to 60	1
White Males under 21 & over 60	5
White Females	5

Names	Daniel Finlay
White Males from 21 to 60	1
White Males under 21 & over 60	1

Names	Mary Nieal
White Males under 21 & over 60	3
White Females	4

Names	Thomas Lock
White Males from 21 to 60	1
White Males under 21 & over 60	2
White Females	3
Blacks from 12 to 50	9
Blacks over 50 & under 12	4

Names	John Lamb
White Males from 21 to 60	1
White Males under 21 & over 60	2
White Females	3
Blacks from 12 to 50	4
Blacks over 50 & under 12	3

Names	Thomas Russ
White Males from 21 to 60	1
White Males under 21 & over 60	2
White Females	5
Blacks from 12 to 50	3
Blacks over 50 & under 12	2

Names	David Lock
White Males from 21 to 60	3
White Males under 21 & over 60	3
White Females	1
Blacks from 12 to 50	2

Chapter 6: Bladen County Tax Lists of 1786

Blacks over 50 & under 12	4

Names	Benjn. Lock
White Males from 21 to 60	1
White Females	2
Blacks from 12 to 50	2
Blacks over 50 & under 12	3

Names	Leonard Lock
White Males from 21 to 60	2
White Males under 21 & over 60	1
White Females	2

Names	Joseph Lock
White Males under 21 & over 60	2
White Females	2
Black Males from 12 to 50	2
Black Males over 50 & under 12	3

Names	Richard Saltar
White Males under 21 & over 60	1
White Females	2

Names	Joseph Russ
White Males from 21 to 60	1
White Females	4

Names	John Singletary
White Males from 21 to 60	1
White Females	2
Blacks from 12 to 50	1

Names	Sophia Smith
White Males under 21 & over 60	2
White Females	2
Blacks from 12 to 50	6
Blacks over 50 & under 12	6

Names	Ceasar August Beloat
White Males from 21 to 60	1
White Females	1
Blacks from 12 to 50	6
Blacks over 50 & under 12	11

Names	Ephm. Mulford
White Males from 21 to 60	1
White Males under 21 & over 60	6
White Females	6
Blacks from 12 to 50	9

A Return from Capt. Mulfords District 31st May 1786 Pr Eph Mulford.

****

BLADEN COUNTY TAX LIST OF 1786

May 1st 1786 - A List of the souls in the first District in Bladen County taken in by Ralph Miller JP

Headings for this list include: Names of the house houlders numbered in their proper Collums, White Males from twenty one years old to Sixty, White Males under 21 years old and over Sixty, White females of Every Age, Blacks of each Sex from twelve to fifty, Blacks upward of fifty and under twelve years old.

[Abbreviations will be used in this list.]

Names	Thos. Brown Esqr
White Males from 21 to 60	1
White Males under 21 & over 60	2
White Females	4
Blacks from 12 to 50	17
Blacks over 50 & under 12	12

Names	Willm. Streety
White Males from 21 to 60	1
White Males under 21 & over 60	2
White Females	1

Names	John Harget
White Males from 21 to 60	1
White Females	1

Names	Jacob Meszick
White Males under 21 & over 60	2
White Females	2
Blacks from 12 to 50	2

Names	John Brown Esqr
White Males from 21 to 60	1
White Females	2
Blacks from 12 to 50	3
Blacks over 50 & under 12	2

Names	James Egleson
White Males from 21 to 60	1
White Females	1
Blacks from 12 to 50	2
Blacks over 50 & under 12	2

Names	Mary Campbell

Chapter 6: Bladen County Tax Lists of 1786

White Males under 21 & over 60	2
White Females	2

Names	Jonadab Russ
White Males from 21 to 60	1
White Males under 21 & over 60	4
White Females	2
Blacks from 12 to 50	1
Blacks over 50 & under 12	2

Names	Edmond Fogartee
White Males from 21 to 60	2
Blacks from 12 to 50	4
Blacks over 50 & under 12	2

Names	Jarymiah Dafron
White Males from 21 to 60	1
White Males under 21 & over 60	2
White Females	3
Blacks from 12 to 50	1

Names	James Dowey
White Males from 21 to 60	1
White Males under 21 & over 60	1
White Females	2
Blacks from 12 to 50	1
Blacks over 50 & under 12	1

Names	John Darrach
White Males from 21 to 60	2
White Males under 21 & over 60	1
White Females	2
Blacks from 12 to 50	1

Names	Margaret Pemperton
White Males under 21 & over 60	1
White Females	2
Blacks from 12 to 50	4
Blacks over 50 & under 12	5

Names	Daniel Downney
White Males from 21 to 60	1
White Males under 21 & over 60	2
White Females	3

Names	John Campbell
White Males from 21 to 60	1
White Males under 21 & over 60	1
White Females	7

Names	Solomon Spears
White Males from 21 to 60	1
White Males under 21 & over 60	1

White Females	4

Names	John Pemperton
White Males from 21 to 60	1
White Males under 21 & over 60	2
White Females	2

Names	Harber Taylor
White Males from 21 to 60	1
White Males under 21 & over 60	4
White Females	2

Names	Bassell Manley
White Males from 21 to 60	3
White Females	5
Blacks from 12 to 50	6

Names	John Tayler
White Males from 21 to 60	1
White Males under 21 & over 60	3
White Females	3

Names	Daniel Macown
White Males from 21 to 60	1
White Males under 21 & over 60	1
White Females	2

Names	Archibell Mackethon
White Males under 21 & over 60	3
White Females	3

Names	William Davis
White Males from 21 to 60	1
White Males under 21 & over 60	3
White Females	2
Blacks from 12 to 50	1
Blacks over 50 & under 12	2

Names	Archabell Macfater
White Males under 21 & over 60	4
White Females	3

Names	James Maulthby
White Males from 21 to 60	1
Blacks from 12 to 50	4
Blacks over 50 & under 12	3

Names	John McVickers
White Males from 21 to 60	1
White Females	1

Names	Duncan Mackethon
White Males from 21 to 60	1

Chapter 6: Bladen County Tax Lists of 1786

White Males under 21 & over 60	1
White Females	2
Blacks from 12 to 50	1

Names   Daniel Mackethon
White Males from 21 to 60	1
White Males under 21 & over 60	1
White Females	4

Names   Benoni Clayton
| White Males from 21 to 60 | 2 |
| White Females | 3 |

Names   Alexdr Ballantine
| White Males from 21 to 60 | 2 |
| White Females | 3 |

Names   Ralph Miller
White Males from 21 to 60	1
White Males under 21 & over 60	2
White Females	5
Blacks from 12 to 50	1
Blacks over 50 & under 12	1

Names   John Poynter
White Males under 21 & over 60	1
White Females	2
Blacks from 12 to 50	3
Blacks over 50 & under 12	2

Names   Ann Mackay
White Males from 21 to 60	1
White Males under 21 & over 60	4
White Females	2
Blacks from 12 to 50	8
Blacks over 50 & under 12	6

Names   Turner Davis
White Males from 21 to 60	1
White Males under 21 & over 60	3
White Females	4

Names   Samuel Swindel
White Males from 21 to 60	1
White Males under 21 & over 60	4
White Females	2
Blacks from 12 to 50	3
Blacks over 50 & under 12	1

Names   Mary Singletary
White Males under 21 & over 60	1
White Females	3
Blacks from 12 to 50	2

| Blacks over 50 & under 12 | 4 |

Names   Mary Smith & Tho. Smith
White Males from 21 to 60	1
White Males under 21 & over 60	1
White Females	3
Blacks from 12 to 50	7
Blacks over 50 & under 12	8

Names   Moses Holms
White Males from 21 to 60	1
White Males under 21 & over 60	4
White Females	4

Names   [?] Semore
White Males under 21 & over 60	1
White Females	1
Blacks over 50 & under 12	1

Names   Willm. Jones
White Males from 21 to 60	2
White Males under 21 & over 60	1
White Females	1
Blacks from 12 to 50	3
Blacks over 50 & under 12	2

Names   Daniel MacFatter
White Males from 21 to 60	1
White Males under 21 & over 60	1
White Females	3

Names   Joel[?] Allen
White Males from 21 to 60	1
White Males under 21 & over 60	2
White Females	2
Blacks from 12 to 50	4

Names   Elizabeth Lucus
White Males under 21 & over 60	3
White Females	3
Blacks from 12 to 50	3
Blacks over 50 & under 12	4

Names   Charles Robeson
White Males from 21 to 60	1
White Males under 21 & over 60	2
White Females	4

Names   Benjamin[?] Singletary
White Males from 21 to 60	1
Blacks from 12 to 50	2
Blacks over 50 & under 12	3

Chapter 6: Bladen County Tax Lists of 1786

Names	Richard Singletary
White Males from 21 to 60	1
Blacks from 12 to 50	2

Names	Willm. Smith Senr.
White Males from 21 to 60	2
White Males under 21 & over 60	2
White Females	4
Blacks over 50 & under 12	4

Names	Willm. Smith
White Males from 21 to 60	1
White Females	2

Names	Simond Smith
White Males from 21 to 60	1
White Males under 21 & over 60	1
White Females	2

Names	Goodin Elletson
White Males from 21 to 60	2
White Males under 21 & over 60	1
White Females	3
Blacks from 12 to 50	46
Blacks over 50 & under 12	39

Names	Neil McLarty

Names	
White Males from 21 to 60	1
White Males under 21 & over 60	2
White Females	2

Names	Willm. Oliphant
White Males from 21 to 60	1
White Males under 21 & over 60	3
White Females	2
Blacks from 12 to 50	2
Blacks over 50 & under 12	1

Names	Benj Singletary
White Males from 21 to 60	1
Blacks from 12 to 50	2
Blacks over 50 & under 12	3

Names	Richd Singletary
White Males from 21 to 60	1
Blacks from 12 to 50	2

Names	Schenching[?] Moore
White Males from 21 to 60	5
White Females	3
Blacks from 12 to 50	12
Blacks over 50 & under 12	8

CHAPTER 7

BLADEN COUNTY TAX LISTS OF 1787

BLADEN COUNTY TAX LIST OF 1787

Headings fro this list include: Mens Names, White Males from 21 to 60, White Males under Twenty one & above 60, White Females of every Age, Blacks of each Sex from Twelve to Fifty, Blacks upwards of Fifty & under Twelve.

[Abbreviations will be used for this list.]

Names	Danl Shipman
White Males from 21 to 60	1
White Females	3
Blacks from 12 to 50	7
Blacks over 50 & under 12	5

Names	Dennis Lennon
White Males from 21 to 60	1
White Males under 21 & over 60	3
White Females	2
Blacks from 12 to 50	3
Blacks over 50 & under 12	3

Names	William Bryan
White Males from 21 to 60	1
White Females	4
Blacks from 12 to 50	3
Blacks over 50 & under 12	1

Names	Thomas Simson
White Males from 21 to 60	2
White Females	3
Blacks from 12 to 50	5
Blacks over 50 & under 12	3

Names	William Burney
White Males from 21 to 60	1
White Males under 21 & over 60	7
White Females	3
Blacks from 12 to 50	2
Blacks over 50 & under 12	3

Names	Joshua Lee
White Males from 21 to 60	2
White Males under 21 & over 60	5
White Females	3
Blacks from 12 to 50	1

Names	Joseph Davis
White Males from 21 to 60	1
White Males under 21 & over 60	2
White Females	2

Names	Daniel Taylor
White Males from 21 to 60	1
White Males under 21 & over 60	1
White Females	1

Names	John McKethan
White Males from 21 to 60	1
White Males under 21 & over 60	2
White Females	2

Names	Dugald Blue
White Males from 21 to 60	1
White Males under 21 & over 60	2
White Females	2

Names	Duncan McCall
White Males from 21 to 60	1
White Females	1

Names	Wm McNiell
White Males from 21 to 60	1
White Females	1
Blacks from 12 to 50	6
Blacks over 50 & under 12	5

Names	Jean Ray
White Males from 21 to 60	1
White Males under 21 & over 60	3
White Females	3

Names	Archd McBride
White Males from 21 to 60	1
White Males under 21 & over 60	4
White Females	2

Names	Duncan Lariman
White Males from 21 to 60	1
White Males under 21 & over 60	3
White Females	3

Chapter 7: Bladen County Tax Lists of 1787

Names	Flora McKay
White Males under 21 & over 60	2
White Females	2

Names	John Purkeypine
White Males from 21 to 60	1
White Males under 21 & over 60	1
White Females	3

Names	William Bigford
White Males from 21 to 60	1
White Females	2
Blacks from 12 to 50	2
Blacks over 50 & under 12	6

Names	Rolly Mills
White Males from 21 to 60	1
White Males under 21 & over 60	6
White Females	2

Names	Charles McNaughton
White Males from 21 to 60	1
White Males under 21 & over 60	2
White Females	3

Names	John Blue
White Males from 21 to 60	1
White Males under 21 & over 60	1
White Females	6

Names	Daniel Taylor
White Males from 21 to 60	1
White Males under 21 & over 60	2
White Females	2

Names	Joseph Wiggins
White Males from 21 to 60	1
White Males under 21 & over 60	3
White Females	6

Names	Archd. Bradley
White Males from 21 to 60	1
White Males under 21 & over 60	4
White Females	1

Names	Thomas Kerr
White Males from 21 to 60	1

Names	John McLerran
White Males from 21 to 60	1
White Females	1
Blacks from 12 to 50	1
Blacks over 50 & under 12	1

Names	William Foster
White Males from 21 to 60	1
White Females	2

Names	Isam Wiggins
White Males from 21 to 60	1

Names	David Bloodworth
White Males from 21 to 60	1

Names	George McKay
White Males from 21 to 60	2
White Males under 21 & over 60	5
White Females	2

Names	Wm Mooney
White Males from 21 to 60	1
White Females	4

Names	Mathew Kelly
White Males from 21 to 60	1
White Males under 21 & over 60	4
White Females	4
Blacks from 12 to 50	8
Blacks over 50 & under 12	12

Names	John kelly
White Males from 21 to 60	2
White Females	1
Blacks from 12 to 50	1
Blacks over 50 & under 12	1

Names	Archd. Kelly
White Males from 21 to 60	1
White Males under 21 & over 60	2
White Females	3

Names	Robt. McEwen
White Males from 21 to 60	1
White Males under 21 & over 60	2
White Females	2

Names	Moses Lewis
White Males from 21 to 60	1
White Females	1

Names	Gideon Hankins
White Males from 21 to 60	1
White Males under 21 & over 60	2
White Females	4

Chapter 7: Bladen County Tax Lists of 1787

Names	Cornelius Farrell
White Females	1

Names	Elizth. Hardcastle
White Males under 21 & over 60	1
White Females	3

Names	Duncan Henderson
White Males from 21 to 60	1
White Males under 21 & over 60	5
White Females	1

Names	Alice Curry
White Males under 21 & over 60	3
White Females	2

Names	Saul Smith
White Males from 21 to 60	1
White Males under 21 & over 60	1
White Females	2

Names	Archd. Shaw
White Males from 21 to 60	1
White Males under 21 & over 60	1
White Females	2

Names	Simon Green
White Males from 21 to 60	1
White Females	5
Blacks from 12 to 50	3

Names	Jas. Murphy
White Males from 21 to 60	1
White Females	4

Names	Joseph Powers
White Males from 21 to 60	1
White Males under 21 & over 60	3
White Females	4
Blacks from 12 to 50	1

Names	Alexr. McCall
White Males from 21 to 60	1
White Males under 21 & over 60	2
White Females	3

Names	Danl McCallum
White Males from 21 to 60	1
White Males under 21 & over 60	4
White Females	5

Names	John Gilbert
White Males from 21 to 60	1
White Males under 21 & over 60	1
White Females	1

Names	John Laslet
White Males from 21 to 60	1
White Males under 21 & over 60	1
White Females	3

Names	Malcolm Shaw
White Males from 21 to 60	1
White Females	1
Blacks from 12 to 50	1
Blacks over 50 & under 12	2

Names	Neill McCoulsky
White Males from 21 to 60	1
White Females	4
Blacks from 12 to 50	5

Names	Thomas Browder
White Males from 21 to 60	1
White Males under 21 & over 60	4
White Females	5
Blacks from 12 to 50	1

Names	Angus McKay
White Males from 21 to 60	1
White Females	1
Blacks from 12 to 50	1

Names	John McKay
White Males from 21 to 60	1
White Males under 21 & over 60	1
White Females	2
Blacks from 12 to 50	1

Names	Dugal McMillan
White Males from 21 to 60	1
White Males under 21 & over 60	1
White Females	5

Names	James Campbell
White Males from 21 to 60	1
White Males under 21 & over 60	1
White Females	1

Names	Cathn. Campbell
White Males under 21 & over 60	2
White Females	1

Names	John Campbell
White Males from 21 to 60	1
White Males under 21 & over 60	1

Chapter 7: Bladen County Tax Lists of 1787

White Females	3

Names	Archd. Campbell
White Males from 21 to 60	1
White Females	2

Names	Thomas Simpson Jr.
White Males from 21 to 60	1
White Females	1
Blacks from 12 to 50	2

Names	George Brown
White Males from 21 to 60	2
White Males under 21 & over 60	1
White Females	3
Blacks from 12 to 50	1

Names	*Gills Chavous*
Blacks from 12 to 50	4
Blacks over 50 & under 12	7

Names	John McMillan
White Males from 21 to 60	1

Names	Jos. Lewis Senr.
White Males from 21 to 60	2
White Males under 21 & over 60	1
White Females	3
Blacks from 12 to 50	3
Blacks over 50 & under 12	2

Names	Absalom Powell
White Males from 21 to 60	1
White Males under 21 & over 60	3
White Females	2
Blacks from 12 to 50	1
Blacks over 50 & under 12	1

Names	William Brown
White Males from 21 to 60	1
White Males under 21 & over 60	6
White Females	5

Names	Aaron Lewis
White Males from 21 to 60	1
White Males under 21 & over 60	1
White Females	1

Names	Joshua Hayes
White Males from 21 to 60	1
White Females	5
Blacks from 12 to 50	2
Blacks over 50 & under 12	1

Names	Abram Stevens
White Males from 21 to 60	1
White Males under 21 & over 60	2
White Females	3
Blacks from 12 to 50	2
Blacks over 50 & under 12	1

Names	Thos. Johnston
White Males from 21 to 60	2
White Males under 21 & over 60	1
White Females	1

Names	Donald Bain
White Males from 21 to 60	1
White Females	2
Blacks from 12 to 50	8
Blacks over 50 & under 12	11

Names	Thomas Sessions
White Males from 21 to 60	3
White Males under 21 & over 60	9
White Females	3
Blacks from 12 to 50	4
Blacks over 50 & under 12	1

Names	William Ellis
White Males from 21 to 60	1

Names	Robert Hodge
White Males from 21 to 60	1
White Females	1
Blacks from 12 to 50	1

Names	John Young
White Males from 21 to 60	1
White Males under 21 & over 60	2
White Females	2

Names	Thomas Mims
White Males from 21 to 60	1
White Males under 21 & over 60	2
White Females	4
Blacks from 12 to 50	2

In Captain Shipman's District July 27th 1787
-- Thomas Sessions JP

CHAPTER 8

BLADEN COUNTY TAX LISTS OF 1789

BLADEN COUNTY TAX LIST OF 1789

Capt Johnsons District for the Year 1789

Headings for this list include: Names, Poles Negroes, Lands, Town Lots

Names	James Smith
Poles	1
Names	John Cashwell
Poles	1
Negroes	1
Lands	200
Names	Thomas Bedsole
Poles	1
Lands	200
Names	Stephen Hollowell[?]
Poles	1
Lands	400
Names	John Suggs
Poles	1
Lands	100
Names	Samuel Pharis
Poles	1
Lands	800
Names	John Melvin
Poles	1
Lands	225
Names	John Bedsole
Poles	1
Lands	300
Names	John Parker
Poles	1
Lands	150
Names	Zekel Suggs
Poles	1
Lands	100
Names	Jeremiah Simmons
Poles	1
Lands	100
Names	John McGee
Poles	1
Names	[?]arde Clark
Poles	1
Lands	100
Names	Henry Davis
Poles	1
Names	Richard Singletary
Poles	1
Lands	650
Names	Thomas Smith
Poles	1
Lands	100
Names	John Edge
Lands	75
Names	William Edge
Poles	1
Lands	250
Names	Isaac Gesop
Lands	400
Names	John Pharis
Poles	1
Lands	400
Names	Isaac Pharis
Poles	1
Names	Ann Haer
Lands	200

Chapter 8: Bladen County Tax Lists of 1789

Names	John Sellers
Poles	1
Negroes	1
Lands	321

Names	John Cain
Poles	1
Lands	75

Names	James Gardner
Lands	100

Names	Jonathan Sikes
Poles	1
Lands	300

Names	Samuel Rowan
Poles	1

Names	Daniel Johnson
Poles	1
Lands	740

Names	[Torn]ard Weatherbee
Negroes	5
Lands	200

Names	James Richardson
Negroes	6
Lands	1200

Names	Bartram Bryant
Poles	1
Negroes	1
Lands	250

Names	Thomas Cashwell
Poles	1
Lands	200

Names	Peter McLane
Poles	1
Lands	100

Names	Dunkin Sellers
Poles	1
Lands	350

Names	Henry Clark
Poles	1
Lands	200

Names	George Thagart

Poles	1
Lands	100

Names	James Carr
Poles	1
Lands	100

Names	Edward Curry
Poles	1

Names	Baseman Clifton
Poles	1
Lands	150

Names	William Smith
Lands	100

Names	John Davis
Poles	1
Lands	250

Names	Samuel Sessums
Poles	1
Lands	300

Names	Culmoor[?] Sessoms
Poles	1
Lands	200

Names	Hezekiah Johens[?]
Poles	1
Lands	450

Names	Archibald McDaniel
Poles	1
Lands	470

Names	William Edge
Poles	1
Lands	100

Names	William Ellis
Poles	2
Lands	350

Names	Rachel McCollum
Poles	1
Lands	230

Names	Baxter Davis
Poles	1
Lands	100

Chapter 8: Bladen County Tax Lists of 1789

Names	William Suggs
Poles	1
Lands	50

Names	William Avritt
Poles	1
Lands	400

Names	Alle Good Suggs
Poles	1
Lands	100

Names	James West
Poles	1
Lands	200

Names	James Cashwell
Poles	1
Lands	50

Names	Charles Johnson
Poles	1
Lands	450

Names	Sampson Davis
Poles	1
Lands	100

Names	Mikel Thommas
Poles	1
Lands	450

Names	Sanders Simmons
Poles	1
Lands	50

Names	John Smith
Lands	580

Names	James Cain
Poles	1
Lands	150

Names	Neal Cain
Poles	1

Names	Samuel Cain
Poles	1

Names	William Smith Junr.
Poles	1
Lands	150

Names	Robert McRee
Negroes	1
Lands	790

Names	Solomon Davis
Poles	1
Lands	100

Names	Jesse Blackiel
Poles	1

Names	William McRee Junr.
Poles	1
Lands	400

****

BLADEN COUNTY TAX LIST OF 1789

A List of Taxable property in the District of John Yates 1789

Headings for this list include: Persons Names, Acres of Land, Free Polls, Black Polls.

Abbreviations will be used in this list.

Names	[Torn]leman Nukols
Acres	870
Free Polls	1
Black Polls	1

Names	John Baldwin
Acres	300
Free Polls	1
Black Polls	6

Names	Simon Smith
Acres	150

Names	John Money
Acres	300
Free Polls	1

Names	Daniel Raborn
Free Polls	1

Names	Mark Lofton
Acres	50
Free Polls	1

Names	Alexander Godwin

197

Chapter 8: Bladen County Tax Lists of 1789

Acres	100
Free Polls	1
Names	Stephen Godwin
Acres	480
Free Polls	1
Names	Thomas Bessell
Acres	100
Free Polls	1
Names	Henry Bessell
Acres	200
Black Polls	1
Names	John Young
Acres	200
Free Polls	1
Black Polls	1
Names	William Sibbett
Acres	300
Free Polls	1
Names	Edward G. Davis
Acres	150
Free Polls	1
Names	Simon Bright Junr.
Acres	250
Free Polls	1
Names	Macajah Hill
Acres	440
Free Polls	1
Names	Daniel Flinn
Acres	360
Names	John Flinn
Free Polls	1
Names	Simon Bright Senr.
Acres	500
Names	Robert Bright
Free Polls	1
Names	John Coleman Junr.
Free Polls	1
Names	Joshua Lee
Acres	1225

Free Polls	1
Black Polls	2
Names	Jethro Robbins
Acres	50
Free Polls	1
Names	Sothey Hays
Acres	450
Free Polls	1
Black Polls	2
Names	William Bessell
Acres	300
Free Polls	1
Names	Leonard Dyson
Acres	200
Free Polls	1
Names	Allen Hardwick
Acres	150
Free Polls	1
Names	Thomas Johnson
Acres	200
Names	Jacob Fokes
Acres	66
Free Polls	1
Names	Andrew Millican
Acres	100
Free Polls	1
Names	Edward Willson Junr.
Free Polls	1
Names	John Wingate
Acres	1235
Free Polls	1
Black Polls	16
Names	Simon Green
Acres	300
Free Polls	1
Black Polls	3
Names	Thomas Mims
Acres	200
Free Polls	1
Black Polls	2

Chapter 8: Bladen County Tax Lists of 1789

Names	William Fokes
Acres	164
Free Polls	1

Names	John Fokes
Acres	216
Free Polls	1

Names	John Best
Acres	315
Free Polls	1

Names	Josiah Fokes
Free Polls	1

Names	William Runnalds
Acres	350
Black Polls	4

Names	Thomas Sanders
Acres	200
Free Polls	1

Names	Edward Willson Senr.
Acres	100

Names	Joseph Cartwright
Free Polls	1

Names	Lewis Williamson
Acres	950
Free Polls	1

Names	Benjamin Sellers
Acres	100
Free Polls	1

Names	Alexander Stevens
Acres	350
Free Polls	1
Black Polls	1

Names	Archibald Cannon
Acres	150
Free Polls	2

Names	Joel Wells
Acres	150
Free Polls	1

Names	[Torn] Tillman
Acres	750
Free Polls	2

Black Polls	1

Names	Samuel Pope
Acres	500
Free Polls	1
Black Polls	1

Names	Averit Nickols
Acres	463
Free Polls	1

Names	William Stevens
Acres	1100
Free Polls	1
Black Polls	3

Names	William Register
Free Polls	1

Names	Charles Powers
Free Polls	1

Names	Ezekiel Parker
Acres	500
Free Polls	1

Names	Waltar Wingate
Free Polls	1
Black Polls	1

Names	Richard Tatham
Acres	200
Free Polls	1

Names	James Bright
Acres	50
Free Polls	1

Names	George Clark
Acres	100
Free Polls	2

Names	Moses Coleman
Acres	700
Free Polls	1

Names	Theophilus Coleman
Free Polls	1

Names	John Coleman
Acres	1440
Free Polls	1

Chapter 8: Bladen County Tax Lists of 1789

Names	John Green
Acres	500
Free Polls	1
Black Polls	2

Names	Ignatious Flowers
Acres	400
Free Polls	2
Black Polls	2

Names	Joseph Powers
Acres	400
Free Polls	1

Names	Philip Faulk
Free Polls	1

Names	Thomas Jordan
Free Polls	1

Names	Edward Wall
Acres	200
Free Polls	1

Names	Philip Strickland
Acres	300
Free Polls	1

Names	Philip Perry
Free Polls	1

Names	Francis Lawson
Acres	40

Names	Pierce Godwin
Acres	160
Free Polls	1

Names	Alexander Campbell
Acres	100
Free Polls	1

Names	David Strickland
Acres	100
Free Polls	1

Names	Benjamin Eason
Free Polls	1

Names	Joshua Hays
Acres	500
Black Polls	2

Names	John Chavious
Acres	150
Free Polls	1

Names	Richard Faulk
Acres	670
Free Poll	1

Names	Luke Yates
Free Polls	1

Names	John Padget
Acres	350
Free Polls	1
Black Polls	1

Names	William Peters
Free Polls	1

Names	Frederick Lofton

Names	Stephen Barefield
Free Polls	1
Black Polls	3

Names	Abraham Stevens
Acres	350
Free Polls	2

Names	Joseph Noble
Acres	1000
Free Polls	2

Names	Tennetson Noble
Free Polls	1

Names	Maturin Branton
Acres	200
Free Polls	1

Names	Robert Hodge
Acres	300
Free Polls	1

Names	Thomas Sessions
Acres	1050
Free Polls	2
Black Polls	4

Names	Josiah Lewis Senr.
Acres	70
Black Polls	1

Chapter 8: Bladen County Tax Lists of 1789

Names	Jesse Jones
Acres	250
Free Polls	1

Names	Wm. Summerset
Acres	300

Names	Absalom Powell
Acres	1150
Free Polls	1
Black Polls	3

Names	Saul Smith
Free Polls	1

Names	John Yates
Acres	1920
Free Polls	1
Black Polls	1

Names	Samuel Leonard
Acres	1500
Free Polls	2

Names	Burrill Hall
Acres	910
Free Polls	1
Black Polls	1

Returned by John Yates

****

BLADEN COUNTY TAX LIST OF 1789

List of Taxable Property for the Lake District for the Year 1789

Headings for this list include: Persons Names, Whites, Blacks & Acres of Land.

Names	John Jackson
Whites	1
Acres	35

Names	Jeremiah Bigford
Whites	1

Names	Abraham Rynolds
Whites	1
Acres	200

Names	William Wilkinson
Whites	1
Acres	570

Names	Demsey Chancey
Whites	1
Acres	250

Names	John Dimory
Acres	450

Names	Barnas Powell
Whites	1
Blacks	1

Names	William Betts
Whites	1
Blacks	2

Names	James Du Pee
Whites	2
Blacks	12
Acres	3228

Names	John Lambert
Whites	1
Blacks	3

Names	Micajah Cohoon
Whites	3

Names	Thos. Penny
Whites	1
Acres	200

Names	Joseph Blassingale
Whites	1
Acres	100

Names	John Smith
Whites	1
Acres	350

Names	Joannah Smith
Blacks	1
Acres	900

Names	John Ellis
Whites	1
Blacks	1
Acres	100

Names	Simon Simpson
Whites	1

Chapter 8: Bladen County Tax Lists of 1789

Acres	100
Names	Estate Brittain Jones Deceas'd
Acres	450
Names	John falk
Acres	550
Names	William White
Whites	1
Acres	200
Names	Zachariah Chansey
Whites	1
Acres	100
Names	Geo. Gibbs
Blacks	4
Acres	720
Names	Josiah Gibbs
Blacks	4
Names	Robert Gibbs
Whites	1
Blacks	3
Acres	840
Names	Samuel Carman
Acres	300
Names	Mary White
Blacks	3
Acres	150
Names	John Gibbs One Town Lot
Whites	1
Blacks	3
Acres	960
Names	John Blanks
Whites	1
Acres	100
Names	William Webb
Whites	1
Acres	50
Names	Joseph Hobbs
Whites	1
Names	Thos. Richardson
Whites	1

Blacks	1
Acres	1510
Names	Hanson Lewis
Blacks	1
Acres	340
Names	William Bryan Senr.
Blacks	2
Acres	240
Names	Estate John [Torn]
Names	Moses Pitman
Whites	1
Blacks	1
Acres	100
Names	William Green
Whites	1
Blacks	1
Acres	200
Names	John Lamb
Whites	1
Names	Isaac Hobbs
Whites	1
Acres	100
Names	Surrell Simpson
Whites	1
Acres	125
Names	Richard Collum 1 Town Lot
Whites	1
Acres	950
Names	John Clark
Whites	1
Acres	600
Names	Caleb Green
Whites	1
Blacks	1
Acres	220
Names	Joseph Baldwin
Whites	1
Blacks	1
Acres	650
Names	Archibald Warren

Chapter 8: Bladen County Tax Lists of 1789

Names	
Whites	1

Names	Brittain Hargrove
Whites	1
Blacks	2
Acres	400

Names	John Stubbs
Whites	1

Names	Jacob Simpson
Whites	1
Acres	155

Names	Edmond Homes
Whites	1
Blacks	3
Acres	1150

Names	Seymore Simpson
Whites	1
Acres	100

Names	Samuel Swindall
Blacks	6
Acres	400

Names	James Clardy
Whites	1
Blacks	6
Acres	1050

Names	Drury Haddock
Whites	1
Acres	100

Names	David Council
Whites	1
Acres	450

Names	David Mims
Whites	1
Blacks	4
Acres	550

Names	William Parker
Whites	1
Acres	300

Names	John Baldwin Senr.
Blacks	8
Acres	450

Names	William Baldwin
Whites	1
Blacks	3
Acres	100

Names	Micajah Fitchet
Whites	1
Acres	200

Names	Daniel Shipman
Whites	1
Blacks	9
Acres	1120

Names	John Simpson
Whites	1
Acres	100

Names	James Wilson
Whites	1

Names	George Raiburn
Whites	1

Names	Thomas Richardson
Whites	1
Acres	100

Names	John Gibbert
Whites	1

Names	James Foke
Whites	1
Acres	340

Names	Josiah Ray
Whites	1

Names	Jessey Ray
Whites	1

Names	George Stubbs
Whites	1
Acres	80

Names	James Lewis
Whites	1
Acres	250

Names	Charles Edward
Whites	1
Acres	150

Chapter 8: Bladen County Tax Lists of 1789

Names	James Moore
Acres	100

Names	Hugh Johnston
Whites	1
Blacks	4
Acres	700

Names	Elijah Rynolds
Whites	1

Names	Eli Smith
Whites	1
Acres	100

Names	Demsey Rynolds
Whites	1
Blacks	1
Acres	300

Names	John Webb
Whites	1
Acres	200

Names	Richard Lambert
Whites	1
Blacks	1
Acres	300

Names	Catharine McGillip
Acres	100

Names	Warren Baldwin
Whites	1
Acres	200

Names	Nathaniel Baldwin
Whites	1
Acres	50

Names	John Doors
Whites	1
Blacks	1

Names	William Bryan
Whites	1
Blacks	2
Acres	1140

Names	James Mims
Whites	1
Acres	250

Names	Charles Baldwin
Whites	1
Blacks	5
Acres	300

Names	Richard Stubbs
Whites	1
Acres	230

Names	Abraham Beesly
Whites	1
Acres	200

Names	James Ellis
Whites	1
Blacks	3
Acres	100

Names	Isaac Wolf
Whites	1
Acres	100

Names	Brittain Pope
Whites	1

Names	Arthur Smith
Whites	1
Blacks	1
Acres	200

Names	William Swindall
Whites	1

Names	Burril Hairgroves
Whites	1
Acres	300

Names	Duncan King
Whites	2
Blacks	1
Acres	250

Names	James Green
Whites	1
Acres	450

Names	Jacob Whitehead
Whites	1

Names	Thos. Jones
Whites	1

Names	Isaack Powell

Chapter 8: Bladen County Tax Lists of 1789

Whites	1
Blacks	2
Acres	100

Names	Estate John Powell Deceas'd
Blacks	5
Acres	400

Return'd by me 3rd November 1789 Jos. G. DuPee

****

BLADEN TAX LIST OF 1789

A List of Taxable Property belonging to the District of Capt. George Brown for the Year of 1789.

Headings for this list include: Persons Names, Lands, Slaves & Poles.

Names	Dugald Blue
Lands	906
Poles	1

Names	Aaron Lewis
Lands	250
Poles	1

Names	Archibald McBride
Lands	150
Poles	1

Names	Charles McNaughton
Lands	200
Poles	1

Names	Duncan Lennon
Lands	161
Poles	1

Names	Wm. Mcneal
Lands	540
Slaves	6
Poles	1

Names	John McKeithan
Lands	257
Poles	1

Names	Archibald Schaw
Lands	100

Slaves	1

Names	John McKeithan Junr.
Lands	280

Names	Floria McKay

Names	Archibald Kelley
Lands	450
Slaves	1
Poles	2

Names	John McLeran
Lands	200
Slaves	1
Poles	1

Names	Dugal Wray
Lands	200
Poles	1

Names	Joseph Laslie
Lands	400
Poles	1

Names	Alex. McColl
Lands	100
Poles	1

Names	Neil McColsky
Lands	1300
Slaves	5
Poles	1

Names	Mathew Kelley
Lands	1000
Slaves	10
Poles	1

Names	Thos. Fitzgerald
Lands	640
Slaves	2
Poles	1

Names	Wm. McEwen
Poles	1

Names	Dugal McMillen
Lands	650
Poles	1

Names	Daniel Turner
Lands	250

Chapter 8: Bladen County Tax Lists of 1789

Poles	1
Names	Thomas Simpson Senr.
Lands	400
Slaves	3
Poles	2
Names	James Shipman
Lands	679
Slaves	2
Poles	1
Names	Robt. McEwen
Lands	200
Poles	1
Names	Archibald Campbell
Lands	300
Poles	1
Names	Dennis Lennon
Lands	800
Slaves	3
Poles	1
Names	Thos. Browder
Lands	200
Poles	1
Names	John Campbell
Lands	530
Poles	1
Names	Duncan McColl
Lands	200
Poles	1
Names	Giddeon Hawkins
Lands	100
Names	Alice Currie
Lands	100
Names	Thos. Simpson Junr.
Lands	500
Slaves	2
Poles	1
Names	Daniel Taylor
Lands	200
Poles	1
Names	Ezekiel Busby

Lands	480
Slaves	1
Poles	1
Names	Moses Lewis
Lands	100
Poles	1
Names	John Blew
Lands	190
Poles	1
Names	Daniel Schaw
Lands	200
Slaves	1
Poles	1
Names	Wm. Hardcastle
Poles	1
Names	John Money
Lands	100
Poles	1
Names	Wm Brown
Lands	700
Poles	1
Names	Wm Ellis
Lands	100
Poles	1
Names	Joseph Griffin
Lands	289
Poles	1
Names	James Campbell
Slaves	2
Poles	1
Names	John Campbell Junr.
Lands	500
Names	Richard Lewis
Lands	350
Slaves	2
Poles	1
Names	George Brown
Lands	380
Slaves	1
Poles	1

Chapter 8: Bladen County Tax Lists of 1789

Names	John Purkepine
200 on white oak Onslow County 38 acres where lives.	
Lands	238
Poles	1

Names	Wm Burney
Lands	580
Slaves	2
Poles	1

Names	John Kelley
Lands	200
Slaves	1
Poles	1

Names	Malkom Shaw
Lands	100
Slaves	1
Poles	1

Names	John McKay
Lands	220
Poles	1

Names	Jacob Lee
Lands	150
Poles	1

Names	Ge[?] McKay
Lands	300

Names	Daniel McCollom
Lands	550
Poles	1

Names	Daniel Taylor
Lands	250
Poles	1

Names	Jesse Jones
Lands	250
Poles	1

Names	Benjamin Adams
Poles	1

Names	Duncan Henderson
Lands	170
Poles	1

Names	Daniel McAllister
Lands	160

Poles	1

Names	Matthew McEwen
Lands	200
Poles	1

Returned By John Yates

****

BLADEN COUNTY TAX LIST OF 1789

A List of Capt Andres District for the Year 1789

Headings for this list include: Whites, Lands, Blacks & Lots.

Rutthey[?] Pridgin
Lands	350

John Pridgin

James Howard   not of age
Blacks	1

William Sutton
Lands	300

Beamon Sutton
Lands	175

John Roberson
Lands	150

Edward Reavs
Lands	710

William Cromerty
Whites	1
Lands	650
Blacks	3

Janet Stewart
Whites	2
Lands	3300
Blacks	7

John Devane
Lands	200
Blacks	4

Hector McAllester

Chapter 8: Bladen County Tax Lists of 1789

Lands	350

Felex McMaster
Lands	250
Blacks	2

John Devane
Lands	1200
Blacks	11

Francis Davis
Lands	35
Blacks	3

Saml Bayman
Lands	900

Alexander Hendry
Lands	350
Blacks	1

John Andres
Lands	200

Drury Smith

Robart McMillian
Lands	700

John Sikes Senr
Lands	450

John Sikes Juner

James Larkins
Whites	2
Lands	900
Blacks	4

Nathen Meradarth
Whites	1
Lands	700

Peter Pridgin
Lands	150

Francis Pridgin

John Pridgin

John Andres
Lands	2332
Blacks	8

Elisha Andres
Lands	200

John Sutton
Lands	400

Josiah Sikes
Whites	1
Lands	140

Allick Strohan
Lands	450
Blacks	3

James Hendry
Lands	50

Danel Cook
Lands	150

James Andres
Lands	900
Blacks	1

Jaremiah Doane
Lands	340

Moses Strahan

John Huffam

Stephen Andres Junr
Lands	300

Wm Mitchell

Bailey Sutton
Lands	300

Stephen Andres
Lands	200
Blacks	3

Samuel Andres
Lands	200

John McMillan
Lands	300

A true List by Stephen Andres

****

Chapter 8: Bladen County Tax Lists of 1789

BLADEN COUNTY TAX LIST OF 1789

A List of the Taxable Property in Captn. Mulford's District for the 1st April 1789

Headings for this list include: Person Names, No. of Acres of Land, No. of Lots in Elizt. Town, No. of White Poles & No. of Black Poles.

Abbreviations will be used in this list.

Names	Edmond Fogarty
Acres	1111
White Poles	1
Black Poles	4

Names	William White
Acres	1000
White Poles	1
Black Poles	1

Names	William Floyd
Acres	120
White Poles	1

Names	Isaiah Sykes
Acres	400
White Poles	1

Names	William Streaty
White Poles	1

Names	David Lloyd
Acres	694
White Poles	1
Black Poles	2

Names	David Lloyd for Richd Loyd's Estate
Acres	610
Black Poles	2

Names	Joseph Russ
White Poles	1

Names	Joseph Davis
Acres	200
White Poles	1
Black Poles	1

Names	Henery Butler
White Poles	1

Names	John Garvin
Acres	172 1/2
White Poles	1

Names	William Saltar
Acres	3342
Town Lots	1
White Poles	1
Black Poles	16

Names	Do. Genl. Waddell's Estate
Acres	12265

Names	Richard Saltar Junr.
White Poles	1

Names	John Parker
White Poles	1

Names	Henery Yerby
White Poles	1

Names	David Lock
Acres	947 1/2
White Poles	1
Black Poles	2

Names	Eunice Lock
Acres	304
White Poles	1
Black Poles	1

Names	Jesse Brown
White Poles	1

Names	Leonard Lock
Acres	950
White Poles	1

Names	Benjamin Elwell
Acres	250
White Poles	1
Black Poles	1

Names	Hezekiah Davis
Acres	982
White Poles	1
Black Poles	8

Names	James Benson Senr.
Acres	140
White Poles	1

Chapter 8: Bladen County Tax Lists of 1789

Names	William Benson
White Poles	1

Names	John Russ
Acres	570
White Poles	1

Names	Thos. Lock & Mother
Acres	1200
White Poles	1
Black Poles	5

Names	Hudnell Huffham
Acres	370
White Poles	2

Names	James Saltar
Acres	900
Town Lots	1
White Poles	1
Black Poles	6

Names	Thomas Russ Senr.
Acres	890
White Poles	1
Black Poles	3

Names	Jesse Oliphant
Acres	850
White Poles	1

Names	George Melvin
White Poles	1

Names	Thomas Russ Junr.
White Poles	1

Names	Joseph Russ Junr.
White Poles	1

Names	John Singletary
Acres	450
White Poles	1
Black Poles	1

Names	James Benson Junr.
White Poles	1

Names	John Benson
White Poles	1

Names	Brayton Singletary
Acres	900
White Poles	1
Black Poles	2

Names	Aleazar Russ
Acres	100
White Poles	1

Names	Thomas Mulford
White Poles	1

Names	George Wilson
Acres	330
White Poles	1

Names	Ambres Wilson
Acres	290
White Poles	1

Names	Benjamin Singletary
Acres	450
White Poles	1
Black Poles	1

Names	James Moorhead for ye Estate of S Smith
Acres	1440
Black Poles	3

Names	John Davis
Acres	350
White Poles	1

Names	Hugh Murphey
Acres	630
White Poles	1
Black Poles	1

Names	Benjn. Lock
Acres	750
White Poles	1
Black Poles	3

Names	George Thomas
Acres	242
White Poles	1
Black Poles	2

Names	John Thomas
Acres	160
White Poles	1
Black Poles	1

Chapter 8: Bladen County Tax Lists of 1789

Names	Ephm. Mulford
Acres	970
White Poles	1
Black Poles	6

Names	Daniel Finlow
White Poles	1

A Coppy from the Original Ephm. Mulford

****

BLADEN COUNTY TAX LIST OF 1789

Taxable property in Capt. Watson's district for 1789

Headings for this list include: Persons Names, Acres of Land, White Polls, Black Polls, Lots in Elizabeth, in Fayetteville, in Wilmington, in Lumberton, Wheels of pleasure, Stud Horses & Lands over the mountains.

Abbreviations will be used in this list.

Names	Elizabeth Allen
Acres	200

Names	Street Ashford
Acres	500
White Polls	1
Black Poles	2

Names	James Bradley & John Cowan
Acres	2028
White Polls	3
Black Polls	17
Lots in Elizabethton	3
Lots in Wilmington	1
Wheels	1

Names	Elizabeth Brown
Black Polls	2

Names	William Bryan
Acres	350
White Polls	1
Black Polls	1

Names	Samuel Baker
Acres	640
White Polls	1

Names	James Blount for self & John Riding
Acres	930
White Polls	1

Names	Phill Bryan
Acres	142
White Polls	1
Black Polls	1

Names	John Bryan
Acres	110
White Polls	1
Black Polls	1

Names	Stephen Bryan
Acres	250
White Polls	1

Names	Phillip [Faded]
Acres	52
White Polls	1

Names	William Cheshire
Acres	160
White Polls	1

Names	John Cabeen[?]
White Polls	1

Names Richd. Cheshire for self & George Lyons estate	
Acres	427
White Polls	1
Black Polls	1

Names	John Decamp
Acres	400
White Polls	1

Names	William Dowlas
Acres	300
White Polls	1

Names	John Ellis
Acres	610
White Polls	1

Names	Jarred Ervin
Acres	600
White Polls	1
Black Polls	2

Chapter 8: Bladen County Tax Lists of 1789

Names	James Ervin
Acres	250
White Polls	1

Names	James Evers
Acres	500
White Polls	1

Names	Benjamin Fitzrandolph
Acres	1410
White Polls	1
Black Polls	5

Names	James Faun
Acres	300
White Polls	1

Names	James Guyton
Acres	150
White Polls	1

Names	John Hester
Acres	424
White Polls	1

Names	Josiah Hendon
Acres	1844
White Polls	1
Black Polls	7

Names	Margt. Harison
Acres	248
White Polls	1

Names	Thomas Hester
Acres	350
White Polls	1

Names	John Hillyard
Acres	500
White Polls	1

Names	William Hester
Acres	600
White Polls	1

Names	Joseph Hester
Acres	180
White Polls	1

Names	Jasper Hester
Acres	288
White Polls	1

Names	Stephen Hester
Acres	800
White Polls	1

Names	Isaac Jones
Acres	1500
White Polls	1
Black Polls	2

Names	Musgrove Jones
Acres	1132
White Polls	1
Black Polls	2
Lots in Wilmington	3

Names	Edward Jones
Acres	751
White Polls	1

Names	Joseph Kemp
Acres	1403
Black Polls	3

Names	Joseph Kemp Junr.
Acres	50
White Polls	1

Names	John Kemp
Acres	350
White Polls	1

Names	George Knowls
Acres	250
White Polls	1

Names	Angus Camons
Acres	100
White Polls	1

Names	John Lenox
Acres	510
White Polls	1
Black Polls	3

Names	Samuel McRee
Acres	270
White Polls	1

Names	Robert McConky
Acres	550
Black Polls	2

Chapter 8: Bladen County Tax Lists of 1789

Names	James Moorhead
Acres	3152
White Polls	1
Black Polls	8
Lots in Fayetteville	1
Lots in Lumberton	2
Lands over the Mountains	660

Names	John McMillan
Acres	150
White Polls	1

From this point on in the list, two new headings are listed: Lots in Smithfield & Lots in Chatham.

Names	William McRee Senr.
Acres	1150
White Polls	1
Black Polls	11
Lots in Elizabethton	4

Names	Thomas McLelland
Acres	200
White Polls	1
Black Polls	1

Names	Thomas Moris
Acres	96
White Polls	1

Names	Mathew Months
Acres	88
White Polls	1

Names	Thomas Owen
Acres	7360
White Polls	1
Black Polls	20
Lots in Chatham	1
Lots in Smithfield	2
Lots in Elizabethton	2

Names	Thomas Owen for the estate of John Owen
Acres	2395
Black Polls	9
Lots in Elizabethton	1

Names	Aaron Plumer
Acres	184
White Polls	1
Black Polls	1

Names	Argulus Pointyr
Acres	502
White Polls	1

Names	David Russ
Acres	1340
White Polls	2
Black Polls	1

Names	William Russ
White Polls	1

Names	John Russ Senr.
Acres	300
White Polls	1

Names	Robert Raiford
Acres	2040
White Polls	1
Black Polls	1
Lots in Wilmington	2

Names	William Russ Junr.
White Polls	1
Black Polls	1

Names	Rikum[?] Riding
Acres	400
White Polls	1

Names	Richd. Saltar
Acres	1060
White Polls	3
Black Polls	1

Names	Lucy Smith
Acres	640
Black Polls	3

Names	Daniel Shaw
Acres	350
White Polls	1

Names	Angus Shaw
Acres	500
White Polls	1

Names	William Singletary Senr.
Acres	350
White Polls	1

Names	Joseph Singletary

Chapter 8: Bladen County Tax Lists of 1789

Acres	420
White Polls	1
Black Polls	2

Names	Joseph Singletary
Acres	610
White Polls	2
Black Polls	8

Names	Neill Shaw
Acres	470
White Polls	1
Black Polls	5

Names	Josiah Singletary
Acres	420
[Rest of data torn away]	

Names	John Stanton
Acres	700
[Rest of data torn away]	

Names	John Singletary
[Rest of data torn away]	

Names	Ithamar Singletary
[Rest of data torn away]	

Names	R. Matthew White
Acres	300
White Polls	1
Black Poles	1

Names	John White
Acres	2070
White Polls	2
Black Polls	8

Names	John White for James White
Acres	200

Names	John White for Docter Ross
Acres	420

Names	John White for Mosley estate
Acres	400

Names	William Watson
Acres	2780
White Polls	1
Black Polls	4
Lots in Elizabethton	1
Lots in Fayetteville	1
Lots in Lumberton	2

Names	Mary White
Acres	750
Black Polls	1

Names	Griff: J White
White Polls	1

Names	George Weir
Acres	450
White Polls	1

Names	Wm. Wilkinson
White Polls	1

Names	David White
Acres	1250
White Polls	2
Black Polls	1

Names	Wm. Willey
White Polls	1

A coppy from the Original List P John White

****

BLADEN COUNTY TAX LIST OF 1789

Taxable property in the 2d. dist. for 1789 viz Capt: Watsons Dist.

Headings for this list include: Persons Names, No. of Acres of Land, White polls, Black Polls, Lots in Elizabeth, Wheels of Pleasure, Stud Horses, Lots in Wilmington, Lots in Fayetteville, Military Grants & Land entered in John Armstrongs Office, Lots in Lumberton, Lots in Chatham & Lots in Smithfield.

Abbreviations will be used in this list.

Names	Joseph Kemp
Acres	1403
Black Polls	3

Names	James Bradley & John Cowan
Acres	2028
White Polls	3
Black Polls	17
Lots in Elizabethton	3

Chapter 8: Bladen County Tax Lists of 1789

Wheels of Pleasure	1
Lots in Wilmington	1
Names	David Russ
Acres	1340
White Polls	2
Black Polls	1
Lots in Elizabethton	1
Names	Elizth. Brown
Black Polls	2
Names	Samuel McRee
Acres	270
White Polls	1
Names	John Ellis
Acres	610
White Polls	1
Names	Robert McConkey
Acres	550
Black Polls	2
Names	William Bryan
Acres	350
White Polls	1
Black Polls	1
Names	Samuel Baker
Acres	640
White Polls	1
Names	Joseph Kemp Junr.
Acres	50
White Polls	1
Names	Mathew R. White
Acres	300
White Polls	1
Black Polls	1
Names	Philip Cake
Acres	52
White Polls	1
Names	John White
Acres	2070
White Polls	2
Black Polls	8
Names	John White for James White
Acres	200
Names	John White for the Estate of Wm Ross
Acres	420
Names	John White for the Estate of Dd. Morley
Acres	400
Names	Richard Saltar
Acres	1060
White Polls	3
Black Polls	1
Names	William Chesher
Acres	160
White Polls	1
Names	James Moorhead
Acres	3152
White Polls	1
Black Polls	8
Lots in Wilmington	2
Lots in Fayetteville	1
Military Grants	660
Names	Lucy Smith
Acres	640
Black Polls	3
Names	Isaac Jones
Acres	1500
White Polls	4
Black Polls	2
Names	John Hester
Acres	424
White Polls	1
Names	Jarred Erwin
Acres	600
White Polls	1
Black Polls	2
Military Grants	1280
Names	Danl. Shaw
Acres	350
White Polls	1
Names	William Jas. Watson
Acres	2780
White Polls	1
Black Polls	4
Lots in Elizabethton	1

Chapter 8: Bladen County Tax Lists of 1789

Lots in Lumberton	**2**

Names	Colo. Thos. Owen
Acres	7360
White Polls	1
Black Polls	20
Lots in Elizabethton	**2**
Lots in Chatham	**2**
Lots in Smithfield	**2**

Names	Colo. Thos. Owen for the Estate of Jno. Owen
Acres	2395
Black Polls	9
Lots in Elizabethton	**1**

Names	Mary White
Acres	750
Black Polls	1

Names	Griffeth Jones White
White Polls	1

Names	Angus Shaw
Acres	500
White Polls	1

Names	John McMillin
Acres	150
White Polls	1

Names	John Cobean
White Polls	1

Names	Angus Lammons
Acres	100
White Polls	1

Names	Josiah Hendon
Acres	1844
White Polls	1
Black Polls	7

Names	John Kemp
Acres	350
White Polls	1

Names	William Singletary Senr.
Acres	350
White Polls	1

Names	Margaret Harrison
Acres	248

White Polls	**1**

Names	John Ducamp
Acres	400
White Polls	**1**

Names	William Russ
White Polls	**1**

Names	Aaron Plummer
Acres	184
White Polls	1
Black Polls	**1**

Names	Richd. Chesher for Self and Estate of George Lyons
Acres	427
White Polls	1
Black Polls	**1**

Names	John Russ Siegnr.
Acres	300
White Polls	1

Names	Robert Raiford
Acres	2040
White Polls	1
Black Polls	1

Names	James Erwin
Acres	250
White Polls	**1**

Names	Joseph Singletary
Acres	420
White Polls	1
Black Polls	**2**

Names	Benjn. Fitz. Randolph
Acres	1410
White Polls	1
Black Polls	5

Names	Ezabella Allin
Acres	200

Names	William McRee Esqr.
Acres	1150
White Polls	1
Black Polls	11
Lots in Elizabethton	**4**

Names   James Blount for selfe & John Riding

Chapter 8: Bladen County Tax Lists of 1789

Acres	930
White Polls	1
Names	George Weir
Acres	450
White Polls	1
Names	Musgrove Jones
Acres	1132
White Polls	1
Black Polls	2
Lots in Elizabethton	3
Names	William Wilkinson
White Polls	1
Names	Joseph Singletary
Acres	610
White Polls	1
Black Polls	8
Lots in Elizabethton	1
Names	Neill Shaw
Acres	470
White Polls	1
Black Polls	5
Names	George Knowls
Acres	250
White Polls	1
Names	David White
Acres	1250
White Polls	2
Black Polls	1
Names	Edward Jones
Acres	751
White Polls	1
Names	Philamon Bryan
Acres	142
White Polls	1
Black Polls	1
Names	Sreet[sic] Ashford
Acres	500
White Polls	1
Black Polls	2
Names	John Bryan
Acres	110
White Polls	1
Black Polls	1
Names	Josiah Singletary
Acres	420
White Polls	1
Black Polls	1
Names	Thos. McLelan
Acres	200
White Polls	1
Black Polls	1
Names	Stephen Bryan
Acres	250
White Polls	1
Names	John Stanton
Acres	700
White Polls	2
Black Polls	1
Names	Thomas Hester
Acres	350
White Polls	1
Names	William Wiley
White Polls	1
Names	John Hilliard
Acres	500
White Polls	1
Names	James Fason
Acres	300
White Polls	1
Names	William Russ Junr.
White Polls	1
Black Polls	1
Names	John Singletary
Acres	160
White Polls	1
Names	Argulas Pointer
Acres	502
White Polls	1
Names	William Hestor
Acres	600
White Polls	1
Names	Joseph Hesters

Chapter 8: Bladen County Tax Lists of 1789

Acres	180
White Polls	1

Names	Jasper Hester
Acres	288
White Polls	1

Names	James Evers
Acres	500
White Polls	1

Names	Riham Reding
Acres	400
White Polls	1

Names	Ithamore Singletary
Acres	160
White Polls	1
Black Polls	1

Names	Thomas Morris
Acres	96
White Polls	1

Names	William Dowlas
Acres	800
White Polls	1

Names	James Guiton
Acres	150
White Polls	1

Names	Mathew Months
Acres	88
White Polls	1

Names	John Lennon
Acres	510
White Polls	1
Black Polls	3

****

BLADEN COUNTY TAX LIST OF 1789

Captn. Thims District 1789

Headings for this list include: Persons Names, Lands, Military Grants or Entrys in John Armstrongs Office, Town Lots in Elizabethtown, White Poles, Black Poles, Wheals of Pleasure, Stud Horses, Lots in Fayetteville, Lots in Wilmington.

Abbreviations will be used in this list

Names	Benjn. Sims
Lands	3175
White Poles	1
Black Poles	1

Names	Edward Gates
White Poles	1

Names	Jane Gates
Lands	100

Names	Gedian Prickett
White Poles	1

Names	Thomas Thims
White Poles	1

Names	Agerton Willis
Lands	100
White Poles	1

Names	Joseph Willis Deceased
Lands	530

Names	Joseph Chason
Lands	875
White Poles	1

Names	John Beard
Lands	510
White Poles	1
Black Poles	3

Names	Joseph Willis
Lands	320
Black Poles	3

Names	Neill Black
Lands	200
White Poles	1

Names	John Reves
White Poles	1

Names	Isaac Sims
Lands	1258
White Poles	1
Black Poles	2

Chapter 8: Bladen County Tax Lists of 1789

Names	James Moore
White Poles	1
Stud Horses	1

Names	John Culbreath
Lands	150

Names	Thomas Taylor
Lands	150

Names	Arthur Graham
Lands	377
White Poles	2

Names	John Lock
Lands	1050
White Poles	1
Black Poles	2

Names	Jeremiah Willis
Lands	173
White Poles	1

Names	Peter Byrne
Lands	750
White Poles	1
Black Poles	2

Names	Andrew Andress
Lands	600
White Poles	1

Names	Robert Council
Lands	320
White Poles	1
Black Poles	1

Names	Archabald Bone
Lands	320
White Poles	1

Names	John Newberry
Lands	260
White Poles	1
Black Poles	3

Names	Jeremiah Plummer
White Poles	1

Names	William G. McDanniel
Lands	200
White Poles	1

Black Poles	3

Names	The Estate of James McDanniel Deceased
Lands	600

Names	William Denton
White Poles	1

Names	John Gates
Lands	100
White Poles	1

Names	David Buchan
Lands	104
White Poles	1

Names	Archabald McDanniel
Lands	200
White Poles	1

Names	Danneil McClain
Lands	100
White Poles	1

Names	Jacob Smilie
Lands	890
White Poles	1
Black Poles	1

Names	Thomas Pickett
White Poles	1
Black Poles	6

Names	Abram Ralls
White Poles	1

Names	Robert Rafourd Senr.
Lands	2210
White Poles	1
Black Poles	4

Names	James Singletary (Long)
Lands	240
White Poles	1
Black Poles	2

Names	Elizabeth Rogerson
Lands	600
Black Poles	4

Names	Richard Singletary Senr.
Lands	1000

Chapter 8: Bladen County Tax Lists of 1789

White Poles	1
Black Poles	2

Names	the Estate of Isaac Ray Deceased
Lands	840
Black Poles	11

Names	the Estate of John [?]eler Deceased
Lands	600

Names	John Singletary
Lands	480
White Poles	1
Black Poles	3

Names	John Jackson
Lands	300
White Poles	1

Names	Sanday Carrel
White Poles	1

Names	James Singletary (Short)
Lands	1216
Lots in Elizabethtown	1
White Poles	1

Names	Thomas Averitt
Lands	100
White Poles	1

Names	Elizabeth Lock
Lands	840
Black Poles	4

Names	Frederick Miller
Lands	1070
Lots in Elizabethtown	1
White Poles	1
Black Poles	3
Wheals	2

Names	James Council
Lands	1640
Military Grants	3840
White Poles	1
Black Poles	12
Wheals	2

Names	Eric Lafferstedte
Lands	1635
White Poles	1
Black Poles	12

Names	Campbell Anderson
White Poles	1

Names	Abel Corbit
Lands	200
White Poles	1
Black Poles	1

Names	James Ellis
Lands	1893
Black Poles	3

Names	Benjn. Lansdell
Lands	500
White Poles	1

Names	William Thims
Lands	190
White Poles	1

Names	Jesse Newberry
Lands	2420
White Poles	1
Black Poles	8

Names	William Champion
Lands	100
White Poles	1

Names	Martha Thims
Lands	830
Black Poles	1

Names	Malikiah Burgess
Lands	300
White Poles	1
Black Poles	1

Names	Nathiel Reves
Lands	1025
White Poles	1
Black Poles	4

Names	John Danneil
Lands	200
White Poles	1

Names	Samuel Hollingsworth
Lands	2000
White Poles	2
Black Poles	5

Chapter 8: Bladen County Tax Lists of 1789

Names	Danneil Willis
Lands	1840
White Poles	1
Black Poles	1

Names	Elizabeth Willis
Lands	320
Black Poles	1

Names	James Beard
Lands	700
White Poles	1
Black Poles	1

Names	William Godfrey Senr.
Military Grants	274
White Poles	1

Names	Thomas Lock
Lands	1065
White Poles	1
Black Poles	3

Names	William Clark
Lands	1466
White Poles	1
Black Poles	1

Names	Mary Clark
Lands	1171
Black Poles	4

Names	Rebecca Lock
Lands	360
Black Poles	4

Names	John Moore
Lands	656
White Poles	1
Black Poles	1

Names	Peter Gates
Lands	100
White Poles	1

Names	John Anderson
White Poles	1

Names	David Halloway
Lands	970
White Poles	1
Black Poles	1

Names	William Anderson Senr.
Lands	420
White Poles	1

Names	William Anderson Junr.
White Poles	1

Names	Sherwood Forts
White Poles	1

Names	Danneil Beard
Lands	400
White Poles	1
Black Poles	2

Names	William Plummer
White Poles	1

Names	Moses Plummer
Lands	100
White Poles	1

Names	James Marsh
Lands	160
White Poles	1

Names	Joseph Singletary (Long)
Lands	250
White Poles	1
Black Poles	2

Names	Josiah Prickett
White Poles	1

Names	John Lansedell
White Poles	1

Names	John Plummer
Lands	130
White Poles	1

Names	Zacariah Plummer
Lands	150
White Poles	1

Names	Rachael Johnston
Lands	200

Names	Peter Robeson
Lands	1492
White Poles	1
Black Poles	5

Chapter 8: Bladen County Tax Lists of 1789

Names	Charles Yancie
White Poles	1

Names	John Walker
Lands	348
White Poles	1

Names	Samuel Cain
Lands	670
White Poles	1
Black Poles	3

Names	Joseph Plummer
Lands	86
White Poles	1

Names	Robert Edwards
Lands	4461
White Poles	1
Black Poles	4

Names	Ollives Cain
Lands	250
Black Poles	2

Names	James Cain
Lands	800
White Poles	1
Black Poles	3

Names	John Bennent
Lands	250
White Poles	1

Names	Joseph Butler
Lands	435
White Poles	1
Black Poles	2

Names	Edward Brafford
White Poles	1

Names	Thomas Scriven
Lands	200
White Poles	1

Names	Elizabeth Prickett
Lands	66

Names	Mathew Byrne Senr.
White Poles	1

Names	Lewis Smith
White Poles	1

Names	Malcum McNeil
Lands	490
White Poles	1
Black Poles	2

Names	William Smith
Lands	200
White Poles	1

Names	Benjamin Brassell
White Poles	1

Names	David Smith
Lands	100
White Poles	1

Names	James Jackson
Lands	2340
White Poles	1
Black Poles	9

Names	Bartram Robeson
Lands	6318
Lots in Elizabethtown	4
White Poles	1
Black Poles	7
Bartram for Estate of Joseph Lock	
Lands	561
White Poles	1
Black Poles	1

Names	John Purnell
Lands	250
White Poles	1

Names	Mary Butler for the Estate of J Cooper
Lands	480
White Poles	1

Names	Jesse Carver
Lands	700
White Poles	1
Black Poles	3

Names	Margaret Byrns
Lands	1280
Lots in Elizabethtown	2
White Poles	2
Black Poles	16

Names	Benjamin Willis Estate

Chapter 8: Bladen County Tax Lists of 1789

Lands	1300
Black Poles	3

Names	Benjamin Willis
Lands	500
White Poles	1

Names	John Wilkins
Lands	800
Lots in Elizabethtown	1
White Poles	1
Black Poles	2

Names	John Thims
Lands	1418
White Poles	2
Black Poles	12

Names	Zac Butler
Lands	605
White Poles	1

Names	Samuel Butlers Estate
Lands	960
Black Poles	2

Names	James S. Purdie
Lands	1920
Lots in Elizabethtown	1
White Poles	1
Black Poles	8

Names	Joseph Cain
Lands	1560
Lots in Elizabethtown	2
White Poles	1
Black Poles	6
Wheals	2
Stud Horses	1

Names	William kirkpatrick
Lands	2466
White Poles	1
Black Poles	2
Lots in Fayetteville	1

Names	Maurice Richards
Lands	180
White Poles	1

Names	Joseph Commons

Names	Jesse Thims

Names	Estate of Isham Carver
Names	Theophilus Evens
Names	David Evens
Names	Thos. Howell
Names	Stephen McFadian

Taken Peter Robeson J.P.

****

BLADEN COUNTY TAX LIST OF 1789

[Approximately fifteen names torn from the top of this list.]

Property of the inhabitants [Torn] for the year 1789.

Headings for this list include: White Poles, Black Poles, Lands, Lotts in Fayetteville, ditto Wilmington, ditto Saulsbury, ditto Elizabethtown, Pitts burgh.

Margaret Pemberton
Black Poles	3

John McMillen
White Poles	1
Lands	400

Neal McCullom
White Poles	1

John Darrah
White Poles	1
Lands	500
Lots in Elizabethtown	1

Richd. Singletary
White Poles	1
Black Poles	2
Lands	500

Ann McKay
White Poles	1
Black Poles	10
Lands	2260

Chapter 8: Bladen County Tax Lists of 1789

Lots in Fayetteville	1
Lots in Wilmington	1
Pitts burgh	1

Benjamin Singletary
White Poles	1
Black Poles	1
Lands	[?]120

Daniel McKitchen
White Poles	1
Lands	166

Neal Campble
White Poles	1
Lands	50

John Camble
White Poles	1
Lands	250

Dugald Clarke
White Poles	1
Lands	100

John McVicker
White Poles	1
Lands	158

John Taylor
White Poles	1
Lands	283

Daniel McEwen
White Poles	1
Lands	133

Cornelus Calihan
White Poles	1

Peirce Calihan
White Poles	1

Martain Calihan
White Poles	1

James Maulsby
White Poles	1
Black Poles	1
Lands	352
Lots in Fayetteville	1/2

Thomas Maulsby

White Poles	1
Black Poles	1

Mary Smith & Thos Smith
White Poles	1
Black Poles	11
Lands	900
Lots in Fayetteville	1/2

James Dowey
White Poles	1
Black Poles	2
Lands	100

Duncan McKeithan
White Poles	1
Lands	210

Daniel Downey
White Poles	1
Lands	150

Alexander Ballintine
White Poles	1
Lands	100

Malcom McLeod
White Poles	1

Benoni Clayton
White Poles	3
Black Poles	1

Wm. Andrews
White Poles	1

Ralph Millers
White Poles	1
Black Poles	6
Lands	636

Aga[?]lly Green
White Poles	1

Harbert Taylor
White Poles	1
Lands	150

William Jones
White Poles	2
Black Poles	4
Lots in Saulsbury	1
Lands	1039

Chapter 8: Bladen County Tax Lists of 1789

Charles Oneal
White Poles 1
Black Poles 1

Elizabeth Lucas
Black Poles 7
Lands 1320

James Eagleson
White Poles 1
Black Poles 2
Lands 500

Jonathan Russ
White Poles 1
Black Poles 1
Lands 600

Thomas Brown
White Poles 1
Black Poles 16
Lands on this side Mountains 5971
Lands o West side of Mountains 3420
Lots in Fayetteville 3
Lots in Wilmington 1
Pitts burgh 2

Griffeth McRee
White Poles 1
Black Poles 7
Lands 4024
Lots in Elizabethtown 1 & 1/2

Gooden Elletson
White Poles 3
Black Poles 48
Lands 2600

Abigald Gregory
Black Poles 1
Lands 1757
Lots in Wilmington 1
Lots in Elizabethtown 4

Euphronica Dewey
White Poles 1
Black Poles 6

Wm Oliphant
White Poles 1
Black Poles 2
Lands 350

[Torn] Darrah
White Poles 1

Moses Holms
White Poles 1
Lands 850

John McKay
White Poles 1
Lands 450
Lots in Elizabethtown 1

John Peabody
White Poles 1
Black Poles 1

Richard Brown
White Poles 1
Black Poles 2
Lands 330

Duncan McCullock
Lands 100

Daniel Bain
White Poles 1
Black Poles 5
Lands 320

Arthur Howe
White Poles 2
Black Poles 22
Lands 1960

Jeremiah Daffron
White Poles 1
Lands 134

Anthony Moresby
White Poles 1
Lands 800

Jn Pointer
White Poles 1
Lands 850

Jn Perry
White Poles 1
Lands 100

Mrs Slingsby
Black Poles 3

Chapter 8: Bladen County Tax Lists of 1789

Lands	**982**

Wm. Smith junr.
White Poles	**1**

Jno Brown
White Poles	**1**
Black Poles	**3**
Lands	**570**

Mary Singletary
Black Poles	**2**
Lands	**680**

Josiah R Gautier
White Poles	**1**
Black Poles	**15**
Lands	**920**

Thos. Gautier
White Poles	**1**
Lands	**200**

A true List of the Taxable Property in Captain Thos. Gautiers District, taken by me for the year 1789   Jno. Brown

Appendix A: North Carolina Law

APPENDIX A

NORTH CAROLINA LAW

THE STATE RECORDS OF NORTH CAROLINA
VOLUME XXIV
LAWS 1777-1788
Editor: Walter Clark
Nash Brothers, Book and Job Printers
Goldsboro, N.C., 1905

Pages 9-12
Chapter III.
An Act declaring what Crimes and Practices against the State shall be Treason, and what shall be Misprision of Treason, and providing Punishments adequate to Crimes of both Classes, and for preventing the Dangers which may arise from the persons disaffected to the State.

I. Be it Enacted by the General Assembly of the State of North Carolina, and it is hereby enacted by the Authority of the same, That all and every Person or Persons (Prisoners of War excepted) now inhabiting or residing within the limits of the State of North Carolina, or who shall voluntarily come into the same hereafter to inhabit or reside, do owe, and shall pay Allegiance to the State of North Carolina.

II. And be it further enacted by the Authority aforesaid, That if any Person or Persons belonging to, or residing within this State, and under the Protection of its Laws, shall take a Commission or Commissions from the King of Great Brittain, or any under his Authority, or other the Enemies of this State, or of the United States of America; or shall levy War against this State, or the Government thereof; or knowingly and willingly shall aid or assist any Enemies at open War against this State, or the United States of America, by joining their Armies, or by inlisting, or procuring or persuading others to inlist for that Purpose, or by furnishing such Enemies with Arms, Ammunition, Provision, or any other Article for their Aid or Comfort; or shall form, or be in any way concerned in forming any Combination, Plot, or Conspiracy, for betraying this State, or the United States of America, into the Hands of Power of any foreign Enemy; or shall give or send any Intelligence to the Enemies of this State for that Purpose; every Person so offending, and being thereof legally convicted by the Evidence of two sufficient Witnesses, or standing mute, or peremptorily challenging more than thirty five Jurors, in any Court of Oyer and Terminer, or other Court that shall and may be established for the Trial of such Offences, shall be adjudged guilty of High Treason, and shall suffer Death without Benefit of Clergy, and his or her Estate shall be forfeited to the State. Provided, That the Judge or Judges of the Court wherein such Conviction may be, shall and may order and appropriate so much of the Traitor's Estate, as to him or them may appear sufficient, for the Support of his or her Family.

III. And be it further Enacted, by the Authority aforesaid, That if any Person or Persons within this State shall attempt to convey Intelligence to the Enemies of this State or of the United States; or shall publicly and deliberately speak or write against our public Defence; or shall maliciously and advisedly endeavour to excite the People to resist the Government of this State, or persuade them to return to a Dependence on the Crown of Great Brittain; or shall knowingly spread false and dispiriting News, or maliciously and advisedly terrify and discourage the People from inlisting into the Service of the State; or shall stir up or excite Tumults, Disorders or Insurrections in the State; or dispose the People to favour the Enemy, or oppose and endeavour to prevent the Measures carrying on in Support of the Freedom and Independence of the said United States; every such Person or Persons being thereof legally convicted by

Appendix A: North Carolina Law

the Evidence of two or more creditable Witnesses, or other sufficient Testimony, shall be adjudged guilty of Misprision of Treason, and shall suffer Imprisonment during the War, and forfeit to the State one Half of his, her or their Lands, Tenements, Goods and Chattels.

IV. And be it further enacted by the Authority aforesaid, That all Offences by this Act declared Misprision of Treason shall be cognizable before any Justice of the Peace of the County where the Offence was committed, or where the Offender can be found; and every Justice of the Peace within this State, on Complaint to him made on the Oath or Affirmation of one or more credible Person or Persons, shall cause such Offender to come before him, and enter into a Recognizance, with one or more sufficient Surety or Sureties, to be and appear at the next County Court of the County wherein the Offence was committed, and abide the Judgment of the said Court, and in the mean Time to be of the Peace and good Behaviour toward all People in the State; and for Want of such Surety or Sureties, the said Justice shall and may commit such Offender either to the Gaol of the County or District where the Offence was committed, and appoint a Guard for the safe conveying of him to such Gaol. And all Persons charged on Oath or Affirmation with any Crime or Crimes by this Act declared to be Treason against the State, shall be dealt with and proceeded against in like Manner as the Law directs in respect of other capital Crimes.

V. And whereas the safety of the State, and the present critical Situation of Affairs, make it necessary that all Persons who owe or acknowledge Allegiance or Obedience to the King of Great Brittain, should be removed out of the State; Be it enacted by the Authority aforesaid, That all the late Officers of the King of Great Britain, and all Persons (Quakers excepted) being Subjects of this State, and now living therein, or who shall hereafter come to live therein, who have traded immediately to Great Britain or Ireland within ten Years last past, in their own Right, or acted as Factors, Storekeepers, or Agents, here or in any of United States of America, for Merchants residing in Great Brittain or Ireland, shall take the following Oath of Abjuration and Allegiance, or depart out of the State, viz. I will bear faithful and true Allegiance to the State of North Carolina, and will to the utmost of my Power, support and maintain, and defend the independent Government thereof, against George the Third, King of Great Brittain, and his Successors, and the Attempts of any other Person, Prince, Power, State, or Potentate, who by secret Arts, Treasons, Conspiracies, or by open Force, shall attempt to subvert the same, and will in every Respect conduct myself as a peaceful, orderly Subject; and that I will disclose and make known to the Governor, some Member of the Council of State, or some Justice of the State, all Treasons, Conspiracies, and Attempts, committed or intended against the State, which shall come to my Knowledge. And that all Persons being Quakers, and under the Circumstances above mentioned, shall make the following Affirmation, or depart out of the State: I, A. B. do solemnly and sincere declare and affirm, that I will bear true Allegiance to the Independent State of North Carolina, and to the Powers and Authorities which are or may be established for the good Government thereof; and I do renounce any Allegiance to the present King of Great Brittain, his Heirs and Successors; and that I will disclose and make known to the Governor, some Member of the Council of State, or Justice of the Peace, all Treasons, Conspiracies, or Attempts, committed or intended against the same, which shall come to my knowledge. And the said Oath or Affirmation shall be taken and subscribed in open Court in the County where the Person or Persons taking the same, shall or do usually reside.

VI. And be it further enacted by the Authority aforesaid, That the County Court in each and every County, and every Justice of the Peace in each respective County, shall have full Power to issue Citations against Persons coming within the above Description, as Officers, Merchants, Traders, Factors, Storekeepers, or Agents, and to demand Surety on Recognizance, if necessary, and to require their Attendance at the next ensuing Court to be held for the County; and if any Person so cited (due Proof being made thereof) shall fail or neglect to attend, or attending shall refuse to take the said Oath or Affirmation (as the Case may be) then the said Court shall and may have full Power and Authority to order such Person to depart out of this State to Europe or the West Indies, within Sixty days, and may take Bond and Security, in the Name of the Governor, for the Benefit of the State, for faithful Compliance with such Order. And if any Person so ordered, shall fail or neglect to depart within the limited Time, such Bond shall be forfeited to the State, without good and sufficient Reason shewn to and approved of by the Governor and Council; and the Justices, or any of them, in the County wherein the Person so failing or neglecting to depart shall be found, shall and may cause him to be apprehended and brought before the Court of the County where the Order was made; and the said Court shall in sucg Case send the Person so

Appendix A: North Carolina Law

offending, as speedily as may be out of the State, either to Europe or the West Indies, at the Cost and Charges of such Offender. Provided nevertheless, That all and every such Person and Persons shall have Liberty to sell and dispose of his or their Estates, and after satisfying all just Demands, to export the amount in Produce (Provisions and Naval Stores excepted) and may also nominate and appoint an Attorney or Attornies to sell and dispose of his or their Estates, for his or their Use and Benefit; but in Case any Real Estate belonging to any such Person, shall remain unsold for more than three Months next after the Owner thereof hath departed this State, the same shall be forfeited to and for the Use of the Public.

VII. And be it further Enacted by the Authority aforesaid, That if any Person so departing or sent off from this State, shall return to the same, then such Person shall be adjudged guilty of Treason against the State, and shall and may be proceeded against in like Manner as is herein directed in Cases of Treason.

VIII. And be it further enacted by the Authority aforesaid, That each and every Justice in each respective County may cite any Person or Persons to appear before the County Court where such Person or Persons usually reside, and take the aforesaid Oath or Affirmation, and in Case of Non Attendance or Refusal, the said Court shall and may have full Power to compel such Person or Persons to leave the State, under the same Regulations herein mentioned in other Cases.

****

Pages 16-17
Chapter IX.
An Act to empower the Justices of Bladen County to take into their Possession the Records of said County, now in Possession of Maturin Colville.

I. Whereas, it is represented by the Justices of Bladen County that Maturin Colville, heretofore Clerk of the same County, upon the appointment of Alfred Moore to that office in the year one thousand seven hundred and seventy four refused to deliver up to the Court the Records and other papers belonging to the County. That among the said records are many Wills, Indentures, and settlements of Estates which contain the only evidence of the property of great numbers of persons, particularly of orphans, and that on the Dockets are many suits yet undetermined, and many Judgments which remain unsatisfied, besides divers sums of money paid into the office, belonging to sundry persons, yet unaccounted for to the great injury of the Inhabitants of the said County and others.

II. In order therefore that the records may be restored to the proper office that the injured may be Redressed and that the obstinate and wilful brought to a sense of their Duty and a proper respect for the Law.

III. Be it enacted by the General Assembly of the State of North Carolina, That the Justices of the said County be appointed, and they or any three or more of them are hereby authorized and empowered to demand and receive of and from the said Maturin Colville, and of and from every other person or persons who are or may be in possession of the same, the Records and other papers of the said County and upon refusal or neglect to deliver the same, then the said Justices, or any three or more of them shall and may issue their Warrant directed to the Sheriff to take with him such force as he may think necessary and to apprehend the said Maturin Colville and such other Person or Persons as may have the said Records, or any of them, in possession, and him or them commit to the common jail of the said County until the records shall be produced and delivered up, and also empowering the Sheriff and other officers of the said county to make diligent search in all suspected places within the same County for the said Records and papers and for that purpose to break open doors and locks where they are suspected to be concealed.

IV. And be it further Enacted by the Authority aforesaid, That all fees and sums of money which may hereafter be paid into the Court of Bladen County, upon any suit depending or Judgment not satisfied on the Dockets, detained by the said Maturin Colville, as well as such Fees and Monies which are due to him the said Maturin Colville as to others, shall be paid by the Clerk of Court for the time being to the person or persons to whom the same shall appear to be due.

****

Appendix A: North Carolina Law

Pages 84-89
Chapter VI.
An Act to ament an Act for declaring what Crimes and Practices against the State shall be Treason, and what shall be Misprision of Treason, and providing Punishments adequate to Crimes of both Classes, and for preventing the Dangers which may arise from Persons disaffected to the State.

I.   Be it Enacted by the General Assembly of the State of North Carolina, and it is hereby Enacted by the Authority of the same, That all and every Person or Persons (Prisoners of War excepted) now inhabiting or residing within the Limits of the State of North Carolina, or who shall voluntarily come into the same hereafter to inhabit or reside, do owe and shall pay Allegiance to the State of North Carolina.

II.   And be it further Enacted, by the Authority aforesaid, That if any Person or Persons belonging to, or residing within this State, and under the Protection of its Laws, shall take a Commission or Commissions from the King of Great Britain, or any under his Authority, or other the Enemies of this State, or the United States of America, or shall levy war against this State, or the Government thereof, or knowingly or wilfully shall aid or assist any Enemies at open War against this State, or the United States of America, by joining their Armies, or by inlisting, or procuring or persuading others to inlist for that purpose, or by furnishing such Enemies with Arms, Ammunition, Provision, or any other Article for their Aid or Comfort, or shall form, or be in any wise concerned in forming, any Combination, Plot or Conspiracy, for betraying this State, or the United States of America, inyo the Hands or Power of any Foreign Enemy, or shall give any Intelligence to the Enemies of this State for that Purpose, every Person so Offending, and being thereof legally convicted by the Evidence of Two sufficient Witnesses, or standing mute, or peremptorily challenging more than Thirty Five Jurors, in any Court of Oyer and Terminer, or other Court that shall and may be established for the Trial of such Offences, shall be adjudged guilty of High Treason, and shall suffer Death without the Benefit of Clergy, and his or her Estate shall be forfeited to the State. Provided, That the Judge or Judges of the Court wherein such Conviction may be, shall and may order and appropriate so much of the Traitor's Estate as to him or them may appear sufficient for the Support of his or her Family.

III.   And be it further Enacted, by the Authority aforesaid, That if any Person or Persons within this State shall attempt to convey intelligence to the Enemies of this State, or of the United States, or shall Publickly and deliberately speak or write against the Public Defence, or shall maliciously and advisedly endeavour to excite the People to resist the Government of this State, or persuade them to return to a Dependence on the Crown of Great Britain, or shall knowingly spread false and dispiriting News, or maliciously and advisedly terrify and discourage the People from inlisting into the Service of this State, or the United States, or shall stir up or excite Tumults, Disorders, or Insurrections in the State, or dispose the People to favour the Enemy, or oppose, or endeavour to prevent the Measures carrying on in Support of the Election of the Freedom and Independence of the said United States, every such Person or Persons, being thereof legally convicted by the Evidence of Two or more creditable Witnesses, or other sufficient Testimony, shall be adjudged guilty of Misprision of Treason, and shall suffer Imprisonment during the War, and forfeit to the State one Half of his, her, or their Lands, Tenements, Goods and Chattels.

IV.   And be it further Enacted, by the Authority aforesaid, That all Offences by this Act declared Misprision of Treason, shall be cognizable before any Justice of the Peace of the County where the Offence was committed, or where the Offender can be found; and every Justice of the Peace within this State, on Complaint to him made on the Oath or Affirmation of one or more creditable Person or Persons, shall cause such Offender to come before him, and enter into a Recognizance, with one or more sufficient Surety or Sureties, to be and appear at the next Superior Court of the District wherein the Offence was committed, and abide the Judgment of the said Court, and in the mean Time to be of the Peace and good Behaviour to all People within the State; and for want of such Surety or Sureties, the said Justice shall and may commit such Offender either to the Gaol of the County or District where the Offence was committed, and appoint a Guard for the safe conveying him to such Gaol; and all Persons charged on Oath or Affirmation with any Crime or Crimes by this Act declared to be Treason against the State, shall be dealt with, and proceeded against, in like Manner as the Law directs in Respect of other Capital Crimes.

Appendix A: North Carolina Law

V. And whereas the safety of the State, and the present critical Situation of Affairs, make it necessary that all Persons who owe or acknowledge Allegiance or Obedience to the King of Great Britain should be removed out of the State; Be it Enacted, by the Authority aforesaid, That all the late Officers of the King of Great Britain, and all Persons (Quakers excepted) being Subjects of this State, and now living therein, or who shall hereafter come to live therein, who have traded immediately to Great Britain or Ireland within Ten Years last past, in their own Right, or acted as Factors, Storekeepers or Agents, here or in any of the United States of America or Ireland, shall take the following Oath of Abjuration or Allegiance, or depart out of the State, viz.

I will bear faithful and true Allegiance to the State of North Carolina, and will truly endeavour to support, maintain, and defend the independent Government thereof, against George the Third, King of Great Britain, and his Successors, and the Attempts of any other Person, Prince, Power, State or Potentate, who by secret Arts, Treasons, Conspiracies, or by open Force, shall attempt to subvert the same, and will in every Respect conduct myself as a peaceful orderly Subject; and that I will disclose and make known to the Governor, some Member of the Council of State, or some Justice of the Superior Courts or of the Peace, all Treasons, Conspiracies, and Attempts, committed or intended against the State, which shall come to my knowledge.

And that all Persons being Quakers, Moravians, Menonists, and Dunkards, and under the Circumstances above mentioned, shall make the following Affirmation, or depart the State:

I, A. B. do solemnly and sincerely declare and affirm, that I will bear true Fidelity to the independent State of North Carolina, and to the Powers and Authorities which are or may be established for the good Government thereof; and I do renounce any Fidelity to the present King of Great Britain, His Heirs and Successors; and that I will disclose and make known to the Governor, some Member of the Council of State, Judge of the Superior Court, or Justice of the Peace, all Treasons, Conspiracies, or Attempts, committed or intended against the same, which shall come to my knowledge.

And the said Oath or Affirmation shall be taken and subscribed in open Court, in the County where the Person or Persons taking the same shall or do usually reside.

VI. And be it further Enacted, by the Authority aforesaid, That the County Courts in each and every County, and every Justice of the Peace in each respective County, shall have full Power to issue Citations against Persons coming within the above Description, as Officers, Merchants, Traders, Factors, Storekeepers, or Agents, and to demand Surety on Recognizance if necessary, and to require their Attendance at the next ensuing Court to be held for the County: And if any Person so cited (due proof being made thereof), shall fail or neglect to attend, or attending shall refuse to take the Oath or Affirmation (as the Case may be) then the said Court shall and may have full Power and Authority to order such Person to depart out of this State, to Europe or the West Indies, within Sixty Days, and may take Bond and Security, in the Name of the Governor, for the Benefit of the State, for faithful Compliance with such Order; and if any Person so ordered shall fail or neglect to depart within the limited Time such Bond shall be forfeited to the State, without good and sufficient Reasons shewn to, and approved of by the Governor and Council; and the Justices, or any of them, in the County wherein the Person so failing or neglecting to depart shall be found, shall and may cause him to be apprehended and brought before the Court of the County where the Order was made; and the said Court shall in such Case send the Person so offending as speedily as may be out of the State, either to Europe or the West Indies, at the Cost and Charges of such Offender, and to this End shall and may direct the Clerk of the Court to issue an Order or Orders to any Sheriff in the State to seize and sell so much of the Goods and Chattels, Lands and Tenements, of such Person within his Bailiwick, as may be judged necessary by said Court to defray such Costs and Charges, together with the Costs and Charges of apprehending and confining such Person until he shall be sent out of the State; and the Sheriff to whom such Order of Court shall be directed, is hereby required to obey the same, and to execute proper Conveyances, and to return the Money arising by any Sale made by Virtue of such Order, after deducting his Fees and Commissions as in other Cases, to the next County Court of the County from whence such Order issued, under the Penalty of Five Hundred Pounds current Money; to be recovered by Action of Debt, in any Court having Cognizance thereof, one Half for the Use of the State, the other Half to the Person that shall sue for the same; and if any Surplus shall remain after paying all Costs and Charges for apprehending, confining, and sending such Person out of the State, then the County Court shall cause such Surplus to be paid the Owner. Provided nevertheless,

Appendix A: North Carolina Law

That all and every such Person or Persons shall have Liberty to sell and dispose of his or their Estates, and after satisfying all just Demands, to export the Amount in Produce (Provisions and Naval Stores excepted) and may also nominate and appoint an Attorney or Attornies to sell and dispose of his or their Estates, for his or their Use and Benefit; but in Case any real Estate belonging to any such Person shall remain unsold for more than Three Months next after the Owner thereof hath departed this State, the same shall be forfeited to and for the Use of the Public.

VII. And be it further Enacted, That if any Person so departing, or sent off from this State, shall return to the same, then such Persons shall be adjudged guilty of Treason against the State, and shall and may be proceeded against in like Manner as is herein directed in Cases of Treason.

VIII. And whereas among other Things it was enacted in an Act, intituled, An Act for declaring what Crimes and Practices against the State, shall be Treason and what shall be Misprison of Treason, and Providing Punishments adequate to Crimes of both Classes, and for preventing the Dangers which may arise from Persons disaffected to the State, that each and every Justice in each respective County may cite any Person or Persons to appear before the County Court where such person or persons usually reside, and take the aforesaid Oath or Affirmation; and in Case of non Attendance or Refusal, the said Court shall and may have full Power to Compel such Person or Persons to leave the State, under the same Regulations herein mentioned in other Cases. And as some Scruples have arisen with Respect to the Manner by Law required for the Service of such Citations, and as by many it has been held that a Service upon the Person of him intended to be cited was necessary, before his Attendance in Court could be legally compelled, as many suspected Persons, by Continual Absence from their Place of Abode, or frequently removing from thence, have rendered the Service of such personal Citations difficult, and in some Cases impracticable, whereby they evade the Intentions of the said Act, and cannot be obliged to take the said Oath prescribed, nor be made subject to the Penalties ordained for neglecting or refusing the same: And whereas there is great Reason to believe that there are divers persons whose intentions are inimical to the State, who would in Case of Invasion by our Enemies, or the Expectation of immediate Support of them, carry such Intentions into Practice, but who artfully in their open Demeanor and Deportment betray no such design, whereby from not incurring particular Suspicion, they have escaped being cited; and as it becomes the Duty of every Member of Society to give proper assurance of fidelity to the Government from which he enjoys Protection, and by their Refusal so to do, the Voice of Reason and Justice, confirmed by the Practice of all Nations, proclaim that they should no longer enjoy the Privileges of Freemen of the said State; and as the Penalties ordained by the said Act have been in great Measure evaded by the Difficulty or Impossibility of procuring Vessels to transport all such Recusants beyond Sea, or from their being unable to pay the Expence of the Voyage, by which Means such Persons still remain within this State, without suffering the Penalties they have justly deserved; Be it further Enacted, by the Authority aforesaid, That the County Court of each respective County which shall sit after the last Day of February, shall divide the County into several Districts, in each of which shall reside one or more Justices of the Peace, which said Justices within their respective Districts are hereby enjoined and required to administer such Oath of Allegiance or Affirmation, as the Case may be, to all free Male Persons above Sixteen Years of Age (Persons non compos Mentis, Prisoners of War, only excepted) and such Justice or Justices in their respective Districts so allotted to him or them, shall immediately after the Sitting of the said Court, in different Parts of the said County, one of which shall be the Court House of the same, and also upon the Church, if any there be, post and publish a Notice in Writing of the Places and Times when and where he or they will attend within their respective Districts to administer such Oath or Affirmation; and all such Persons who are inhabitants of the said Districts respectively (and it is declared that a Residence of one Week shall in this Instance constitute any Person an Inhabitant, seafaring Persons and foreign Traders excepted) being above the Age of Sixteen Years, and of sound Mind, shall at such Time attend upon such Justice of the Peace, and take the Oath or Affirmation required, as the case may be, and subscribe the same in a book which such Justice or Justices shall keep for that Purpose, or in Case of such Juror or Affirmant's Name, which Book or List shall at the next succeeding Court be returned to the said Court, together with the Names of those within his or their respective District refusing or neglecting the same; and if any Person (such only as are by this Act excepted) shall fail to attend, or attending at such Time and Place as he shall have been warned by such public Notice, shall refuse to take the Oath, or make such Affirmation, as the Case may be, except as excused by Sickness or unavoidable Necessity, or other

Appendix A: North Carolina Law

sufficient Reason, to be adjudged of by the next County Court, the Party offering such Excuse proffering at the same Time to take such Oath or Affirmation, as the Case may be, which in this Case such County Court are directed to administer, such Person or Persons so offering, shall be ordered by the said County Court next after such Failure or Neglect, to take the said Oath, or quit the said State, and depart to the West Indies or Europe in Sixty Days; and if he or they shall fail so to do, and shall at the Expiration of such Term be found within this State, then the County Court shall and may, at their Discretion, either exercise the same Power and Authority with Respect to such Person or Persons, in order to compel his or their Departure out of the State, as is herein before provided, with Regard to the late Officers of the King of Great Britain, and Persons who have traded to Great Britain or Ireland within Ten Years last past, or been concerned for, or employed by Persons trading thereto, within the Time aforesaid, or permit him to remain within the State.

IX. And be it further Enacted, by the Authority aforesaid, That all Persons failing or refusing to take the Oath of Allegiance, and permitted by the County Courts, as immediately aforesaid, to remain in the State, shall be adjudged incapable and disabled in Law to have, occupy or enjoy, any Office, Appointment, License, or Election of Trust or Profit, civil or Military, within this State, and shall not be capable of being elected to, or aiding by their Votes to elect another to be a Member of Assembly, and shall not by themselves, or by Deputy, Attorney or Trustee, execute any such Office, Trust or Appointment, and shall be disabled to prosecute any Suit at Law or Equity, or to be Guardians, Executors or Administrators, or capable of any Legacy, or Deed of Gift of Lands, and shall be disabled from taking any Lands by Descent or Purchase, or conveying Lands to others for any Term longer than for one year, and shall not keep Guns or other Arms within his or their house, but the same may be seized by a written Order of a Justice of the County in which he or they reside; and after the Expiration of the said Sixty Days, he or they shall not be permitted to depart this State without Permission first had and obtained from the Governor and Council; and in Case of being suffered to depart, shall give Bond and sufficient Security, if such shall be required, , not to be aiding to the Enemies of this State during his or their Absence; and in Case of their Departure without such Permission had, he or they shall forfeit all their Goods and Chattels, Lands and Tenements, to the Use of the State. Provided nevertheless, That all and every Person who has already taken the Oath, or made the Affirmation prescribed, before any Authority competent by Law to receive the same, upon his producing a Certificate of the same to the Justice or Justices appointed to administer the said Oath or Affirmation in their respective District where he resides, shall be held and deemed a good Subject of the State, and shall enjoy the Privileges thereof, as if he had made such Oath or Affirmation in Manner as by this Law directed.

X. And be it further Enacted, by the Authority aforesaid, That if any Person who has been banished this State for not having taken the Oath of Allegiance, or made the Affirmation agreeable to the aforesaid Act, passed the last Session of Assembly, shall return hither, or who may be banished in Consequence of this Act, then such Persons shall be held and deemed guilty of Treason against the State, and shall and may be dealt with in like Manner as in herein directed in Cases of Treason.

XI. And be it further Enacted, by the Authority aforesaid, That all and every other Act or Acts, and every Clause and Article thereof, heretofore made, within the Purview of this Act, is and are hereby repealed and made void, to all Intents and Purposes.

XII. And be it further Enacted, by the Authority aforesaid, That this Act shall be published in all the Newspapers of this State, as soon as the same shall have obtained the Sanction of both Houses of Assembly.

INDEX

[

[Brantly?]
  Charles, 60
[Torn]hson
  Laml., 36
  Richd., 36
[Torn]llis
  Robert, 137
[Torn]ntagard
  Danold, 40

A

Adair
  John, 33, 54, 69, 99
Adams
  Benjamin, 207
Adare
  John, 39
Adkins
  Silas, 68, 70
Agelston
  James, 57
Aitkin
  James, 59, 70
Aitkins
  Howell, 141
Alford
  [Faded], 119
  Jacob, 33, 62, 70, 101, 112, 113, 119
  Thos., 158
Alfords
  Jacob, 113
Allen
  Elizabeth, 211
  James, 115
  Joel, 57, 69, 159
  Joel[?], 189
  John, 153
Allin
  Ezabella, 216
Amis
  Mary, 133
  Thomas, 33, 70, 119
  Thos., 48
  Thos. Esqr., 133
  Thos., Assessor, 105, 126, 134
Anders
  Captn. Stephen, 102
  John, 34, 105, 107
  John Senr., 34
  Joseph, 34
  Stephen, 33, 105
  William, 70
  Willm., 34
Anderson
  Campbell, 220
  John, 221
  William, 150, 181
  William Junr., 221
  William Senr., 221
Andres
  Capt., 207
  Elisha, 208
  James, 208
  John, 50, 51, 70, 208
  Joseph, 51, 70
  Samuel, 8, 208
  Stephen, 51, 70, 208
  Stephen Junr., 208
Andress
  Andrew, 219
  Saml., 6, 22
Andrew
  Samuel, 10
Andrews
  Absalom, 67
  Asa, 65
  John, 65, 128
  Robert, 65
  Saml., Constable, 70
  Samuel, 33, 65, 70
  Samuel, Constable, 33
  Samuel, Constbl., 65
  Wm., 224
Apley
  Jacob, 164
Aranton
  Benjamin, 44
Ard
  Captain, 161
  James, 34, 41, 60, 65
  Patty, 60, 70
  Reuben, 34
  Ruben, 41
  Simon, 65
  Thomas, 34, 41, 65, 70, 102, 162
Arington
  Benjamin, 33
Armstrong
  John, 218
Arrenton
  Benjamin, 69
Arrington
  Benjn., 122
Ash
  Genl., 5
Ashburn
  Wm., 4
Ashburns
  William, 3
Ashford
  Sreet[sic], 217
  Street, 211
Atkins
  Jesse, 111
  John, 33, 142
  Thomas, 34, 41
Atkinson
  Benjn., 180
  John, 47, 70
  Joseph, 182
  William, 33
Avent
  Thos., 156
Averit
  Lewes, 158
Averitt
  Thomas, 220
Avert
  Thomas, 70
  Thos., 54
Avritt
  William, 197

B

B[?]wn
  David, 55
Bacon
  Job, 31
Badget
  John, 131
Bagget
  Joseph, 73
Baggett
  Joseph, 65
Bailey
  Elizabeth, 39, 55, 70
  James, 29
  Richard, 74
Bain

Index

Daniel, 110, 225
Donald, 50, 194
Baker
Jesse, 66, 74
Robert, 8, 34, 71
Robt., 30, 57, 150
Saml., 28, 57
Samson, 167
Samuel, 28, 211, 215
Baldwand
John, 30
Baldwin
[Torn], 35
Charles, 11, 17, 22, 34, 35, 46, 72, 136, 173, 204
James, 34, 45, 72
John, 17, 30, 35, 36, 49, 173, 197
John Junr, 17
John Junr., 73, 132
John Senr., 35, 46, 72, 136, 203
Joseph, 30, 35, 46, 72, 141, 171, 202
Nathaniel, 34, 35, 72, 170, 204
Nathl., 137
Warren, 139, 173, 204
Will, 35
William, 203
Willm., 142
Baley
Richard, 66
Ballantine
Alexdr., 1, 189
Alexr., 1
Ballintine
Alexander, 224
Barefield
Charles, 74
David, 184
Dempsey, 74
John, 40, 59, 73
Lucke, 129
Luke, 33, 72
Stephen, 128, 200
Barefoot
Jesse, 51
Jessey, 73
William, 35
Barfield
Charles, 67, 118
Dempsey, 67, 118
Luke, 47
Barfil
Willis, 153
Bargwin[?]
John Esqr., 133
Barker

Charles, 66, 74, 183
Barkley
James, 12
Barlow
Jno., 164
Reff[?], 164
William, 101
Wm., 164
Barnes
Abraham, 64, 65
Abram, 185
Elias, 64
Josiah, 64, 112, 113
Micael, 69
Michael, 74, 118, 185
William, 116
William Senr., 172
Barns
Abram, 71
Bartley
James, 12
Bartly
James, 9
Barton
Owel John, 72
Baughard
John, 60, 73
Baxley
Edmund, 65, 73
John, 66, 73
William, 65, 73
Bayman
Saml., 208
Beard
Daniel, 72, 145, 180
Danneil, 221
James, 53, 72, 144, 181, 221
John, 53, 72, 144, 176, 218
Bearfoot
Melea, 171
Beasley
Benjamin, 72
Robert, 72
Beasly
Robert, 31
Beaton
Beaton, 101
Beatty
Willm., 71
Beaty
William, 63
Beaven
Isom, 172
Mary, 172
Bedsoal
John, 158
Thos., 157
Bedsole
John, 195

Thomas, 195
Beesley
Benjamin, 47
Benjn., 134
Robert, 47
Beesly
Abraham, 204
Bell
John, 66, 74, 182
Beloat
Ceasar August, 187
Benbow
Benjamin, 37, 38, 71
Thomas, 37, 71
Thos., 38
Bennent
John, 222
Bennet
James, 54, 72
John, 175
Joseph, 119
Benson
James, 49, 73, 105, 185
James Junr., 210
James Senr., 209
John, 210
William, 210
Bentley
John, 57
Bently
John, 39, 71
Berry
John, 40
Bessell
Henry, 198
Thomas, 198
William, 198
Best
Bryan, 163
John, 161, 199
Beton
David, 114
Betts
William, 201
Betty
William, 101
Beven
Morria, 35
Bevens
Morris, 72
Bevins
Morriss, 47
Bigford
Jeremiah, 44, 71, 143, 172, 201
William, 44, 192
Wm., 125
Biggs
James, 61, 163
Bigs

Index

James, 73
Bird
  Elexander, 30
  Isaac, 184
  William, 18, 67, 74
Biven
  Morris, 135
Black
  Jas, 165, 166
  Neill, 218
Blackiel
  Jesse, 197
Bland
  James, 108
Blankes
  John, 36
Blanks
  John, 142, 169, 202
Blassingale
  Joseph, 201
Blenning
  Elizabeth, 12
    Estate of, 12
Bleu
  Dugald, 39
Blew
  Dugald, 124
  Duncan, 1
  John, 124, 206
  Wm., 167
Blocker
  John, 111
Bloeker
  John, 27
Bloodworth
  David, 192
Blount
  Jacob, 67, 74
  James, 66, 74, 211, 216
  John, 66, 74
  Philip, 18, 74
  Phillip, 66
Blue
  Dugal, 25, 43
  Dugald, 34, 71, 191, 205
  John, 192
  William, 40
Blyth
  John, 105
Boazman
  Joseph, 54
  Sa[Torn], 52
  Saml., 54
  Saml. Junr., 54
  Samuel, 72
Bodiford
  Green, 67, 161
  Greens, 73
Boice

William, 131
Boiey
  Duncan, 60
Bone
  Archabald, 219
  Archd., 180
  Archebald, 42
Bosey
  Duncan, 41
Bosman
  Saml., 6
  Samuel, 105
Bossell
  Henry, Constable, 35
Bosswell
  Henry, 133
Boswell
  Henry, 33
  Henry, Constable, 72
Bourdoux
  Israel, 50
Bovey
  Malcolm, 42
Bowen
  Sarah, 71, 111
Bowman
  Joshua, 12, 34
Boyces
  William, 33
Boyd
  [Torn], 39
  John, 57, 71, 109
  Jon, 57
Boyit
  William, 33
Boyswell
  Henry, Constable, 34
Bozeman
  Samuel, 103
Bozman
  Saml., 72
  Samuel, 5
Bradford
  William, 146
Bradley
  Archd., 39, 71, 192
  Archibald, 34
  Asbell, 121
  James, 211, 214
  Richard, 14
Bradly
  Archibald, 43
Brafford
  Edward, 222
  William, 180
Branches
  David Gam branch, 2
Brantly
  Benjamin, 60, 73

Thomas, 30
Branton
  John, 33, 34, 47, 72
  John Junr., 128
  John Senr., 129
  Maturin, 200
  Saml., 35
  Saml. Jr., 35
Branty
  Benjamin, 146
Brassel
  Nathan, 168
Brassel[?]
  Benjamin, 168
Brassell
  Benjamin, 222
Braveboy
  David, 67, 74
Bridges
  Bluff Bridge, 18
  Jesse [?], 31
Brigers
  Joseph, 67
Briggers
  Joseph, 74
Bright
  James, 131, 199
  Richd., 129
  Robert, 198
  simon, 34
  Simon, 33, 71, 131
  Simon Junr., 198
  Simon Senr., 198
Brit
  Isams, 44
  Lemuel, 69
  Richard, 44
  Simon, 44
Britt
  Benja., 184
  Benjamin, 41
  Lamuel, 184
  Samuel, 74
Brittish, 16
Broades
  Peter, 50, 73
Brodie
  Alexander, 71
  Alexr., 59
Broom
  Mark, 161
Browder
  Thomas, 44, 193
  Thoms., 71
  Thos., 120, 206
Brown
  Anguish, 7, 14, 25
  Angus, 101, 162
  Capt. George, 205

Index

Colo, 17
Colo., 17
Edmund, 68, 74
Elisha, 183
Elizabeth, 211
Elizth., 215
George, 39, 43, 55, 70, 99, 106, 194, 206
George Esqr, 34
George Esqr., 154
Hugh, 18, 20, 65, 73, 164, 168
Hugh Junr., 163
Jesse, 209
Jno, 226
John, 38, 106, 109, 117
John Esqr., 187
Neil, 114
Neill, 63, 65, 71, 73, 102, 162
Richard, 225
Thomas, 17, 38, 68, 71, 109, 225
    Claim against Tories, 17
Thos., 37, 38
Thos. Esqr., 187
William, 17, 34, 44, 65, 71, 121, 194
Wm., 163, 206
Brown Marsh, 23
Brumble
Elisabeth, 117
Eliza., 183
Brumlow
James, 147
Brumpton Plantation, 11
Brunswick County, 12, 27
Bryan
Amey, 39, 71
Ammey, 57
Bennet, 30
David, 70
Edward, 39, 70
Edwd., 56
Idam[?], 56
Jean, 39
John, 43, 125, 211, 217
Jonathan, 30
Philamon, 217
Philemon, 25
Phill., 211
Phillemon, 70
Phillm., 56
Stephen, 55, 70, 211, 217
Thomas, 44, 71
William, 25, 43, 191, 204, 211, 215
William Junr., 125
William Senr., 202

Willm., 71
Wm. Senr., 125
Bryant
Bartram, 196
Ezekiel, 45, 72, 127
John, 170
Bryon
[Torn], 100
David, 156
Edward, 155
Elizth., 152
John, 152
Philemon, 156
Steaphen, 151
William, 151
Buchan
David, 165, 219
Buchar
Jno., 164
Bud
Thomas, 101
Buey
Duncan, 73
Malcom, 63, 71
Buie
Archd., 166
Dun., 167
John, 161, 163
Bullard
Henry, 54, 72
John, 68, 74
Bullock
Charles, 67, 74, 118, 185
Buoie
Malcum, Soldier, 101
Burdox
Peter, 185
Burges
Malaciah, 176
Malica, 146
Burgess
Malikiah, 220
Burley [Busby?]
Ezekiel, 121
Burney
Simon, 34, 39, 71, 122
Will Senr., 35
William, 172, 191
William Junr., 35, 48, 73, 140
William Senr., 46, 72, 135
Willm. Senr., 34
Wm., 207
Burns
Capt., 182
Burny
Simon, 43
Busby
Ezekiel, 44, 206

William, 45, 72
Butlar
Joseph, 61
Saml., 181
Stephen, 61
Butler
Henery, 209
John, 33, 34, 73, 101
Joseph, 73, 148, 174, 222
Mary, 222
Moses, 65, 73
Saml., 150
Samuel, 59, 73
Stephen, 73
William, 40, 59, 73
Zac, 223
Butlers
Samuel, 223
Buttler
John, 48
Buzby
Ezekiel, 71
Byar
Edward, 30
Byrd
William, 18
Byrn
Capt., 174
Lawrence, 72
Margaret, 70, 177
Margt., 55
Peter, 72
Byrne
Laurance, 143
Lawrence, 53
Margaret, 149
Mathew, 180
Mathew Senr., 222
Matthew, 53, 145
Peter, 53, 144, 180, 219
Byrns
Margaret, 222
Byrns[?]
Peter, 11

C

Cabeen[?]
John, 211
Cade
Elizabeth, 20
John, 20, 64, 75
John Esqr, 20
Cahoon
Micajah, 76
Cain
James, 58, 75, 152, 156, 175, 197, 222
John, 58, 159, 196

Index

Jos., 59
Joseph, 75, 150, 181, 223
Mrs. Olive, 16
Neal, 197
Olive, 16, 176, 222
    Claim against Peter
      Mallett[?], 16
    Claim against Tories, 16
Saml, 16
Saml., 7, 9, 11, 58, 159, 174, 182
Saml., Assessor, 143, 159
Samuel, 74, 197, 222
William, 16, 74, 75, 149, 156, 158
Wm., 54, 58

Cairsey
Jacob, 62
John, 62

Cake
Philip, 215

Calihan
Cornelus, 224
Martain, 224
Peirce, 224

Callum
Donald, 24
Richd., 19

Cambell
Anguish, 37
John, 37

Cambelson
Duncan, 75

Cambeskon
John, 30

Camble
John, 224

Cameron
Anguish, 75
Lach, 165

Cammeron
Anguish, 62

Camons
Angus, 212

Camp
Joseph, 151

Campbel
Anguish, 38

Campbell
A.G., 29
Alexander, 200
Anguish, 57
Angus, 74
Archd., 21, 75, 123, 194
Archibald, 21, 43, 206
Cathn., 193
Daniel, 50, 59, 162
Danl., 76
Danold, 101

Dun., 167
Duncan, 63
Hugh, 63
James, 21, 24, 38, 193, 206
Jo, 57
John, 24, 38, 74, 75, 106, 108, 123, 188, 193, 206
John Junr., 57, 74, 206
Laughlan, 63
Laughlin, 75
M[?], 167
Martha, 50, 77
Mary, 187
Wm., 106

Campble
Neal, 224

Campell
John, 43

Camren
Lauthren, 41

Canady
Isaac, 40
John, 38
Samuel, 59
Samuel Senr., 41

Cane
Samuel, 118

Cannady
Samuel, 76

Cannon
Archibald, 199

Caps
William, 69, 76, 112

Caright
Joseph, 27

Carlile
Alex, 161

Carman
Saml., 54, 75, 142
Samuel, 202

Carpenter
Deter, 105

Carr
James, 196

Carrel
Sanday, 220

Carright
Clo[?] S, 27
Richard, 27

Carsey
John, 75
Thomas, 66, 76

Carslile
Robert, 161

Carter
Henry, 61, 77
Isaac, 68, 184
James, 76
James Junr., 68, 76, 183

James Senr., 68, 183
Jesse, 61, 77, 158
John, 61, 77, 147
Joseph, 61, 77, 157
Luke, 182
Mark, 68, 182
William, 119

Cartright
Solomon, 27

Cartwright
Joseph, 199

Carver
[?], 35
Isham, 223
James, 37, 148, 149
Jesse, 148, 149, 181, 222
John, 148, 149
Mary, 148, 149
Sam, 148
Saml., 148
Sampson, 41, 147, 181

Cashwell
James, 197
John, 156, 195
Thomas, 196
Thos., 157

Caswell
Richard, 6, 26
Richard Esqr., 19, 20, 21, 26
Richard Esquire Governor, 5

Cessome
Thos., 156

Champin
William, 145

Champion
William, 220

Chancey
Demsey, 201
Edmund, 39
John, 48, 136
Miriam, 172
Thomas, 31
Zachariah, 139, 172
Zachriah, 36

Chancy
Edmund, 75
John, 76

Chang
John, 30

Chansey
Edmond, 58
Zachariah, 202

Chason
Joseph, 75, 179, 218

Chavers
Bud, 68
William, 31

Chavious
John, 200

239

Index

Chavous
Gills, 194
John, 31
Cheser
Richard, 61
Chesher
Richard, 152
Richd., 216
William, 215
Cheshire
Richard, 77
Richd., 211
William, 211
Chester
Nickson, 136
Cheves
John, 64, 75
Chicken
John, 35
Child
Francis, 39
Chisher
William, 152
Chishire
Wm., 24
Clarady
Capt., 105
Clardy
Capt., 134
James, 48, 76, 140, 172, 203
Clark
[?]arde, 195
Archd., 63
Benja., 53
Benjamin, 75, 145
Benjamin Jnr., 158
Benjn., 158
Charles, 158
David, 30, 33, 130
George, 199
Henry, 61, 77, 158, 196
Jno., 30
John, 46, 76, 135, 171, 202
Mary, 179, 221
William, 8, 10, 178, 221
Claim against Tories, 10
Wm, 10
Wm., 8
Clarke
Dugald, 224
James, 30
Claton
Benoni, 108
Benony, 37, 38
Clayton
Benoni, 75, 189, 224
Cliburn
Joshua, 68
Nathan, 69, 76
Robert, 68, 76
William, 68, 76, 117
Clifton
Baseman, 196
Clyburn
John, 62, 75
Cobean
John, 216
Cohone
John, 35
Will, 35
Cohoon
John, 46, 138, 171
Mary[?], 174
Micajah, 46, 141, 170, 201
William, 138
Wm., 169
Colbert
Abel, 42
Coleman
Dennis, 75
Jno, 33
Jno., 6, 22, 33
John, 28, 127, 199
John Junr., 198
John, Constable, 45, 76
Moses, 6, 22, 33, 45, 76, 126, 199
Theophilus, 27, 199
Collemn
[Torn]is, 52
Collom
Dennis, 151
Collum
Richard, 202
Colvil
Maturin, 8
Colvill
Maturin, 9, 13, 39, 76
Confiscation of Estate, 9
Colville
Maturin, 15, 119
Colvills Estate, 9
Commissioners of Confiscated Property, 9
Commons
Joseph, 223
Conerly
John, 37
Connelley
John, 112
Connelly
Cullen, 19
Conner
Tarrance, 175
Cook
Danel, 208
Daniel, 51, 77
James, 29
John, 18
Mr. James, 29
Stephen, 29
William, 65, 76
Willm., 100
Cooke
Danel, 103
Cooper
Benjamin, 147
Joseph, 41, 61, 76
Mary, 147
Sellers, 105
Corbet
Abel, 177
Able, 144
James, 59
Judith, 41, 59
Corbins
Reuben, 172
Corbit
Abel, 220
Judith, 76
Cordel
Absolam, 146
Correnton
Mary, 153
Corry
John, 105
Council
Davd., 171
David, 203
James, 9, 147, 171, 175, 220
James Esquire, 9
James, Trustee for Fred. Grage, 147
Jams., trustee for James Brumlow, 147
Jas., 143
Mr., 18
Robert, 13, 219
Claim against Levi Glass, 13
Robt., 180
Councill
Chas., 167
James Esquire, 18
Jno., 167
John, 18, 146
Counsel
David, 31
Cowan
John, 24, 211, 214
Cox
Gilbert, 68, 76, 117, 183
John, 68, 76, 183
Simon, 68, 76, 116, 184
Thomas, 39
Craft
Jas., 166

Index

Crawford
 Da[?], 161
Creal
 Lazarus, 63
Creek
 Whites Creek, 38
Creeks
 Drowning Creek, 106
 Rockford Creek, 18
 Whites Creek, 37, 38
Creel
 Lazarus, 75
 Thomas, 61, 76
Crews
 John, 47, 76
Cromarte
 James, 24
Cromartie
 William, 24
 Wm., 24
Cromarty
 William, 51, 105
Cromerty
 William, 75, 207
Crometey
 William, 104
Crowson
 Jacob, 27, 28
 William, 75
Cruis
 William, 42
Cudington
 John, 58
Culbreath
 John, 219
 Neal, 40
Cumberland County, 9, 15, 18
Cumbo
 Cannon, 55, 74, 162
 Gibeon, 162
Currey
 Archd., 114
Currie
 Alice, 206
 Even, 24
Curry
 Alexr, 164
 Alice, 193
 Daniel, 37, 38, 39, 75
 Edward, 196
 Neil, 23, 120
 Saml., 55, 150
 Samuel, 74

D

Daffor
 Jeremiah, 38
Daffron
 Jeremiah, 225
Dafron
 Jarymiah, 188
Daniel
 Benjamin, 69
 Enoch, 29
 John, 29, 69
 Margaret, 169
 O., 28
 Overton, 28
 Robert, 140
 Sarah, 139
 Shadrach, 30
 Stephen, 138
Danneil
 John, 220
Dannel
 David, 179
Daragh
 Arch., 56
 John, 56
Darrach
 Archd., 78
 John, 188
Darrah
 [Torn], 225
 Archd., 154
 Archibald, 39
 John, 154, 223
Davice
 Turner, 38
Davidson
 Richd., 110
Davis
 Abram, 113
 Baxter, 157, 196
 Edward, 39, 55, 77, 151
 Edward G., 198
 Ezekiah, 37
 Ezekiel, 105
 Francis, 156, 208
 Henry, 195
 Hezekiah, 185
 Hezekiah, 50, 77, 209
 John, 110, 157, 196, 210
 Joseph, 173, 191, 209
 Sampson, 156, 197
 Solomon, 197
 Thomas, 137
 Turner, 37, 77, 107, 185, 189
 William, 39, 78, 188
 Wm., 58, 112
Dawson
 Dempsey, 33, 126
 Thomas, 77
 Thos., 36
Decamp
 John, 211
Demery
 Allen, 174
 John, 142
Demry
 John, 171
Demsy
 Dawson, 77
Den
 John, 7
Denton
 William, 219
Devane
 John, 207, 208
Dewey
 Euphronica, 225
Dimery
 John, 30
Dimory
 John, 201
Doan
 Ester, 39
Doane
 Ephraim, 51
 Jaremiah, 208
 Jeremiah, 51, 77
Doboys
 Demcey, 47
 Demsey, 77
Dofford
 Jeremiah, 37
Done
 Hezekiah, 14
 Jeremiah, 105
 John, 105
Donelley
 John, 113
Donnelly
 John, 112
Doors
 John, 204
Dore
 John, 172
Dores
 Frederick, 35
 John, 35, 47, 77, 137
Dormand
 John, 40
Douge
 Talley, 41
Douglass
 Kei[?], 163
Dowey
 James, 77, 107, 188, 224
Dowlace[?]
 William, 39
Dowlas
 William, 77, 211, 218
 Wilm., 55
Dowles
 William, 150

Index

Downey
Daniel, 110, 224
Donald, 78
Donnal, 57
Downney
Daniel, 188
Dowy
James, 50
Dridin
John, 155
Driggers
Ephraim, 64, 77
Drinkwater
Daniel, 182
Drurie
Evie, 168
Drybrow
Thos., 37
Drydand
John, 56
Dryden
John, 77
Drydon
John, 39
Du Pee
James, 201
Dubois
Jane, 77, 110
William, 142
Wm., 173
Duboise
Jean, 50
Ducamp
John, 216
DuCamp
John, 143
Due
Seth, 40, 142
Dula[?]
Seth, 171
Duncan
David, 127
Dunkin
James, 119
DuPee
Jos. G., 205
Dupre
James, 134, 172
Lewis, 135
Dupree
James, 77
Jas., 48
Dye
Avery, 179
Dyson
Leonard, 198
Solomon, 35, 45, 77, 132
Thomas, 45, 77
Thos., 129

E

Eagleson
James, 225
Earrd
Jas, 164
Eason
Benjamin, 200
Edge
John, 158, 195
William, 195, 196
Edward
Charles, 203
Edwards
Charles, 31
John, 27, 29
Mr. John, 29
Newat, 106
Pharibe, 163
Robert, 78, 177, 222
Robt., 53, 145
Samuel, 66, 78
William, 69, 78
Egleson
James, 187
Eglestor
J, 15
James, 15
    Claim against Maturin
        Colville, 15
Eglison
Jas., 108
Eknar
Felix, 164
Eless
James, 35
John, 35
Willm., 35
Eliza. Town, 5, 21
Elizabeth Town, 24, 26
Elless
Robert, 170
Elletson
Gooden, 190, 225
Ellis
Capt., 159
Capt. William, 156
Captain, 143
Evan, 52, 78
Evin, 153
J., 1, 22, 24, 28
James, 30, 42, 47, 78, 135, 149, 173, 177, 204, 220
Jno. esqr, 28
John, 78, 136, 173, 201, 211, 215
John Junr., 35
Thos., 136
William, 21, 52, 194, 196

Willm., 78
Wm., 120, 206
Elliss
John, 47
Elmore
William, 178
Elwell
Benjamin, 50, 78, 185, 209
Richard, 41
Richd., 150
Ervin
James, 58, 155, 212
Jaret, 153
Jarred, 211
Erwin
James, 216
Jarred, 215
Esom
Thos., 50
Estates
Benjamin Willis, 222
Brittain Jones Deceas'd, 202
Dd. Morley's, 215
Doctr. Hall, 110
G. Waddell's, 186
Genl Waddell, 107
Genl. Waddell's, 209
George Lyon's, 211, 216
Isaac Ray, Deceased, 220
Isham Carver's, 223
J. Cooper's, 222
James McDaniel's, 219
Jas. Baldwin's Estate, 142
Jas. Carver, 112
Jno. Owen's, 216
John [?]eler, Deceased, 220
John Bryon, 152
John Owen's, 213
John Powell, Deceas'd, 205
Joseph Lock's, 222
Mosley's, 214
Richd. Lloyd's, 185, 209
S. Smith, 210
Samuel Butler's, 223
Wm. Ross's, 215
Eustace
Judith, 143
Evens
David, 223
Theophilus, 223
Evers
James, 25, 154, 212, 218
Samuel, 41
Evins
Elizth., 148

F

Fair Bluff, 27

Index

Fair Cloth
Lucrecia, 174
Faircloth
Jacob, 68, 79
Fairley
Alexr., 63
Archd., 63
John, 63
Reuben, 63
Fairly
Archibald, 101
John, 78, 102
Falk
John, 202
Faning
David, 10
Fanning
David, 8, 11
Farrell
Cornelius, 193
Fason
James, 217
Faulk
Philip, 200
Richard, 200
Faun
James, 212
Fayetteville, 7
Fayette-Ville, 7
Fayetteville District, 7
Fen
Richard, 7
Ferrell
Richmond, 18
Ferries
Waddles Ferry, 24
Fiels
Michel, 166
Finlay
Daniel, 186
Finlow
Daniel, 211
Finney
Thomas, 41
Fitchet
Christan, 171
Micajah, 203
Fitchrandolph
Benjamin, 61
Fitz. Randolph
Benjn., 150, 216
Fitzgerald
Thos., 205
Fitzrandolph
Benja. Junr., 24
Benja. Senr., 24
Benjamin, 29, 39, 212
Benjamn., 29
Fitz-Randolph
Benjamin, 79

Fiveash
Demsey, 62
John, 62, 78
Flanagan
William, 129
Flin
Daniel, 78
Flinn
Daniel, 8, 35, 44, 127, 198
John, 8, 10, 132, 198
    Claim against William
    White, 10
Flow
Willm., 38
Flowers
Arick[?], 66
Drewry, 66
Edward, 66, 79, 117
Henry, 69, 117
Ignatious, 19, 20, 33, 132, 200
Ignatius, 47, 78
John Senr., 118
William, 66, 69
Floyd
Richard, 49
William, 209
Fogartee
Edmond, 188
Fogarty
Edmond, 209
Foke
James, 203
Fokes
Jacob, 46, 78, 131, 198
James, 46, 139, 169
John, 46, 78, 130, 199
Josiah, 199
William, 131, 199
Folk
James, 169
John, 140, 171
Forgason
Alexander, 116
Elexander, 101
James, 102, 114
Malcom, 115
Malcum, 101
Neill, 101
Niel, 115
Forguson
James, 42
Forrester
William, 39, 79
Forster
Wm., 55
Fort
Elias, 42, 102
John, 162

Joseph, 67, 78, 162
Forts
Sherwood, 221
Foster
William, 192
Fouler
John, 104
fowler
John, 105
Fowler
Edward, 152
Elipha, 175
John, 78
Freeman
[Torn]ham, 36
Abraham, 48, 78, 141
Abram, 31
Benjamin, 65, 79
James, 30
Joseph, 56
Roger, 48, 78, 141
Saml., 79, 141
Samuel, 51
Steaphen, 148
William, 48, 65, 78
Willm., 36, 141
Freman
Roger, 169

G

Gadby
Thomas, 9
Galano
Tobe, 27
Gallaway
Ann, 130
Gape way, 106
Gardner
James, 51, 105, 196
Gardnier
James, 79
Garrat
Mary, 25
William, 25
Garret
Mary, 25, 26
Garvin
John, 209
Gates
Edward, 176, 218
James, 61, 79
Jane, 218
Janet, 149
John, 61, 79, 176, 219
Peter, 176, 221
Gautier
Captain Thos., 226
Josiah R., 226

Index

T.N., 27
Thomas S., 28
Thos., 226
Gay
  James, 51
Gernagan
  Abraham, 28
Gesop
  Isaac, 195
Gibbert
  John, 203
Gibbs
  Geo., 202
  John, 39, 202
  Josiah, 202
  Margaret, 48
  Robert, 202
Gibs
  Margaret, 80
Gibson
  Walter, 5
Giffard
  James, 59
  Jamie, 79
Gilbert
  John, 193
Gilchrist
  John, 63
Gilcrease
  John, 116
  John, Soldier, 101
Gilcriest
  John, 80
Gillis
  John, 102
Glas
  Levi, 12
Glass
  Levey, 41
  Levi, 12, 13, 14, 79
  Levy, 7, 14, 25, 60
  Solomon, 9, 10
Glear
  Stephen, 133
Gleer
  Stephen, 69, 79
Goddin
  David, 11
Godfrey
  William, 40, 177
  William Senr., 221
Goding
  David, 22
Godwin
  Alexander, 6, 22, 197
  Alexr., 126
  David, 12, 17, 18, 33, 35, 48, 80, 126
  Eleazr, 35
  Pierce, 132, 200

Stephen, 6, 22, 132, 198
Godwing
  David, 22
Goff
  Lewis, 31
Goodwin
  Christopher, 39
Grage
  Fred., 147
Graham
  Alexander, 39, 79
  Alexr., 56
  Alxr., 110
  Arthur, 179, 219
  Faith, 59
  Faithful, 107
  Faithfull, 9, 79
  Henry, 13, 38, 39, 79, 111
  Neill, 62, 79
  Rachel, 145
Grange
  John, 38
Grantham
  Edward, 68, 79, 117
  John, 112
  Richard, 79, 119
  Richard, Constable, 68
Graves
  Benja., 105
Gray
  [Torn]ham, 39
  Abraham, 56, 79, 150
Green
  [?], 35
  Aga[?]lly, 224
  Aquilla, 173
  Caleb, 170, 202
  Eliz., 80
  Eliza., 47
  Hill, 35
  James, 136, 170, 204
  Jas, 35
  John, 44, 80, 131, 200
  Simon, 49, 80, 132, 193, 198
  William, 142, 202
  Wm., 169
Gregory
  Abigald, 225
Grice
  Robert, 79
Griffin
  Andrew, 79, 106, 117
  Andrew Junr., 66
  Andrew Senr., 66
  James, 66
  Joseph, 206
  William, 67, 153
Grifin
  Andrew, 113

James, 113
Grimes
  Duncan, 162
  Elexander, 101
Grise
  Robert, 61
Grist
  Robt., 158
Groom
  Isaac, 64, 80
Guiton
  Jacob, 154
  James, 218
  Saml., 155
Gunn
  John, 39
Guyton
  James, 212
  Saml., 79
Gytan
  Sam, 57

H

Haddick
  Drury, 173
haddock
  Drure, 30
  Henry, 31
Haddock
  Drury, 143, 203
Hadley
  Thomas, 8
  Thos, 8
Haer
  Ann, 195
Hails
  Samuel, 61, 80
Hails[?]
  Saml., 157
Hains
  Thos., 22, 100, 154
Hairgrove
  Britton, 174
  Burwell, 82
Hairgroves
  Burril, 204
Hall
  Burrill, 201
  Docter Thos., 12
  Eliza., 12
  Elizabeth, 12
  Enoch, 81, 101
  Enuch, 63
  Isaac, 101, 119
  Isaac Junr., 63, 81
  Isaac Senr., 63
  Lewis, 63, 81, 101
  Lewis Junr., 63, 81, 101

Index

Lues, 119
William, 12
Halloway
David, 145, 221
Hammon
John, 65, 81
Richard, 66
Richd., 81, 183
Hanchey
Jacob, 45, 130
Martain, 27
Hanchy
Jacob, 33
Handen
[Faded] Junr., 101
Handon
Jos., 56
Hankins
Gideon, 192
Hanna
John, 26
Hardcastle
Elizth., 193
Wm., 206
Hardiwick
Allan, 35
Linville, 35
Thomas, 35
Thomas Junr., 35
Hardwick
Allen, 45, 81, 131, 198
Linvill, 130
Saml., 128
Thomas, 45, 81
Thomas Junr., 45
Thoms. Junr., 82
Thos. Junr., 127
Thos. Senr., 127
Harget
John, 187
Hargrove
Britain, 140
Brittain, 30, 203
Burrel, 173
Burrell, 143
Burwell, 47, 172
Harison
Margt., 212
Harper
George, 129
John, 66, 81
Shadrach, 127
Harrel
George, 67
Jesse, 66
Harrell
Elisha, 65, 163
Jesse, 162
Harrison
[Torn] Junr., 55
Captain, 143
Edward, 155
Jno., 7, 22
John, 152
John junr., 11
John Junr., 80, 152
John Senr., 61, 80
Margaret, 216
Prichard, 52
Richard, 81
Richd., 155
William, 11, 152
Harrisons
Capt., 159
Hart
John, 63
Harvey
Alexander, 39
Alexr., 99, 151
John, 28
Robert, 28
Robt., 28
Hase
Isaac, 102
Jacob, 102
Hatcher
Robert, 106
Timothy, 106
Hawkins
Giddion, 206
Hawthorn
Cader, 18
John, 18
Nathaniel, 182
Hayes
Joshua, 121, 194
Joshua Junr., 44
Southy, 47
Suthey, 130
Thos., 44
Haynes
Thomas, 39
Thos., 22
    Claim against Tories, 22
Hays
Balitha, 81
Belitha, 69
Isaac, 51, 81, 105
Joshua, 44, 80, 200
Robert, 69
Sirthy, 33
Sothey, 198
Southy, 82
Thomas, 80
Unity, 39
Henderson
Dun., 166
Duncan, 44, 80, 123, 193, 207
Richard, 7
Thomas, 13
Thos., 13
Hendon
Josiah, 80, 152, 212, 216
William, 39, 80, 155
Wm., 55
Hendry
Alexander, 24, 208
Charles, 24
James, 24, 208
Herrell
Elisha, 81
George, 81
Jesse, 81
Hester
Jasper, 212, 218
John, 154, 212, 215
Joseph, 212
Steaphen, 150, 154
Stephen, 212
Thomas, 39, 212, 217
Thos., 154
Thos. Junr., 154
William, 212
Hesters
Joseph, 217
Hestor
William, 217
Hestors
Stephen, 57, 80
Thos. Junr., 100
high
Esau, 31
Hill
Abram, 119
Ezekiel, 45, 82, 129
George, 107
Joel, 127
John, 39, 154
John, Constable, 55, 80
Macajah, 198
Philip, 24
Hilliard
John, 153, 177, 217
Hillyard
John, 212
Hobbs
Hardy, 134
Isaac, 31, 171, 202
Joseph, 30, 202
Hodge
[Torn], 102
Moses, 102
Robert, 100, 194, 200
Robt., 151
Hogan

Index

Zachariah, 117
Holliman
  Samuel, 27
Hollingsworth
  Elizth., 180
  Isaac, 157
  John, 81, 145
  Sam., 148
  Saml., 148
  Samuel, 177, 220
  Stephen, 81, 179
  Stephen Junr., 52
Holloway
  David, 179
Hollowell[?]
  Stephen, 195
Holmes
  Moses, 38, 80, 111
Holms
  Moses, 189, 225
Holt
  Thomas, 80
  Thos., 58
Homes
  Edmond, 203
  John, 37
  Moses, 37
Horn
  Hardy, 68, 81, 130
  Nathan, 68, 81
  Richard, 68
  William, 66
Horse
  Robert Esqr., 12
How
  William, 80, 108
How[?]
  William, 37
Howard
  Hezekiah, 50, 81
  James, not of age, 207
  Jesse, 4
  John, 4, 51, 81, 105
  Joseph, 3
  Joseph Junr, 4
  Joseph Junr., 3
  Thomas, 39, 57, 80
  Thos., 154
  Titus, 3, 4
  William, 105, 179
Howe
  Arthur, 225
Howell
  Thos., 223
Huffam
  Hudnal, 49, 81
  Hudnall, 105
  John, 208
  Richard, 49, 81

Huffham
  Hudnall, 185
  Hudnell, 210
Hughes
  Samuel, 3
  Samuel Senr., 3
Hull
  Willis, 174
Humphrey
  Benjamin, 150
  Benjm., 58
  Benjn., 99
  Chambers, 67, 81, 161
Humphreys
  Benjamin, 39, 80
Hunchy
  Jacob, 81

I

Ikener
  Michael, 15
Ikner
  Michael, 82
  Philip, 42, 59
  Phillip, 82
Indians
  Indian Wench Hannah. *See* Slaves:Indian Wench Hannah
Inman
  Hardy, 68, 82, 116, 185
  James, 69, 82, 118
Insurgents
  Commanded by David Fanning, 11
Irwin
  Jared, 21, 22
Isham
  James, 52, 83, 152
Ivey
  Adam, 68, 82, 184
  Benjamin, 69, 82
  Curtis, 7
  Francis, 69, 82, 118, 182
  George, 68
  Henry, 146
  Isham, 65, 82
  Jeremiah, 65, 82
  Lewis, 69, 82, 118, 182
  Thomas, 65, 82

J

Jackson
  James, 61, 82, 147, 177, 222
  John, 63, 66, 83, 201, 220
  Thomas, 66, 82

Thos, 65
Jacobs
  James, 31
  Samuel, 31
  Shaderick, 31
James
  Soloman, 82, 183
  Soloman Sr., 183
  Solomon, 67
Jay
  Elisha, 30
Jenkins
  Lewis, 65, 82, 163
Jernigan
  Abraham, 27
Jessop
  Isaac, 83, 145
Jesup
  Isaac, 180
Johens[?]
  Hezekiah, 196
John
  Jacob, 35
John Howard Landing, 4
Johnson
  Capt., 195
  Charles, 197
  Daniel, 196
  John Junr., 35
  John Senr., 35, 45
  Rachel, 181
  Saml., 54
  Simon, 35
  Thomas, 35, 198
  William, 35
  Wm., 54
Johnston
  Alexr., 165
  Angus, 166
  Archd., 166
  Charles, 157
  Dond., 166
  Hugh, 204
  James, 157
  Jno., 165
  John, 40, 60, 63, 82
  John Junr., 45, 83, 128
  John Senr., 83, 129
  Lazarous, 168
  Lazarus, 41, 144
  Nehemiah, 33, 45, 83
  Rachael, 221
  Saml., 157
  Thomas, 45, 83, 131
  Thos., 194
  William, 83, 128
  Wm., 156
Jones
  Brittain, 202

Index

Britton, 138
Chloe, 171
Edward, 24, 54, 154, 212, 217
Ezekiah, 54, 158
Henry, 30
Hezekiah, 83
Isaac, 19, 51, 54, 83, 212, 215
Isaac Esqr., 153
Isaac Junr., 54
Jesse, 21, 22, 201, 207
John, 37, 38, 82
Josiah, 31
Matthew, 17, 113
Musgrove, 24, 212, 217
Robert, 17, 69, 113
Robt., 82
Simon, 30
Stephen, 174
Thomas, 134
Thos, 35
Thos., 172, 204
Will, 65
William, 37, 68, 82, 110, 224
Willm., 189

Jonston
Wm., 58

Jordan
Thomas, 200

K

Kelley
Archibald, 205
Duncan, 163
John, 207
Mathew, 205

kelly
John, 192

Kelly
Archd., 192
Archibald, 44, 83, 123
John, 43, 83, 120
Mathew, 192
Matthew, 43, 83, 120
P., 28
Patrick, 28

Kemp
John, 212, 216
Joseph, 83, 212, 214
Joseph Junr., 212, 215

kenedy
Isaac, 161

Kenedy
Sam., 168

Kennedy
John, 127

Kerr
Margaret, 134
Thomas, 192

Kersey
Mary, 184

Kervin
Thos., 146

Kid
David, 100

Kindlow
Thomas, 55

King
Abraham, 33, 83
Abram, 48
Duncan, 137, 172, 204
John, 5, 9, 58, 83, 159
John, Assessor, 143, 159

Kinlaw
Thos., 151

Kinlow
Thomas, 83

Kirby
William, 176

Kirk Patrick
Willm., 145

kirkpatrick
William, 223

Kirkpatrick
William, 40
Willm., 12
Wm., 12
  Claim against Tories, 12

Knowle
Geo., 21

Knowles
George, 21

Knowls
George, 100, 212, 217
James, 100

Kook
William, 154

Kurry
Neil, 43
Neill, 83

L

Lafferstedte
Eric, 220

Lakes
Waccamaw Lake, 30

Lalleestedt
E., 175

Lam
Arthur, 84

Lamb
Arthur, 68, 182
Campbell, 182
John, 37, 108, 186, 202
Meardy[?], 185

Meedy, 68
William, 67, 84

Lambardson
Uriah, 60

Lamberdson
Uriah, 84

Lambert
John, 201
Richard, 204
Uriah, 168

Lambethson
Benjn., 139
Cortney, 170
Richd., 140

Lammons
Angus, 216

Lamond
Duncan, 124

Landill
William, 119

Lansdell
Benjamin, 176
Benjn., 148, 220
John, 181
William, 175

Lansedell
John, 221

Lariman
Duncan, 191

Larkins
James, 185, 208

Laslet
John, 193

Laslie
Joseph, 205

Lasly
John, 156

Laurance
Cielia, 178

Law
David, 185

Lawson
Demcy, 48
Frances, 43
Francis, 84, 123, 200

Le Compt
John, 11

Led
Wm., 24

Lee
Jacob, 207
Jesse, 117
Jesse Junr., 185
Jesse Senr., 184
John, 66, 84
Joshua, 191, 198
Lucy, Widow, 182
Shadarick, 84
Shadrach, 66
Shadrick, 18

Index

Zachariah, 68, 84
Legett
  Absolem, 41, 61
  David, 144
  John, 41
  Rachel, 61
Leggett
  Absolem, 84
  Rachel, 84
Lemmon
  Duncan, 83
Lennen
  Denis, 84
Lenning
  Dennis, 44
Lennon
  Dennis, 124, 191, 206
  Duncan, 205
  John, 39, 58, 83, 125, 218
Lenox
  John, 212
Leonard
  Samuel, 201
Lesley
  J.S., 55
Lessley
  John, 55, 83
Leveston
  John, 39
Lewes
  Hanson, 30
Lewis
  Aaron, 194, 205
  Benj, 27
  Benj., 28
  D, 27
  H. Junr., 36
  Handson Junr., 140
  Handson Senr., 140
  Hanson, 169, 202
  Hanson Senr., 46, 84
  J., 21
  James, 43, 84, 125, 203
  Jonah, 35
  Jos. Senr., 194
  Josiah, 43, 83
  Josiah Junr., 11, 124
  Josiah Senr., 124, 200
  Moses, 192, 206
  Richard, 206
  Samuel, 27
  Solomon, 43, 84, 123
  William, 30
Lightfoot
  W., 13
Litle
  Thomas, 67
Little
  Alexander, 162
  Arch., 163
  Archd., 84, 167
  Archibald, 40, 60, 84
  Duncan, 64, 84
  John, 40, 60, 84, 161, 184
  Neill, 64
  Thomas, 84, 183
Lloyd
  David, 50, 105, 185, 209
  Richard, 105
  Richd., 209
Lock
  Benj, 28
  Benj., 28, 49
  Benjamin, 25
  Benjn., 187, 210
  David, 85, 105, 186, 209
  David Junior, 49
  David Junr., 105
  David Senior, 49
  Elizabeth, 220
  Elizth., 178
  Eunice, 209
  John, 61, 84, 177, 219
  John Junr., 145
  John Seignr., 147
  John, Constable, 53, 72
  Joseph, 49, 85, 105, 178, 187
  Leonard, 49, 61, 84, 134, 187, 209
  Rebecca, 221
  Rebeckah, 178
  Thomas, 84, 186, 221
  Thos., 143, 178, 210
Locke
  Thomas, 15
    Claim for trespass, 15
  Thos., 15
Lockelair
  Dudley, 84
  Gutterage, 84
Lockeliar
  Dudeley, 64
  Gutterage, 64
Locklear
  Ann, 169
  Jacob, 119
  John, 101, 119
  Robert, 101, 119
  William, 101, 119
Lofton
  Frederick, 200
  Mark, 197
Long
  William, 132
Lord
  Peter, 58, 83, 146, 176
  Wm., 58
Loury
  [Faded], 119
Love
  Elexander, 102
Low
  David, 119
  Thomas, 68
Lowary
  James, 101
Lowery
  James, 115
Lowry
  James, 63, 84
Loyd
  David, 25, 85
Lucas
  Elizabeth, 225
  F., 112
  Frances, 37, 38
  Francis, 25, 85, 107, 112
  George, 38, 85, 109
  John, 107
  Thomas, 109
  Thos., 38
  William, 47, 85
Lucus
  Elizabeth, 189
Lyon
  George, 10, 152
  Mary, 10

M

M Claron
  John, 39
M Clelland
  [Torn], 39
  Thomas, 39
M Conkey
  Robert, 39
M Coulskey
  Archibald, 39
M Fatter
  Mary, 38
M Gillop
  Alexander, 39
M Keithan
  Arch., 39
Mac Ourrich
  William, 24
MacCallum
  Jno., 166
Macfater
  Archabell, 188
MacFatter
  Daniel, 189
Mackay
  Ann, 189
MacKeacharn
  Dand., 165
Mackethon

Index

Archibell, 188
Daniel, 189
Duncan, 188
Maclimore
Drury, 158
Drury Jnr., 158
MacMillan
Neil, 165
Robert, 24
Macown
Daniel, 188
Macteer
William, 26
Mains
John, 157
Malsby
John, 14
Will of, 15
Mangam
Jacob, 66
Manley
Bassell, 188
Manly
Basil, 37
Bassel, 38
Maradith
Nathan, 51
Marlow
David, 35, 120
Marsh
James, 221
Marsh Plantation, 9
Marshall
John, 25
Saml., 111
Sarah, 25
Marshes
Brown Marsh, 106
W. Marsh, 107
White Marsh, 106
Marshingal
Joseph, 31
marten
[?], 31
Mash
James, 178
Mason
David, 51
Massengale
Joseph, 170
Massie
Raymond, 105
Mathies
Dan., 164
Matthias
Daniel, 40
Maulsby
Ann, 56
Anthony, 56
James, 56, 224

Thomas, 224
William, 8
Wm., 8
Maulthby
James, 188
Maultsby
Ann, 39, 89, 107
Jas., 109
John, 151
Saml., 145
Thomas, 37
William, 17, 37, 85
Willm., 38
Wm., 112
Mc aNewer
John, 64
Mc aNewer[?]
Iver, 64
John, 64
McAchen
John, 102
McAlestar
Anguish, 6
Charles, 25
McAlester
Anguish, 105
Angus, 6
Duncan, 6
McAlister
Duncan, 51
McAllester
Duncan, 6
Hector, 207
McAllister
Anguish, 6
Daniel, 207
Duncan, 6, 85
McAlpin
Alexr., 168
Malcum, 102
McAnewer
Daniel, 87
John, 87
McaNewer[?]
John, 63
McArthur
Alexander, 18, 86
Alexr., 63
Danold, 102
Elexander, 101
Elexander, Soldier, 101
John, 102
Peter, 42, 62, 86, 102
Peter, Soldier, 101
McArvie
Neill, 163
McAtter[?]
Peter, 162
McAulay

John, 166
McBean
Peter, 41
McBri[Torn]
Macum, 37
McBride
Archd., 39, 56, 89, 123, 191
Archibald, 205
John, 101, 115, 168
McCall
Alexr., 193
David, 86
Duncan, 86, 191
McCallister
Anguish, 114
McCallum
Daniel, 123
Danl., 193
Iver, 135
McCalpin
Malcom, 115
McCarmaig
Archd., 62
Duncan, 62
Gilbert, 62
John, 62
McCarmig
Archd., 86
Duncan, 86
Gilbert, 86
John, 86
McCarter
Daniel, 115
Elaxander, 114
John, 115
Peter Junr., 114
McCarther
Peter Senr., 116
McClain
Danl. Senr., 87
Danneil, 219
Hector, 115
McClanon
Thos, 100
McCleland
John, 43
McClpan[?]
Neil, 18
McColl
Alex., 205
Alexander, 124
David, 62
Duncan, 62, 206
McCollem
Daniel, 44
McCollemn
John, 53
McCollester
Angus, 102

Index

McCollom
  Daniel, 207
  Danl., 89
  Duncan, 102
  Iver, 21, 89
  John, 86, 158
McCollome
  Dunkin, 114
McCollum
  Donald, 23
  Iver, 21
  Rachel, 196
McColskey
  Archd., 133
  Jas., 133
McColsky
  Neil, 205
McConkey
  Robert, 215
  Robt., 89
McConky
  Robert, 212
  Robt., 153
McCoulskey
  Neil, 39, 122
McCoulsky
  Archd., 58, 89
  Duncan, 25
  James, 58
  Neil, 43
  Neill, 88, 193
McCoya
  John, 174
McCrainey
  John, 63
McCrane
  Hugh, 59
  John, 101
McCraney
  Hugh, 163
  John, 115
McCullam
  Iver, 56
McCullock
  Duncan, 225
McCullom
  Neal, 223
McDaniel
  [Torn], 51
  Alexander, 69, 88
  Archabald, 52
  Archd., 86
  Archibald, 196
  David, 54, 86
  James, 53, 86
  John, 85, 162
  Wm., 53
  Wm. Gray, 180
  Zachariah, 69, 88
McDannel

  John, 179
McDanniel
  Archabald, 219
  William G., 219
McDonald
  Angus, 166
  Dond., 166, 168
  Saggy[?], 164
  William, 21, 41
McDond
  Jno., 168
McDonnel
  Archd., 156
  James, 146
  John, 149
McDonnol
  David, 157
McDougall
  Ronald, 105
McDuffie
  Donald, 166
McDuffy
  Daniel, 41
McDugal
  Alexr., 163
McEacharn
  Duncan, 86
  John, 24
McEachern
  Daniel, 60, 87
  Danold, 40
  Duncan, 62
McEahan
  Robert, 162
McEwen
  Daniel, 224
  Matthew, 207
  Robt., 192, 206
  Wm., 205
McEwin
  John, 121
  Robert, 121
McFadian
  Stephen, 223
McFall
  Donde, 168
  Jno., 167
  John, 18
  Neal, 60
  Neill, 88
  Neill, Soldier, 101
Mcfarshen
  Daniel, 25
McFarsion
  Daniel, 60
  Danl., 88
  Edward, 115
McFarson
  John, 42

McFarter
  Daniel, 110
  John, 111
  Malcom, 108
  William, 115
Mcfashion
  John, 27
McFassion
  Edward, 101
McFater
  Danl., 89
  Danold, 101
  Malcom, 87
  William, 87
McFatter
  Danie, 39
  Donald, 56
  Malcolm, 20
McFaull
  John, 116
  Nial, 116
McFauter
  Daniel, 64
  Malcum, 64
  William, 64
Mcferson
  Danl., 9
Mcfhassion
  Daniel, 20
McFoster
  Mary, 105
McGayer
  Thos., 38
McGee
  Daniel, 68
  George, 44, 89, 122
  John, 195
McGill
  Archd., 62, 86, 163
  Neil, 114
  Neill, 64, 87, 101
  Rodger, 101, 116
McGillip
  Alexr., 141
  Catharine, 204
McGillup
  Archd., 58
McGirt
  Archd., 62, 86
McGlauchlin
  John, 114
McGuire
  Thomas, 85
  Thos., 38, 106
Mcgwier
  Thomas, 111
McKay
  [Torn], 39
  Alexander, 60
  Alexr., 88

Index

Anguish, 43, 88
Angus, 125, 193
Ann, 223
Archibald, 15
Dugald, 124
Flora, 192
Floria, 205
Ge[?], 207
George, 192
Gilbart, 167
Iver, 89, 109
James, 88
Jno., 24, 28
John, 19, 43, 125, 193, 207, 225
Neal, 60
Neill, 87
McKeever
  Alexr., 53
McKeithan
  Archd., 56, 89, 110
  Daniel, 39, 111
  Donald, 89
  Donall, 56
  Dugald, 111
  Duncan, 1, 38, 56, 89, 224
  Gilbert, 39, 49, 85, 105
  Isbell, 112
  John, 205
  John Junr., 205
McKeithen
  Daniel, 1
  Duncan, 1
  Isabella, 1
McKeller
  Peter, 59, 87
McKethan
  John, 191
McKewn
  John, 39
McKey
  Christopher, 41
McKinley
  Dond., 167
McKinsey
  John, 17
McKinzey
  John, 57
Mckinzie
  John, 89
McKinzie
  Gilbart, 165
  John, 109
  Kenneth, 166
McKissack
  Archd., 88
McKissak
  Archd. Jr., 68
  Archibald Sr., 68

McKissaks
  Archd., 62
McKitchen
  Daniel, 224
McKonkey
  Robt., 56, 178
McKorter
  Alexr., 164
Mckown
  John, 44
  Robert, 44
McKown
  John, 89
McKoy
  [Torn], 55
McKree
  Roger, 166
McLachlen
  Jno., 166
McLaine
  John, 86
McLane
  Peter, 196
McLaran
  John, 122
McLaren
  Darby, 44
  John, 44, 89
McLaron
  Duncan, 50
McLartie
  James, 110
McLarty
  Alexr., 154
  Neil, 190
McLary
  Alexander, 38
McLauchlan
  Daniel, 64
  Danold, 101
Mclaughlin
  John, 41
McLaughlin
  Danl., 87
  Dugald, 161
McLean
  Archd., 62, 86, 165
  Daniel Junr., 62, 86
  Hector, 62, 86
  John, 62
  John, Taylor, 63, 87
McLelan
  Malcum, 101
  Thos., 217
Mclelland
  Andrew, 43
McLelland
  Andrew, 89, 124
  John, 89

  Mary, 124
  Thomas, 213
McLenon
  Thos., 155
McLeod
  Malcom, 224
McLeran
  John, 205
McLerran
  John, 192
McLocklan
  John, 102
McLoud
  Elaxander, 114
  Mordach, 42
  Mordoch, 60
  Murdoch, 87
  Murdock, 165
McMaster
  Felex, 208
  Rachel, 149
  William, 86
  Wm., 53
McMillan
  Archd., 166
  Daniel, 6
  Danl., 6
  Dugal, 193
  Dugald, 123
  Dun., 164
  Duncan, 64, 87
  Iver, 6
  Jno., 165, 168
  John, 24, 194, 208, 213
  Malcolm, 165
  Margaret, 126
  Neil, 167
  Robert, 6
  Robt, 6
  Wm., 167
McMillen
  Dugal, 205
  John, 223
  Robert, 5
McMillian
  Robart, 208
McMillin
  John, 216
McMuling
  William, 40
McMullan
  Christan, 115
  Iver, 89
McMullen
  Duncan, 102
  Gibba, 56
  Jno., 56
  John, 102, 151
  Robert, 105
McMullin

Index

Dugal, 44
Dunkin, 114
Ever, 44
John, 39
McNaughten
Charles, 39
McNaughton
Charles, 89, 111, 192, 205
McNauton
Charels, 58
Mcneal
Wm., 205
McNeal
Godfrey, 41, 59
Hecter, 40
Hector, 16, 25
Hector, sailor, 42
James, 40, 60
John, 42
Laughlin, 40
Turtle, 40
McNear
John, 101, 115
McNeel
Hector, 7
McNeil
Dond., 167
Hector, 14
Jas., 165
John, 50, 115
Malcum, 222
Neil, 164
William, 26, 43, 121
Wm., 26
McNeill
Godfrey, 87
Godr., 164
Hecto, 9
Hector, 7, 9, 64
Hector Esqr, 4
Hector, Sailor, 63, 87, 101
Jams., 87
John, 102
Laughlan, 101
Malcom, 87, 168
Neil, 101
Neill, 63, 64, 87
Neill, Weavr., 102
Peter, 64
William, 88
McNemarr
Daniel, 37
McNiell
Wm., 191
McPharsion
Danl., 7
Mcphersion
Daniel, 20
McPhersion
Danl., 14

McPherson
Daniel, 20
John, 168
McRainey
Hugh, 87
John, 87
Mcree
Jamy, 29
McRee
Griffeth, 225
Jamy, 29
Mary, 108
Mr., 9
Robert, 88, 197
Robt., 58, 153
Saml., 85
Samuel, 49, 135, 212, 215
Will., Esqr., 38
William, 26, 39, 85, 99, 150, 175
William Esqr., 5, 216
William esquire, 9
William Junior, 9
William Junr, 5
William Junr., 154, 197
William Senr., 213
Willm., 100
Wm., 11, 26, 54, 58
  Claim against Tories, 11
Wm. Jr., 27
McShaw
Tire, 30
Mcswain
Jno., 164
McSwain
Dand., 165
Mal., 165
McSwainey
Danold, 42
McTigre
William, 64
McViccar
John, 126
McVicker
John, 1, 224
McVickers
John, 188
Meason
Annie, 167
Meglohlen
John, 25
Megloklin
John, 7, 14
Meloy
Charles, 25
Daniel, 7, 14, 25
MeLoy
Charles, 7, 14
Melven
Danel, 103

Melvin
Daniel, 24, 105
Danl., 86
George, 186, 210
John, 195
Meradarth
Nathen, 208
Mercer
Christopher Junr., 67
Henry, 18, 42, 60, 87
Malachi, 67, 88
Noah, 67, 88
Solomon Junr., 67, 88
Solomon Senr., 67, 88
Meredath
Nathan, 104
Meredith
Nathan, 85
Mersingale
Joseph, 137
Mesh[?]
Matthew, 108
Meshaw
Peter, 136
Messack
Jacob, 38
Messar
Petter, 165
Messer
Henri, 164
Meszick
Jacob, 187
Mezick
Jacob, 37, 107
Jacob Junr., 37, 85
Militia
Arbitrators, 5
Commanded by Genl. Ash, 5
Regmt. of, 5
Miller
Frederick, 220
Ralph, 37, 38, 85, 108, 189
Ralph, JP, 187
Millers
Ralph, 224
Millican
Andrew, 198
Mills
Rolly, 192
Stewarts Mill, 18
Mim
James, 30
Mims
David, 46, 86, 140, 173, 203
James, 170, 204
Thomas, 194, 198
Thomas Senr., 46
Thoms. Senr., 86
Thos. Junr., 138

Index

Thos. Senr., 137
Mitchell
  Wm., 208
Mittlester
  John, 105
Mixon
  Michael, 51, 85
Moat
  David, 52
Money
  Benjamin, 35, 132
  James, 35, 46, 85, 132
  John, 35, 129, 197, 206
Monro
  Angus, 23
  Duncan, 23
    Inventory of Estate, 23
    Will of, 23
Monroe
  John, 51
Monrow
  Lewis, 41
Monthe
  Mathew, 155
Months
  Jacob, 155
  Mathew, 213, 218
Mooney
  Wm., 192
Moor
  James Junr., 145
  James Seignr., 147
  John, 144, 176
  Matthew, 10
  William, 40
Moore
  [Torn], 142
  Alfred, 12
  James, 67, 88, 98, 204, 219
  James Junr., 182
  James Senr., 184
  John, 42, 61, 64, 87, 90, 221
  Mary, 38
  Schenching[?], 190
  W, 18
  William, 18, 65
  Willm., 88
  Wm., 16
Moorehead
  James, 19
  Wm., 58
Moorhead
  James, 52, 147, 210, 213, 215
  Moorhead, 89
  William, 157
Moran
  Jas., 3, 4
Moresby

Anthony, 225
Moris
  Thomas, 213
Morison
  Duncan, 49
  Margaret, 172
  Neil, 164
Morley
  Amelia, 35, 46, 85
Morris
  Thomas, 218
Morrison
  Duncan, 11, 17, 35, 86, 119
  Duncan Esqr., 135
  Duncan Esqr., Assessor, 105
  Duncan, Assessor, 126, 134
Morse
  Elisha, 21
Mortimer's Land, 106
Mott
  Joseph, 148
Mulford
  Capt., 185
  Captn., 209
  Ephm., 187, 211
  Ephraim, 50
  Thomas, 210
  Thos, 50
Mullford
  Ephraim, 85
Mulloy
  Anguish, 9
  Charles, 9
Munce
  Jacob, 89
  Mathas, 86
Munro
  Hecter, 60
  Hector, 88
  John, 85
  Malcom, 88
  Malcum, 60
Munroe
  John, 104
Munrow
  Lewes, 164
  Malcom, 114
  Malcum, 101
Muns
  Jacob, 55
Munts
  Jacob, 39
Murffy
  Edward, a criple, 64
Murfy
  Edward, 102
Murpha
  Hugh, 186
Murphey

Edward, 115
Hugh, 210
James, 39, 121
John, 144
Murphy
  Edwd., a criple, 87
  Hugh, 24
  James, 43, 88
  Jas., 193
  Neil, 167
Murray
  Mr., 106
Murrel
  Barnaby, 174
  Samuel, 30
Murrell
  Zakariah, 30
Muselwhite
  Milsby, 65
  Nathan, 65
Musselwhite
  Jesse, 67
  Thomas, 66
Musstlewhite
  Jesse, 88
  Milsby, 88
  Nathan, 88
  Thoms., 88

N

Newberry
  Elizabeth, 42
  Elizth., 144
  Jesse, 42, 90, 145, 220
  John, 42, 90, 149, 177, 219
Newbery
  Jesse, 59, 179
  John, 59, 180
Newcombe
  Robt., 30
Newhanover County, 3, 4
Newton
  Mary, 15
Nichols
  Coleman, 35, 45, 90
Nicholson
  John, 38
Nickleson
  John, 53
Nickols
  Averit, 199
  Coleman, 33, 126
Nicleson
  John, 38
Nieal
  Mary, 186
Noble
  Joseph, 33, 49, 90, 133, 200

253

Index

Tennetson, 200
Nobles
  Joseph, 27
Norton
  Charles M., 106
  Wm., 106
Nowls
  George, 153
  James, 154
Nukols
  [Torn]leman, 197

O

O'Dear
  John, 108
Oates
  Caroway, 68
Oath of Allegiance, 6, 20, 21
Oats
  Caraway, 90
Odom
  Aaron, 67
  Jacob, 64, 67, 90, 185
  John, 90
  John Junr., 67
  John Senr., 67
  William, 67
Odum
  John, 17
Oliphant
  Jesse, 210
  William, 127
  Willm., 190
  Wm., 225
Oliver
  Thomas, 66, 90
Oneal
  Charles, 225
Oquinn
  Tarlor Junr., 162
  Tarlor Senr., 162
Overseers
  William McRee Junior, 9
Overton
  Titus, 90, 146
Oviter
  John, 176
Owel
  John Barton, 53
Owen
  Catheron, 153
  Colo. Thos., 216
  John, 56, 90, 213
  Major Thos., 153
  Thomas, 39, 213
  Thos, Esqr, 57
  Thos., 4, 59
Owens

William, 90, 156
Wm., 54
Oxendine
  Charles, 161

P

Padget
  John, 200
Page
  Joseph, 113
Parker
  [?], 35
  Aaron, 31
  Ezekiel, 199
  Gabriel, 33
  Henry, 30
  James, 169
  John, 31, 157, 195, 209
  Nicholas, 2
  William, 139, 203
  Wm., 173
Parnal
  John, 182
Parnell
  John, 90
Parret
  William, 91
Pate
  Samuel, 113
Paterson
  Alexr, 165
  Daniel, 25, 60
  Dond., 165
  Dun., 165
Patrick
  Daniel, 31
Patterson
  Daniel, 91
  Danl., 7, 9, 14
  Danold, 40
  Jno., 166
Paul
  Abraham, 90
  Abram, 62
  John, Const., 64
  John, Constable, 91
Pavey
  [Torn], 36
Peabody
  John, 225
Pemberton
  [Torn], 39, 56
  James, 37, 56, 108
  John, 39, 91, 108
  Margaret, 223
  Margt., 56, 91, 108
Pemperton
  John, 188

Margaret, 188
Pender
  Jas., 21
Penny
  Thos, 171
  Thos., 201
  William, 30
Perrit
  William, 69
Perry
  Jn., 225
  Philip, 200
Peters
  William, 200
Pevey
  Joshua, 90
Pevy
  Joshua, 47
Pharis
  Isaac, 195
  John, 157, 195
  Samuel, 195
Phillips
  James, 67, 183
  John, 67, 91
  Mark, 29
Pickett
  Thomas, 219
Pierce
  Jonathan, 30
Pitman
  Hannah, 161
  Hardy, 182
  Isam, 182
  Isom, 68
  Jesse, 91, 184
  Joel, 69, 91, 119, 180, 182
  Moses, 202
  Newat, 183
  Sion, 69
  Thomas, 69, 91
  Thomas Senr., 184
Pittman
  Isham, 91
  Jesse, 66
  Moses, 31
Plumer
  Aaron, 213
  John, 53
  Wm., 53
  Zachariah, 16, 25, 53
Plummer
  Aaron, 175, 216
  Elipha, 181
  Elipha [Elisha], 144
  Jeremiah, 90, 143, 180, 219
  Jno, 7
  Jno., 14
    Claim against Tories, 14

Index

John, 7, 14, 90, 143, 181, 221
Joseph, 176, 222
Moses, 221
Nathaniel, 181
Richd., 145
William, 181, 221
Willm., 90
Zacariah, 181, 221
Zachariah, 16, 25
    Claim against Tories, 16, 25
Zacriah, 148
Pointer
Argulas, 217
Argules, 150
Jn., 225
John, 38, 186
John Junr., 37, 90
John Senr., 90
Pointyr
Argulus, 213
Pope
Brittain, 204
Henry, 66, 91, 183
Jacob, 118
Sampson, 66, 91, 117, 183
Samuel, 199
Port[Post?]
Peter, 169
Porter
Saml., 153
Samuel, 184
Powel
Ambrose, 102
Ambruis, 59
Barney, 174
Isaiah, 15
John, 174
Powell
Absalom, 36, 46, 130, 194, 201
Absolem, 90
Ambrois, 40
Ambrose, 91
Ambrouse, 162
Barnas, 201
Charles, 163
Childs, 40
Elijah, 183
Isaack, 204
John, 205
John Junr., 36, 141
John Senr., 138
Tillah, 25
William, 25
Powers
Charles, 199
Joseph, 44, 91, 120, 193, 200
Poynter
John, 108, 189

John Junr., 112
Price
Joseph, 40, 60, 91
Prick
Gidian, 144
Pricket
Gidion, 53, 90
Prickett
Elizabeth, 222
Elizth., 175
Gedian, 218
Josiah, 221
Pridgin
Francis, 208
John, 207, 208
Peter, 208
Rutthey[?], 207
Prigan
Matthew, 105
Prigeon
Matthew, 90
Prigon
Matthew, 50
Pritchet
Kinchen, 30
Public Roads
Work on, 30
Puff
Andr., 164
Andrew, 60, 91
Purcel
William, 39
Purcell
William, 37
Purdie
J S, 1
James S., 223
James Saml., 175
Purkepine
John, 126, 207
Purkeypine
John, 192
Purnell
John, 147, 222

R

Raborn
Daniel, 197
Rafourd
Robert Senr., 219
Raiburn
George, 203
Raiford
Robert, 213, 216
Robt., 19
Ralls
Abram, 219
Ramsey

Gilberd, 41
Gilbert, 93
Ramsy
Gilbird, 60
Randols
Capt., 106
Ratley
Joseph, 184
Ray
[?], 30
Angus, 163
Duncan, 7, 14, 16, 25
Isaac, 54, 92, 149, 220
Jane, 122
Jean, 191
Jemima, 171
Jessey, 203
Joseph, 138
Josiah, 174, 203
Rayford
Robert, 19, 40
Rea
Anguish, 63, 92
Reaves
Nathaniel, 145, 180
Zacariah, 146
Reavs
Edward, 207
Redgister
Jas., 30
John, 30
Redin
[Torn], 101
Reding
Rekum, 58
Riham, 218
Rikam, 151
Reess
John, 39
Reeves
Edward, 6, 52
Edwd., 91
Nathaniel, 53, 92
Regan
John, 65, 92
Joseph, 66, 92
Ralph, 18, 66, 92
Richard, 65
Register
William, 199
Reonalds
Elijah, 170
Richard, 170
Reves
Edward, 5
John, 218
Nathiel, 220
Revill
Edmund, 101
Revils

255

Index

Edmon, 119
Reynalds
   William, 117
Reynolds
   Demsey, 30
   Richd., 30
Rhodes
   Jacob, 7
Rices[?]
   Edward, 105
Richards
   Maurice, 223
   Morris, 177
Richardson
   James, 196
   John, 134, 171
   John Junr., 54, 92
   John Senr., 54, 92
   Majr. Jas., 156
   Robert, 92
   Robt., 54, 138
   Saml., 149
   Samuel, 11
   Thomas, 47, 91, 203
   Thos., 169, 202
Richd. Singletary Land, 109
Richeson
   John, 30
   Moses, 30
   Robert, 174
   Thomas, 30
Richison
   Thomas, 136
Riding
   John, 211, 216
   Rikum[?], 213
Right
   James, 30
Risin
   James, 113
River Plantation, 9
Rivers
   black river, 3
   Black River, 3, 4
   Cape Fear River, 26
   South river, 102
   South River, 52
   Waccamaw River, 30
Robbins
   Jethro, 198
Roberson
   Charles, 24
   John, 207
Roberts
   John, 48, 91, 121
Robertson
   John, 24
Robeson
   Bartram, 222
   Capt. Peter, 11, 143
   Charles, 189
   Col. Thomas, 9
   Colo. Thos., 149
   Daniel, 38, 108
   Donald, 92
   John, 125
   Mary, 181
   Peter, 11, 53, 92, 175, 221
   Peter, JP, 223
   Thomas, 45, 91, 92
   Thomas Senr, 4
   Thos Esqr, 58
   Thos Senr., 4, 5
   Thos., 127
Robeson County, 18
   Temporary Line, 18
Robison
   Capt., 159
   Captain, 143
   Donall, 58
   Thomas, 35
Rogers
   John, 33, 45, 91
   Saml., 14
Rogerson
   [Torn], 52
   Elizabeth, 219
   John, 91, 149, 176
Ronalds
   Dempsey, 139
   Mark, 6, 22
   Richard Senr., 138
   Richd. Junr., 138
Roots
   Saml., 100
   Samuel, 39
Ross
   Docter, 214
Rourk
   Samuel, 46, 91, 143
Rowan
   Apollo, 158
   John, 37, 38
   Saml., 156
   Samuel, 196
Rowan Land, 107
Rowan's Land, 106
Rowland
   Eliza., Widow, 184
   James, 68, 92, 184
   James Junr., 116
   James Senr., 118
   John, 67, 92, 118, 184
   Nathan, 68, 113
   Samuel, 68, 113
   Thomas, 69, 92, 118, 182
Rozar
   Daniel, 67, 161
   David, 66
   Isaac Junr., 67
   Isaac Senr., 67
   John, 65
   Reuben Junr., 66
   Reuben Senr., 66
   Robert, 66
Roziar
   David, 184
   John, 182
Rozier
   David, 92
   Isaac, 92
   John, 92
   Ruben, 92
Runalds
   Mark, 69
   Richard, 30
   William, 69, 92
Runals
   Richard, 36
Runnalds
   William, 199
Runolds
   Abraham, 173
   Dempsy, 173
   Richard Senr., 173
Russ
   Aleazar, 210
   David, 59, 93, 99, 151, 213, 215
   Edmd., 100
   Eleaser, 24
   John, 49, 185, 210
   John Junr., 121
   John Senr., 57, 92, 121, 213
   Jonadab, 37, 188
   Jonathan, 225
   Joseph, 24, 187, 209
   Joseph Junr., 210
   Thomas, 24, 49, 91, 186
   Thomas Junr., 210
   Thomas Senr., 210
   William, 92, 151, 213, 216
   William Junr., 213, 217
   Willm., 99
   Wm., 55, 59
Russel
   [Torn], 36
Russell
   Saml., 142
   Thomas, 68, 92
Rynolds
   Abraham, 201
   Demsey, 204
   Elijah, 204

Index

S

Saltar
James, 105, 186, 210
Richard, 94, 187, 215
Richard Junr., 209
Richd., 24, 213
William, 24, 49, 105, 107, 186, 209
Willm., 96

Salter
[Torn]nard, 52
Richd., 152
William, 105
Wm., 105

Samford
Willm., 101

Sampson County, 7

Sanders
Thomas, 199
Thos., 132
Willm., 36

Sasser
Benja., 30
Frederic, 30
Jas, 30

Saunders
Christopher, 45, 95
Thomas, 45
Thoms., 95

Sawyer
John, 10, 66, 94
William, 67, 94

Scarbrough
Stephen, 105

Schaw
Alexr., 151
Archibald, 205
Daniel, 206
Daniel Esqr., 1
John, 155
Neil, 155
Niel Junr., 151

Scot
Israel, 67, 94
John, 67, 94, 162

Scott
Robert, 110

Scriven
Thomas, 222

Scrivin
Thomas, 93

Scriving
Thos., 148, 176

Sealah
Tobias, 42

Seamore
Sarah, 105
Thomas, 105

Selah
Tobias, 117

Sellars
Angus, 39
Archibald, 6
John, 6, 94, 105

Seller
John, 5

Sellers
Anguish, 57, 93
Angus, 123
Archabald, 52
Archd., 94, 123
Archibald, 6
Benjamin, 19, 199
Benjn., 20
Daniel, 59
Duncan, 52
Dunkin, 196
Joel, 128
John, 6, 196
Simon, 46, 95

Sellors
Archibald, 44

Semes[?]
Robt., 168

Semore
[?], 189

Sessione
Thos., 128

Sessions
Thomas, 194, 200
Thomas, JP, 194

Sessoms
Culmoor[?], 196
Thomas, 53, 95

Sessums
Samuel, 196

Seymore
Sarah, 39

Shaw
Angus, 213, 216
Archd., 93, 122, 193
Archibald, 39, 43
Daniel, 39, 43, 93, 106, 123, 213
Daniel Junr., 31
Danl., 215
Duncan, 43, 125
James, 50, 104
John, 39, 43, 56, 93, 125
Mal., 165
Malcolm, 193
Malkom, 207
Neil, 39, 55
Neill, 93, 214, 217
William, 50, 96

Shephard
Mary, 14

Shepherds Land, 109

Shipman
Capt., 105, 119, 169
Captain, 194
Daniel, 44, 93, 120, 203
Daniel Junr., 44
Danl., 191
James, 44, 119, 174, 206
James Esqr., 119
James, Assessor, 105, 126, 134

Sibbet
William, 131

Sibbett
William, 198

Siegnr
John Siegnr., 216

Sikes
[?], 105
Jacob, 103
John, 103
John Juner, 208
John Senr, 208
Jonathan, 157, 196
Josiah, 24, 102, 105, 208

Sillars
John, 24

Simmonds
Grace, 112
Thomas, 27

Simmons
Demcy, 27
Jeremiah, 158, 195
Jesse, 27
John, 28
Sanders, 197
Thomas, 28

Simms
Isaac, 98

Simpson
Ann, 25
Elinor, 25
Jacob, 30, 137, 169, 203
John, 30, 93, 170, 203
Peter, 42, 148
Richard, 25
Robert, 170
Semore, 138
Seymore, 203
Simon, 136, 171, 201
Solomon, 30
Surrel, 30
Surrell, 202
Thomas, 122
THomas Jr., 194
Thomas Senr., 206
Thoms., 94
Thos. Junr., 206
William, 25

Index

Sims
  Benjamin, 42, 146
  Benjn., 179, 218
  Isaac, 147, 179, 218
  Robert, 41
  Robt., 149
  William, 148, 181
Simson
  John, 43
  Thomas, 44, 191
Sinclair
  John, 60, 93
Sineth
  James, 27
Singaltary
  Benjm., 57
  James, 57
  Joe, 58
  Mary, 58
  Sarah, 58
  Wm., Constable, 57
Singletary
  Benj., 49, 190
  Benja., 111
  Benjamin, 19, 24, 93, 210, 224
  Benjamin[?], 189
  Benjn., 100
  Brayton, 49, 96, 185, 210
  Council, 19
  Eithamon, 152
  Elizabeth, 105
  Ithamar, 24, 214
  Ithamor, 56
  Ithamore, 218
  James, 93
  James (Long), 219
  James (Short), 220
  James Junr., 175
  James Senr., 181
  Jas., 24
  Jas. Junr., 148
  Jas. Seignr., 148
  Jno, 2
  John, 1, 25, 49, 95, 105, 181, 187, 210, 214, 217, 220
  Jos., 24
  Joseph, 52, 155, 175, 213, 214, 216, 217
  Joseph (Long), 221
  Josiah, 214, 217
  Mary, 18, 19, 39, 93, 151, 189, 226
  Richard, 1, 38, 190, 195
    Division of land, 19
  Richard Senr., 219
  Richd., 2, 19, 94, 109, 190, 223
  Richd. Junr., 148
  Richd. Senr., 174
  Richd. Snr., 148
  S., 28
  Sarah, 39, 93
  Snowden, 28
  William, 18, 19, 38
    Estate of, 18
  William Senr., 213, 216
  Willm., 100
Singletary[Faded], 109
Sinkelton
  Jno., 167
Sizemore
  John, 64, 94
Slaughter
  John, 27
Slaves
  Aberdeen, 44
  Addie, 37
  Agnis, 38
  Albrow, 38
  Alfred, 38
  Amaretta, 44
  Ambor, 37
  Ameritta, 37
  Amilia, 38
  Amy, 38, 69
  Aro, 44
  Attey, 38
  Balindah, 38
  Bandy, 66
  Beck, 66
  Belinda, 38
  Bellah, 38
  Bellow, 37
  Bess, 29, 67
  Besse, 38
  Bet, 37
  Billy, 63
  Binah, 69
  Black Billy, 37
  Bob, 37, 44
  Bobbit, 38
  Boltimoor, 69
  Boy Ned, 38
  Brigs, 69
  Bristoe, 37
  Brunswick, 62
  Cane, 38
  Care, 37
  Casar, 14
  Casinda, 38
  Cater, 38
  Cato, 14
  Catoe, 37, 38
  Cesar, 38
  Champion, 63
  Clareda, 38
  Cloe, 38, 63, 64, 69
  Clorey, 43
  Cockney, 37
  Cuffey, 38
  Cymen, 38
  Dan, 63
  Daniel, 69
  Darcus, 37
  Dianna, 38
  Dick, 37, 43, 66
  Dill, 69
  Dilly, 38
  Dinah, 44
  Dirnboe, 38
  Doll, 37, 69
  Duncan, 43
  Elsey, 38
  Emanuel, 38
  Febe, 43
  Feebe, 69
  Fiby, 63
  Filis, 43
  Flora, 14
  Florow, 37
  Fortune, 67
  George, 67
  Glasgow, 38
  Grace, 38, 44
  Greenwick, 38
  Hagar, 37
  Hampton, 68
  Hannah, 38, 69
  Hansom, 63
  Hardy, 62
  Harglus, 44
  Harris, 37
  Harry, 44, 66, 67
  Haywood, 69
  Hendrick, 37
  Indian Wench Hannah, 12
  Isaac, 38
  Isaik, 37
  Isick, 37
  Jack, 38, 43, 63, 64, 69
  Jackoe, 38
  Jacob, 64, 67
  James, 37
  Jamy, 29
  Jane, 69
  Jean, 44
  Jemmy, 38
  Jenney, 69
  Jenny, 37
  Jetang, 38
  Jo, 44
  Joan, 44
  Joe, 38, 66
  Joney, 37, 38
  Joseph, 69
  Jubah, 38
  Juda, 37

Index

Judah, 38
Jude, 44, 67
Judey, 38
Jupiter, 37
Kate, 38
Katherin, 64
Len, 37
Letice, 59
Lettice, 62
Lewis, 43
Limrick, 67
Lingo, 63
Little Cloe, 38
London, 43
Lonzoe, 38
Lucy, 37, 38, 66, 69
Luke, 66
Manuel, 37
March, 38
Markes, 44
Marky, 43
Mary, 37
Mingo, 69
Moll, 37
Molly, 37, 38, 43, 44
Monday, 59
Money, 37
Mood, 37
Moriah, 37
Nan, 37
Nancey, 37
Nancy, 37, 38
Nat, 38
Natt, 69
Nell, 37, 64, 69
Noco, 37
Old Betty, 38
Old Cloe, 38
Old Frank, 69
Old Jack, 38
Old Nany, 38
Old Pompy, 69
Old Toney, 38
Patience, 66
Patt, 67
Peg, 29
Pegg, 64
Peggy, 38
Penney, 37
Perthene, 38
Peter, 37, 38, 63, 69
Philis, 38
Phillis, 65, 67, 68, 69
Poiny, 37
Poja, 37
pomp, 18
Pomp, 38
Pompey, 14, 37
Priscilla, 38
Quaco, 38

Quacoe, 37
Quash, 18, 38, 63, 66
Quocco, 66
Rentes, 38
Robin, 38
Sall, 65, 69
Sam, 38, 44, 63, 66, 68
Samboe, 37
Samson, 67
Sanco, 37
Sarah, 37, 38
Secas, 37
Selah, 38
Seley, 67
Sesar, 44
Sethra, 38
Shields, 38
Silvia, 37, 38
Siras, 43
Spencer, 66
Stepny, 37
Sue, 64
Sutina, 37
Tamer, 69
Tinah, 69
Tinis, 64
Tock, 66
Tom, 37, 44, 69
Tomboy, 37
Toney, 38
Tony, 37
Tull, 66
Veanus, 43, 44
Venter, 37
Wat, 69
Will, 37, 38, 66, 67
York, 37, 66
Young Frank, 69
Young Nanny, 38
Young Pompy, 69
Slingbley
  John, 17
Slingsbey
  Colo. John, 14
  John, 14
Slingsby
  John, 11, 26, 50, 96, 112
  Mrs., 225
Sloan
  William, 51
  Willm., 95
Small
  John, 178
  Richard, 39, 96, 134
Smart
  Jno., 166
Smilie
  Jacob, 219
Smith
  [Torn], 36

[Torn] Junr., 52
Archd., 115, 116, 161
Archelaus, 102
Arthur, 48, 95, 135, 170, 204
Capt. Saml., 112
Claraday, 35
Daniel, 114
Danold, 102
David, 168, 222
Drury, 208
Eley, 170
Eli, 204
Elisha, 139
Grace, 46, 95, 134
Henry, 31
Iam, 59
James, 30, 39, 42, 60, 93, 99, 134, 168, 195
Jas, 5
Jas., 167
Jese, 31
Jno Esqr, 98
Jno., 167, 168
Jno. Seignr., 158
Joannah, 201
John, 24, 26, 27, 39, 42, 49, 66, 69, 94, 96, 108, 110, 113, 173, 197, 201
John Junr., 140, 144, 156
John Senr., So. River, 94
John Siegnr., 143
John Sr., 141
Jos., 25, 35
Joseph, 66
Lewis, 222
Lucy, 213, 215
Mary, 189, 224
Neal, 25
Neil, 166
Newit, 31
Peter, 116
Petter, 164
Richard, 17
  Claim against Tories, 17
Richd., 64, 94
Richd. Esqr., 153
Sam, 59
Saml., 94
Samuel, 26, 30, 69, 105, 168
Samuel Esqr., 117
Saul, 193, 201
Simmon, 27
Simon, 110, 127, 197
Simond, 190
Sophia, 187
Stephen, 137
Steven, 48, 95
T Arthur, 30
T C, 26

Index

Tho, 1
Tho., 189
Thomas, 66, 94, 195
Thos, 224
William, 14, 38, 41, 52, 54, 93, 111, 144, 156, 196, 222
   Claim against Tories, 14
William Junr., 197, 226
William Sr., 14
Willm., 190
Willm. Senr., 190
Wm., 168, 172
Zachariah, 170
Sojourner
John, 127
Sols
Benjamin, 27
Joseph, 27
Sommerset
Willm., 106
Sorevin
Thomas, 57
Soules
Benj., 28
Spear
Harriss, 184
Moore, 183
Spears
Solomon, 188
Speller
J., 15
Standfast
Willm., 37
Stanton
John, 214, 217
Stapbleton
Joab, 64
Solomon, 64
Stapleton
Joab, 94
Starkey
Will, 35
William, 46
Wm., 125
Starky
William, 95
Starling
Isaac, 67
John, 67, 113
Thomas, 66
Steavens
Abraham, 44
Barneby, 44
Stener[?]
George, 162
Stephens
Moab, 68
Oliver, 35

Thomas, 40
Stepto
John, 180
Thomas, 179
Sterling
John, 94
Thomas, 94
Stevens
Abraham, 131, 200
Abram, 194
Alexander, 199
Barnabas, 7, 22, 36
Barnabass, 94, 120
Charity, 6, 22
   Claim against Tories, 22
Henry [?], 30
James, 18
Joshua, 33, 35, 48, 95, 106
Moat, 94
William, 21, 30, 49, 128, 199
Willm., 36, 95
Stevenson
Alexr., 107
Stewart
Alexander, 3
James, 116
Janet, 207
John, 18, 60, 93
Robert, 6, 50, 95
William, 105
Willm., 95
Stone
Benj, 11
Benj., 58
Benjamin, 39, 93, 155
Elias, 144
James, 148, 179
John, 101, 152
Stons
Mr., 11
Storm
John, 61, 93, 145
Mary, 146, 175
Strahan
Alexr., 24
Moses, 208
Straughan
Othniel, 95
Streaty
William, 209
Streetey[?]
William, 109
Streety
Willm., 187
Streite[?]
William, 49
Strickland
Aaron, 94, 101
Abram, 101

David, 200
Elias, 133
Philip, 200
Phillip, 129
Philon, 28
William, 33, 47
William Junr., 6, 22
Willm., 95, 126
Stricklin
Abram, 114
Aron, 114
Philip, 35
William, 35
William Junr., 35
Strikland
Aaron, 64
Abram, 64
David, 64
Strohan
Allick, 208
Strohon
Alex Sr., 103
Othneal, 102
Stuart
William, 50
Stubbs
George, 30, 170, 203
John, 170, 203
John Junr., 139
John Senr., 47, 139
Richard, 30, 204
Richd., 95, 139, 171
Stubs
John Senr., 95
Sugg
John, 2
Suggs
Alle Good, 197
John, 2, 61, 93, 156, 157, 195
Thomas, 53, 95
Thos., 156
William, 53, 197
Zekel, 195
Suggs Hundred Acre Survey, 2
Summerset
Wm., 201
Sutton
Bailey, 24, 208
Beamon, 207
Beaumont, 51, 95
Bemen, 104
Christopher, 5, 6, 52, 94, 103
James, 36, 44
John, 24, 104, 208
John, Constable, 51, 95
William, 51, 207
Swamps
Bryan Swamp, 106
Great Swamp, 18

Index

Mitchell Swamp, 20
Sweetin
  Elisha, 64, 94
Swindall
  Henry, 31
  Samuel, 31, 203
  William, 204
Swindel
  Samuel, 189
Swindle
  Saml., 107
Sykes
  [Torn]iah, 51
  Isaiah, 51, 209
  Jacob, 95
  James, 51
  John, 95
  Josiah, 95

T

Tailor
  Archible, 37
  Harbert, 38
  John, 38
  John, Constable, 37
Tarel
  Philemon, 10
Tatham
  Richard, 199
Tayler
  John, 188
Taylor
  Anguis, 112
  Archd., 57, 96, 110
  Archibald, 17, 39
  Damse[?], 167
  Daniel, 191, 192, 206, 207
  Harber, 188
  Harbert, 224
  Harbet, 110
  Henry, 18
  Henry Junr., 65
  Henry Senr., 65, 96
  John, 25, 39, 57, 96, 108, 224
  John Junr., 111
  John McKay, 124
  Jonathan, 68, 96, 113
  Thomas, 65, 219
  William, 41, 68
Terrel
  Philemon, 96
Terrell
  Cornelius, 120
Terril
  Philemon, 65
Thagart
  George, 196
Themes

  Jesse, 97
  Joseph, 96
Thime
  Joseph, 144
Thimes
  Jesse, 60
  Joseph, 59
Thims
  Captn., 218
  Jesse, 42, 147, 177, 223
  John, 223
  Joseph, 39, 177
  Martha, 177, 220
  Thomas, 179, 218
  William, 179, 220
Thomas
  Benjn., 152
  David, 50, 107
  Francis, 24
  George, 25, 49, 96, 186, 210
  George Jr., 105
  George Senior, 49
  George Senr., 96
  George Sr., 105
  John, 49, 105, 186, 210
  Lewis, 55, 96
  Mical, 158
  Michael, 96
  Michal, 54
  Nathen, 32
  Richd., 56
  Th[?], 24
Thomlinson
  Israel, 35
Thommas
  Mikel, 197
Thompson
  Charles, 68, 96, 182
  John, 17
  Neill, 97
  Niel, 39
  Wm., 183
Thomson
  Neal, 60
  Neil, 167
Thygert
  George, 180
Tillman
  [Torn], 199
Tokes
  John, 30
Tolar
  William, 116
Toler
  William, 69
Toller
  William, 96
Tolor
  John, Constable, 35

Tomlinson
  Aaron, 35, 128
  Aaron Senr., 45, 96
  Israel, 45, 96, 130
Tories
  Commanded by John
    Slingsby, 14
  under the Command of David
    Fanning, 8
  under the Command of
    Hector McNeal, 16
Torry
  Geo., 165
Torys, 7, 8, 11, 14, 16, 22
  under the Command of David
    Fanning, 8
Townsend
  Thomas, 68, 96
Travers
  P., 25
  Patk, 9
  Patrick, 9, 10, 25
    Claim against Tories, 25
Treadway
  Moses, 50, 104
Treadwell
  Ruben, 50
Tredaway
  Moses, 96, 105
Tredwell
  Benjn., 129
Trul
  Thomas, 25
Trull
  Thos., 25
Truman
  William, 169
Turnbull, 2
Turner
  Daniel, 96, 122, 186, 205
  Jn., 36
  John, 44, 169, 172
  John Esqr., 97, 135, 172
  Mr. John, 33
Turner[?]
  Daniel, 44
Tyler
  Moses, 28
Tyrell
  Philemon, 15

U

Upton
  Robert, 65, 97

Index

V

Vail
  Jeremiah, 106
Virginia
  Common Wealth of, 25

W

Waccamaw Stream, 30
Waddell
  Genl., 107
  H, 3
  Hugh, 3
Waddells
  Genl., 107
Walker
  Chas., 166
  John, 43, 222
  Mary, free Negro, 175
  Moses, 39
  Robert, 43, 97
Wall
  Edward, 35, 45, 129, 200
  Edwd., 97
  Richard, 35
Walters
  John, 35
  Tho., 35
Ward
  John, 59, 98
Warren
  Archibald, 202
Washburn
  James, 56, 98
Washbyrne
  James, 152
Watson
  Capt., 211, 214
  James, 101, 114
  Jane, 101
  William, 214
  William Jas., 215
Watters
  S., 12
  Saml., 12
  Samuel, 12
Watts
  Berryman, 27, 28
Weatherbee
  [Torn]ard, 196
Weathersby
  Cade, 157
  James, 157
Web
  John, 97
Webb
  [Torn], 36

John, 48, 141, 169, 204
William, 202
Willm., 141
Wm., 173
Weir
  George, 214, 217
  Margt., 99
  Mary, 39
Wells
  Joel, 67, 117, 199
  Robert, 98
  Robt., 58, 153
  Samuel, 31
West
  James, 158, 197
White
  [Torn], Widow, 52
  Capt., 163, 168
  David, 39, 58, 98, 160, 214, 217
  David L., 14
  David Lenze, 144
  David Lindsay, 11, 14, 20, 54, 98
    Claim against Levi Glass, 14
  David, Assessor, 143, 159
  Docter James, 13
  Griff. J., 214
  Griffeth Jones, 216
  Griffith Jones, 155
  James, 39, 50, 57, 97, 214, 215
  Jams, Weaver, 98
  Jno, 5
  John, 20, 21, 23, 26, 27, 38, 39, 55, 100, 152, 214, 215
  John Senr., 5, 6, 20, 98
  John, Mercht., 39
  Joseph, 15, 38, 39, 97, 109
  Joseph, Patroller, 37
  M.R., 11
  Marah, 172
  Mary, 97, 155, 178, 202, 214, 216
  Mathew, 186
  Mathew R., 215
  Matthew Rone, 154
  R. Matthew, 214
  Sarah, 105
  Stephen, 39
  Thomas, 14, 183
  Thos., 14, 153, 166
  V [?], 24
  White, 52
  William, 8, 10, 11, 17, 137, 154, 186, 202, 209
  William, Constable, 48
  Willm., Constable, 97

Whitehead
  Jacob, 204
Whiteman
  Michael, 129
Whitley
  Solomn., 184
Whitly
  Solomon, 65
Whitman
  Michael, 33, 47, 97
Wier
  George, 151
Wigens
  Joseph, 44
Wiggins
  Isam, 192
  Issum, 120
  Joseph, 98, 120, 192
  Major, 68
Wilearson[?]
  Wm., 169
Wiley
  Solomon, 97
  William, 217
Wilkins
  John, 223
  William & wife Constant, 68
Wilkinson
  Anguish, 63, 97
  Angus, 102
  Archd., 63
  Archebald, 102
  Edward, 102
  James, 62, 97
  Neill, 63, 102
  Richd., 146
  William, 31, 48, 62, 137, 150, 201, 217
  Willm., 97
  Wm., 214
Wilks
  Isaac, 101
Willey
  Wm., 214
Williams
  Benedict, 27
  George, 163
  John, 46, 97
  Joseph, 66, 97
  Joshua, 27, 28, 106
  Samuel, 27
Williamson
  Lewis, 199
Willis
  Agerton, 61, 98, 146, 176, 218
  Agerton Junr., 150
  Benjamin, 61, 98, 176, 223
  Benjamin Junr., 146

Index

Benjamin Snr., 146
Daniel, 178
Daniel Junr., Constable, 68
Daniel Senr., 68
Danl., 97, 147
Danl. Junr., 147
Danl. Seignr., Trustee, 147
Danneil, 221
Elizabeth, 221
Elizth., 178
George, 61, 98, 150
Jeremiah, 177, 219
John, 68, 161
Joseph, 176, 178, 218
Joseph, Deceased, 218
Sarah, 178
Willkinson
Wm., 56
Willson
Edward, 47, 97, 130
Edward Junr., 198
Edward Senr., 199
Eliza, 183
James, 47
Jams., 97
John, 97, 98, 131
John Junr., 47
Sarah, 97
Wilson
Ambres, 210
Ambross, 24
Edward, 33
George, 186, 210
James, 33, 128, 203
John, 29, 61, 103, 150
John Senr., 28, 29
Mary, 176
Rebekah, 178

Robert, 179
Saml. Carver, 182
Sarah, 49
Silvanus, 146
Solomon, 146
Wingat
John, 35
Wingate
John, 198
John Senr., 130
Joseph, 21
Waltar, 199
Wishart
William, 55
Willm., 98
Withers
Malc., 164
Wolf
Isaac, 204
Wood
Benjamin, 9, 12
Benjn., 12
Francis, 37
James, 37
Jo, 56
Joseph, 4, 98, 148
Philip, 148
Phillip, 57, 98
Woodard
Benjn., 138
Woods
Capt. Joseph, 101
Woodside
Alexr., 35
Woodward
Garat, 178
Woolf
Isaac, 171

Work
James, 112
Worley
Ni., 27
Nicholas, 27
Wray
Dugal, 205
Wright
[?], 31
Jonn, 30
Josiah, 31

Y

Yancie
Charles, 222
Yates
Capt., 105, 126
Jane, 4
John, 8, 9, 20, 33, 46, 98, 132, 197, 201, 207
John esquire, 19
Luke, 200
Yeats
John, 35
Yerby
Henery, 209
Young
David, 40, 59, 98
George, 98
George Jr., 67
George Sr., 67
John, 50, 100, 109, 194, 198
Leavy, 149
Levi, 37, 98
Mary, Widow, 162
Wm., 163

www.ingramcontent.com/pod-product-compliance
Lightning Source LLC
Chambersburg PA
CBHW081348230426
43667CB00017B/2755